TRUE FOR THE CAUSE OF LIBERTY

TRUE FOR THE CAUSE OF LIBERTY

*The Second Spartan Regiment
in the American Revolution*

BY OSCAR E. GILBERT &
CATHERINE R. GILBERT

CASEMATE

Philadelphia & Oxford

Published in the United States of America and Great Britain in 2015 by
CASEMATE PUBLISHERS
1950 Lawrence Road, Havertown, PA 19083
and
10 Hythe Bridge Street, Oxford OX1 2EW

Copyright 2015 © Oscar E. Gilbert & Catherine R. Gilbert

ISBN 978-1-61200-327-6
Digital Edition: ISBN 978-1-61200-328-3

Cataloging-in-publication data is available from the Library of Congress and
the British Library.

10 9 8 7 6 5 4 3 2 1

Printed and bound in the United States of America.

For a complete list of Casemate titles please contact:

CASEMATE PUBLISHERS (US)
Telephone (610) 853-9131, Fax (610) 853-9146
E-mail: casemate@casematepublishing.com

CASEMATE PUBLISHERS (UK)
Telephone (01865) 241249, Fax (01865) 794449
E-mail: casemate-uk@casematepublishing.co.uk

CONTENTS

[Thomas Brandon] knew very well the game that suited himself and his command; and it is probable that they did as much hard fighting and swift running as any of their contemporaries.

GEORGE HOWE, "History of the Presbyterian
Church in South Carolina"

For the South Carolina and Georgia refugee militia.
In the most desperate days, they never wavered.

ACKNOWLEDGMENTS

WE WOULD LIKE TO ACKNOWLEDGE THE INVALUABLE cooperation of several individuals, notably Martin Mongiello and staff, Inn of the Patriots and The American Revolutionary War Living History Association, Grover NC; Elizabeth J. Gilbert-Hillier; Michael Scoggins, Southern Revolutionary War Institute, York SC; Charles Baxley; Will Graves; Brent Holcombe; and Joe Epley.

Historical resources were provided by the various facilities of the National Archives and Records Administration (NARA); the Houston Texas Public Library System, particularly the Clayton Library Center for Genealogical Research; the Fondren Library, Rice University, Houston TX; the Daughters of the American Revolution records center, Washington DC; The British National Archives (formerly the Public Records Office), Kew, Surrey; The Library of Congress, Washington DC; the Montgomery County Public Library, Conroe TX; the Anne S. K. Brown Military Collection, Brown University, Providence RI; and the US Marine Corps History Division, MCB Quantico VA.

Steve Smith and Libby Braden of Casemate Publishing edited the final manuscript and oversaw preparation of the illustrations, respectively.

SOURCES AND
ADDITIONAL
RESOURCES

A PRIMARY RESOURCE IS THE FEDERAL PENSION APPLI-cation (FPA) records of veterans preserved by the National Archives and Records Administration (NARA). Individual records can be ordered by name at http://www.archives.gov/veterans/military-service-records/pre-ww-1-records.html, and microfilm copies are available at participating libraries. Many but by no means all can now be viewed online at www.fold3.com or in transcript form at revwarapps.org. Researchers masochistic enough to delve into the original records should be aware that the length of a file ranges from ten to one hundred thirty or more pages, and averages about forty pages of handwritten script. Considerable information may be buried within supporting letters, affidavits, or depositions. The authors have also utilized microfilm records of the "Accounts audited of claims growing out of the Revolution in South Carolina," and the "stub indents," records of reimbursement for military expenses. To our best knowledge the latter are available only at the South Carolina State Archives, the Southern Revolutionary War Institute in York SC, and at the Daughters of the American Revolution records center in Washington D. C.

Veterans' FPA depositions were for the most part recorded by court clerks, some of whom were semi-literate. In addition, most first-person depositions were recorded as a sort of "stream of consciousness" as the veteran talked. Punctuation and breaks in sentences were sometimes completely lost as the clerk struggled to keep up with the speaker. Some clerks used abbreviations: ampersands or plus-marks (+) were commonly substituted for "and," &c for "and so forth/on." In some cases quotations within quotations—"'nnnn'"—have been revised for clarity.

Creative spellings of unfamiliar place names or unusual family names were quite common, and even simple names were subject to misspelling; Colonel Thomas Brandon quite often became Brannon, Brannen, Branhan, or Branden. More complex names were hopeless. Cornwallis became Corn Wallis or Corn Wallace, and in Henry Deshasure's FPA his name is spelled three different ways.

We have for the most part preserved original spellings and grammatical errors. The primary exception is the insertion of periods at obvious sentence breaks, for ease of reading. Where information has been inserted for clarity, where known errors have been corrected, or where our interpretation of period documents are uncertain, are all indicated by brackets [xxx].

Other problems include the varying quality of pens and paper with blots caused by quill pens on rough paper, poor (or rushed) penmanship, and poor preservation because of subsequent damage.

The FPA of one William Kennedy serves as an example. Note that there were three William Kennedys: Kennedy Senior, Junior, and an unspecified Kennedy. Some researchers have lumped the unspecified Kennedy's account into the father-son, but detailed examination of the chronology, i.e. battles participated in, indicates he was a "third William Kennedy." From his pension application, S2695:

> That during the Revolutionary war between the United States and Great Brittain and in the year 1776. he inlisted for the Term of 18 months in the State of South Carolina, in the service of the United States, whether this were called the united States Troops or the Carolina Line he cannot now Be certain—But knows he inlisted under Major William Henderson was in the company commanded by Captain John Blasingim—in the Regiment commanded by Col Sumpter the number of the Regiment he does not recollect But believes it was either 4th or That he was mustered into service at Charlston from there to Savannah; from there to Altamaha River and was stationed at Fort Barrington. from hier they were marched to Charlestown to the Barracks. and from then to Hadleys. point was there when fort Moutrie was attacked—the Brittish

attempted to Land at Hadlys point where this petitioner was with the American army; the Enemy was repulsed From there; they were marched to Seneca against the Cherokee Indians and was in the Battle of Squaw Creek—then they were marched through the nation destroying the Idean towns &c.

Additional useful sources are narratives recorded by amateur historians, ministers, and family members. Such stories inevitably became garbled in repeated retellings, a problem not limited to former centuries. The reader interested in this issue may wish to refer to an exhaustive analysis of the various retellings of Major Joseph McJunkin's memoirs at http://southern-campaign.org/newsletter/v2n11.pdf. We have taken some care to track such stories back toward original sources as far as possible.

Some classical resources must be used *very* judiciously. Examination of the collection of raw data compiled by Lyman C. Draper, whose admirable *King's Mountain and Its Heroes* has long been considered *the* primary source, reveals inconsistencies, outright contradictions (many of which are over-looked as the reader plows through 593 pages of very small type), and in-tentional elaboration to make a better story. These issues are discussed in the main text where significant.

An example is a letter from politician Daniel Wallace to the prolific historical novelist William Gilmore Simms which recounts tales told to Wallace (an invalid at the time) by his elderly neighbor Christopher Brandon. There are certain factual errors noted by Draper, and at the end of the letter Wallace makes it clear that he is suggesting fictional plot elements based on local lore. Such sources have truth buried within them, but must be corroborated by other evidence. For example, Wallace recounts one actual skirmish but inserts "Horse-shoe Robinson"—a fictional character from John P. Kennedy's 1835 novel *Horse-Shoe Robinson: A Tale of the Tory Ascendency*—as a participant. The Robinson character was loosely based on James Robertson, a well-known local teller of tall tales. Robertson's FPA, taken under oath, is far more mundane. The novels of Simms and Kennedy, and Draper's hagiography, did much to firmly embed the myth of the buckskin-clad frontiersman and his unerring rifle into popular history.

Draper's original Manuscript Collection, held by the Wisconsin His-torical Society, is available on microfilm at a number of libraries; there are several different versions of the microfilm collection with varying reel numbers, and some libraries do not have the complete collection. They are sometimes referred to as the "King's Mountain Papers" or the "Sumter Papers." Like the FPAs, plowing through thousands of pages of Draper's correspondence, newspaper clippings, transcriptions of documents, and interview notes is a Herculean task. Several not very exhaustive indices have been compiled, but do not always match the reel numbers for different microfilm editions of the collection.

A project that provides additional useful detail in locating specific sites mentioned in the text is *The Global Gazetteer of the Revolutionary War* by John A. Robertson and others (http://gaz.jrshelby.com/). An additional printed map resource that readers may find useful is Savas and Dameron's *Guide to the Battles of the American Revolution*, though our analyses of the relevant battles may differ significantly.

This project deals only peripherally with the weapons, clothing, and equipment of the ordinary militiaman. Most artwork depicting the militia was produced long after the war, and was considerably romanticized, often showing the militia dressed in elaborate European-style uniforms or in the fancy dress of wealthy city folk. For those interested in more accurate pictorial depictions of the back country militia uniforms and equipment, see Gilbert and Gilbert, *Patriot Militiaman in the American Revolution, 1775–82*.

AUTHORS' PREFACE

IN THE EARLY NINETEENTH CENTURY BOTH AMERICAN
and British historians regarded the failure of the British Southern Campaign as the decisive final phase of the American War of Independence.
More battles, sieges, skirmishes, raids, ambushes and assassinations occurred in South Carolina than in any other colony. Many of the now little-
known battles rivaled or exceeded the scope and strategic significance of
far more famous battles fought in the northern colonies. The climactic
assault (9 October 1779) that ended the joint Franco-American siege of
Savannah, Georgia was the single bloodiest day of the entire war. Political
and military authorities on both sides agreed that the Battle of King's
Mountain (7 October 1780) marked the beginning of the end for the
British in America. A devastating defeat at The Cowpens (17 January 1781)
nailed the coffin shut on British hopes. Even British tactical victories at
Guilford Courthouse (15 March 1781) and Eutaw Springs (8 September
1781) proved to be strategic defeats as diminished British forces were
subsequently driven north into Virginia, or penned into impotent coastal
enclaves.

Most wars are ended when one or both sides simply grow weary of
fighting. Ultimately it was the cumulative moral, political, and financial
effects of these defeats and Pyrrhic victories that ground down the will of
the powerful British Empire, turning public opinion and eventually Parliament against the war.

Then in the mid-nineteenth century the war in the south began to be
willfully ignored. After South Carolina's secession triggered the American
Civil War of 1861–1865, the Revolutionary War in the south virtually disappeared from mainstream American history. Battles in the northern and

middle colonies assumed primacy; the war was fought chiefly in the northern colonies until Cornwallis inexplicably found himself trapped at Yorktown. One recently published popular history devoted only six of nearly 400 pages to the Southern Campaign. King's Mountain was mentioned in a figure caption. Cowpens, considered by military historians to be "the most [tactically] perfect battle fought in the Americas," and still studied by military professionals, rated less than a single page.

Treatment of the Southern Campaign in the mass media that now shapes most Americans' perception of their own history is vastly worse. As we were completing this project we took time to view a multi-hour historical television epic on the War of Independence. The entire war in the south was reduced to less than two minutes (replete with twanging banjo music) on the Battle of King's Mountain, treating it as a slightly more upscale version of the Hatfield-McCoy feud.

The war in the south has gained a bit more historical traction, notably with the publication of John Buchanan's 1997 book *The Road to Guilford Courthouse*. But on the whole the Southern Campaign remains the province of a relatively small but admittedly rich regional and academic literature.

Fortunately the dominantly Scots-Irish regional culture, with its strong emphasis on family tradition and oral history, left a rich collection of surprisingly literate accounts of the savage war in the southern colonies, as recorded in military pension applications, interviews, and family histories.

This work does not pretend to be a complete history of the Revolutionary War, or even the war in the south. It is simply a record of the role of one unit, the Second Spartan Regiment of the South Carolina State Militia, and their role in some of the pivotal battles of the war. It is brutal partisan warfare as seen from the bottom up by officers, soldiers, and family members. It is an attempt to depict the birth of a nation as seen by the common people.

ED AND CATHY GILBERT
Katy Texas, July 2015

PROLOGUE

William Blackstock's Plantation,
South Carolina, 20 November 1780

THE TEMPERATURE WAS FALLING RAPIDLY AS NIGHTFALL
approached, and the sweaty, ill-clad rebel militiamen shivered in the growing chill. They had marched far and fast for days, but now they were trapped, their backs to the cold, swift-flowing Tyger River. Successfully fording the river might bring a brief respite, but being caught in the act of crossing would spell absolute disaster.

Close on their heels—and gaining fast—was the hard-charging Lieutenant Colonel Banastre Tarleton's British Legion. Recruited in the northern colonies and sent south to terrorize and subdue their fellow colonists, the battle efficiency of Tarleton's Legion was exceeded only by its mindless brutality. Ambitious, vain, cruel, and without doubt a talented leader, Tarleton had never lost a battle. General Charles Cornwallis had assigned his most trusted subordinate the explicit mission of eliminating the vainglorious but troublesome Thomas Sumter and his ragtag rebel back-country militia. He had given Tarleton two additional regiments of regulars, one his elite Fraser's Highlanders, to complete the task.

"Bloody Ban" always went straight for the kill, and this was no gentleman's war. The specialty—and the joy—of his favored Green Dragoons were to ride down and slaughter the remnants of rebel formations broken by the equally ruthless green-clad Legion infantry and red-coated British regulars. For the rebels, surrender was an iffy proposition. The Legion had earned a reputation for butchery, literally hacking apart men who threw down their arms in surrender, and mutilating rebel wounded. Those who—

on the Legion's whim—were allowed to live would be sent to the prison at Ninety Six, where prisoners subsisted on the leavings of the garrison's horses, and most died. That was still better than the British prison hulks anchored in Charleston Harbor. There prisoners endured a lingering death from disease and starvation in conditions far worse than on any slave ship. Slaves had value, but rebel prisoners were a liability.

The rebel force outnumbered Tarleton, but his every experience dictated that this was no problem. The rebels would break and run in the face of a British bayonet charge, to be ridden down and destroyed utterly by the Green Dragoons.

Pressed into a corner the senior rebel colonel, Thomas Sumter, was in his usual headstrong fashion ready to go head-on at the enemy, a trait that had earned him the nickname Gamecock. But shrewd rebel Colonel Thomas Brandon of the Second Spartan Regiment was familiar with the local country. From hard-won experience he advised that this farm was as good a place as any to fight the type of defensive battle the Gamecock disdained. Dense woods ringed the farm, preventing the Green Dragoons from flanking the position. Blackstock's unusually sturdy fences and equally massive buildings would serve as an impromptu fort, crucial shelter against a British bayonet charge and the onrushing dragoons.

Now the prize was within Tarleton's grasp. He had as usual driven his troops hard in pursuit along the crude roads. His tired men would have to charge uphill across a hundred yards of open fields left barren after the tobacco harvest. In Tarleton's eyes this presented no problem for his hardened veterans.

The first of Tarleton's scouts emerged into the opening in the forest. The rebel pickets fired a ragged volley and scampered back up the hillside into the protection of trees and fences. Nervous but confident rebels shoved wire picks in to clear the vents of their muskets and rifles, blew old and possibly damp powder out of the pans, and re-primed.

The next hour would tell the tale. It would also help decide the fate of an infant nation.

CHAPTER 1

INTRODUCTION

Hell is empty, and all the devils are here.
—WILLIAM SHAKESPEARE

IT WAS WAR, AND IT WAS NOT AT ALL PRETTY.

It was not the war of colorful lace-trimmed uniforms, squealing fifes, and courtly gestures so beloved of artists and Hollywood costume dramas. A new and nobler form of government was being born, but its birthing pangs were mud, broiling heat, bitter cold, disease, famine, plunder, arson, rape, torture, massacre, and murder.

Historians have written that the American Revolution marked a transition from European dynastic wars to nationalistic wars. But as with most things it was far more complex, in part a cultural conflict rivaling anything the twenty-first century has to offer. And it was equally vicious.

The leadership on the British side arose from a system where the ruthless and ambitious could most easily rise—economically and socially—by serving the king as officers in the brutal suppression of those who were not lucky enough to be true Englishmen.

Their tools were soldiers recruited from the lower classes of a ruthlessly stratified society. They were paid a pittance, subjected to arbitrary and cruel discipline, and had no realistic expectation of surviving to see the end of their term of service. Their path to a slightly better life—defined by abundant alcohol and money for whoring and gambling—was looting. When their government ran short of recruits, it rented conscripts hired out by a German prince to fight another country's war. They were paid a pittance, and the prince profited handsomely.

The most reliable British allies—and ruthlessly exploited tools—were the Cherokee and Creek tribes, with their own history of brutal inter-tribal warfare.

All these were pitted against the descendants of immigrants from one of the most violent cockpits of Western Europe, who had resisted outside rule since Roman times, built an entire culture based on raiding and cattle rustling, and been ruthlessly used by kings and local lords to either resist or suppress the peoples of neighboring lands.

It was a religious war, where the clergy of a state church served as agents of a king who ruled by "divine right." Pitted against them were adherents of new faiths that emphasized equality in the eyes of God, equal human rights, personal independence, and that kings most definitely did *not* rule by divine right. Each sought to suppress the other.

It was part of a protracted struggle in which European powers vied for control of colonies around the globe. The British and French were the primary contenders, and the French were only too happy to exploit an internecine war between England and its colonies. Spain was waiting in the wings for the British to stumble. British colonial raiders from Georgia had plagued Spanish Florida for a century, then, humiliated in the aftermath of the Seven Years War, Spain had been forced to cede Florida to Britain. Even the native tribes were joining the colonizing binge. After disease and Spanish repression destroyed the native tribes of Florida, the Southern Creeks expanded southward to fill the void (they would eventually become a separate tribe, the Seminole). Despite treaty agreements the colonists were pushing relentlessly against the poorly-defined eastern boundaries of territories guaranteed to the Creeks and Cherokee by the British government.

Perhaps the miracle is that it was not worse.

CHAPTER 2

A PEOPLE BRED TO WAR

The migration of predominantly Scots-Irish settlers transformed the lower South, and, in the final analysis, was key to America's triumph over Great Britain in the Revolution. —WALTER EDGAR

TO UNDERSTAND ANY WAR IT IS NECESSARY TO FIRST understand the culture of the warriors—the reasons they fight and the ways in which they fight. The rebels in the southern back country who called themselves Whigs, and later Patriots, prided themselves on a long tradition of resistance to authority, and a stubborn personal pride—reinforced by religion—that decreed following one's conscience no matter what the cost. Casually reaching back two centuries into his own family's history, Revolutionary War soldier Robert Long said that ". . . his father's people lived in Scotland, originally, & in Charles the First's time opposed his Tariff or ship money—and being of that kind of Presbyterians, called Covenanters, in Charles the Second's time, fled to Ireland to escape his persecution. Being left at his father's death in a neighborhood of whigs in the revolutionary war between them and his father's policy, & above all the all wise providence of God, he was a whig, too, that [He] made his way perfect."[1]

The roots of these men in fact reached back centuries into one of the most violent regions of Europe. They were descendants of a people from an ancient borderland so turbulent that in 122 A.D. the exasperated Romans built Hadrian's Wall in an ultimately futile attempt to hold them at bay.

In the period between 1717 and the beginnings of the American Revolution an unprecedented wave of immigration reshaped both the character and boundaries of England's American colonies. A quarter of a million people, the first great wave of immigrants who traveled as extended families and even entire communities, arrived in the American colonies. In general these diverse immigrants originated from the areas around the Irish Sea: true Ulstermen, Lowland Scots, borderers from the northern counties of England, and French Huguenots (Calvinist Protestants) who had fled France for safety in Ulster and Scotland.[2] The Ulstermen were in turn descended from Lowland Scots, English settlers, and remnants of the "riding families" or reivers who flourished along both sides of the chaotic and disputed border of Scotland and England between 1300 and 1600.

During the Revolutionary War these people were generally referred to as "Irish," but by the mid-eighteen hundreds the term "Scotch-Irish" and much later, "Scots-Irish" began to stick. The men were of distinctive appearance: tall, lean, with unusual habits of dress that marked them as strangers to the colonists from southern England who had settled along the Atlantic seaboard. The Scots-Irish were quick to take offense, stubborn, careful of their honor, and fought readily when offended. The vast majority of these peculiar immigrants were Presbyterians, Covenanters, and people of "New Light" persuasions, and the refusal to accept their position in the bottom rungs of colonial society was directly tied to their perceived "arrogance."

The Covenanters were a group who rejected any government interference in their religious practices. During the reigns of Charles II and James II, Covenanters were often executed or banished for their steadfast refusal to acknowledge the King's divine authority in religious matters. "Non-Subscribers" or "New Light" Presbyterians rejected unquestioning acceptance of any religious dogma—even their own. Their fundamental tenet was "faith guided by reason and conscience."[3] These radicals thought all men equal in the eyes of God, a heretical concept in an era when the nobility were regarded as God's agents on earth. Calvinist theology in Ulster had evolved to a point where revolt against an earthly King was a duty if the monarch's actions were believed to violate the will of God.[4]

Entering through the ports of Philadelphia and Baltimore, the Scots-Irish flooded west across Pennsylvania and then began their journey north and south along the spine of the Appalachians. They spread south through the Piedmont region of modern day North and South Carolina, and eventually spilled over the mountains into modern day Tennessee and Kentucky. It made perfect sense that they headed for the frontiers: these were a people who had been frontiersmen for centuries.

Prior to the great migrations the Scots-Irish had survived hundreds of years of violence by bonding in extended families or clans. Their warrior culture, unique fighting styles, distrust of government, and reliance on extended family were forged from harsh experience in two of the deadliest environments of the British Isles: the Anglo-Scottish borderlands and the province of Ulster.

THE STEEL BONNETS

Prior to 1600 Scotland lacked any effective national government. The lowland Scots, sandwiched between Gaelic Highlanders to the north and the English to the south, were routinely subjected to robbery and mayhem by reivers, the cattle rustling families who lived on both sides of the disputed border. The center of the border was dominated by the Cheviot Hills, notoriously difficult to traverse. For centuries armies marched north or south through the rich farm country of the west or around the mountains to the east. The locals, who knew hidden ways through the mountains often made use of that superior knowledge when war came to them.

Malcolm Frazer described the border between Scotland and England as "the ring in which the champions met; armies marched and countermarched and fought and fled across it; it was wasted and burned and despoiled, its people harried and robbed and slaughtered on both sides by both sides. Whatever the rights and wrongs, the Borderers were the people who bore the brunt, for almost 300 years, from the late thirteenth century to the middle of the sixteenth, they lived on a battlefield that stretched from the Solway to the North Sea. War after war was fought on it, and this to put it mildly, had an effect on the folk who lived there."[5] The Bishop of Ross, John Leslie, wrote of the border people in his 16th century *History of Scotland that* ". . . in time of war they are readily reduced to extreme poverty by the almost daily inroads of the enemy, so, on the restoration of peace, they entirely neglect to cultivate their lands, though fertile, from fear of the fruits of their labour being immediately destroyed by a new war . . . whence it happens that they seek their subsistence by robberies, or rather by plundering and rapine."[6]

Traditional economic systems on the border also made farming unprofitable. Scottish tradition decreed that land owners divide their land equally among their sons, so that in time even the most prosperous farms were subdivided into unprofitable plots. The strip-rig system used to parcel out the feudal lord's rental farm land ensured that none of the lease holders could improve contiguous plots, or even count on having the same strip of land for longer than the duration of a short lease. Most men were hard put to feed their families, and military service and other work for the local lord provided constant interruptions in attempts to make a living.[7]

Continual fighting across their lands made improving their homes pointless, so the poorest among them built turf and peat "cabbins" so simple that they could be abandoned and rebuilt quickly when the enemy departed. For the poor farmer obligatory military service was beyond his control. There was no nationwide judicial system, and all justice was local. If a man's laird was just, there would be some attempt at redress when wronged; if the local laird was unjust, people suffered without hope. The system came to depend solely upon which local lords could field the largest armies, and were the most aggressive in ruthlessly striking against any threat to themselves or those who swore fealty.

Recognition of the instability and danger along the borders eventually produced an agreement between the English and Scottish governments, and establishment of the Laws of the Marches. Northern England and Southern Scotland were divided into East, West, and Middle Marches, and strongmen, or March Wardens, were selected to govern the turbulent territories. The Border Laws were drawn up to reflect the needs of the area, including laws against treasonous acts: selling weapons, armor, and horses across the border; assisting raiders from the other kingdom; refusal to follow the "fray" (pursuit of raiders across the border to regain your neighbors' stolen property); marriage to a woman from the opposing kingdom without permission; or refusal to assume assigned defensive duties. Keith Durham noted that ". . . because the March Wardens were operating in what was essentially a bandit-ridden war zone, they often proved ineffective in protecting the law abiding Borderer and his family from the sudden violence that could descend upon them.

"On both sides of the Border people of all social classes lived in constant fear of their lives and banded together in their own *graynes* to whom they gave a loyalty that transcended any national allegiance."[8] Borderers relied only upon their own kinsmen and community.[9] By the mid-sixteenth century the Anglo-Scottish border was still locked in medieval warfare, dotted with castles, *peles* (fortified structures built of dirt and timber), and *bastles* (fortified farm houses). "Alongside them had evolved a formidable race of light horsemen, skilled in the art of raiding, scouting, ambush, feint and skirmish." Border officials complained of their "wildness and disorder," but also called them "fine soldiers who were 'able with horse and harness,' 'a military kind of men, nimble, wilie, and always in readiness for any service.'"[10] With friends and kin they "rode with the moonlight, and with 'lance and steel bonnet,' engaged in the nightly mayhem that 'shook loose the Border.'"[11]

The reiving culture dominated all social classes on both sides of the Border. Reiving families fought blood feuds against families both across the border and within their own countries. Hermitage Castle was built to protect the Lyddesdale Valley from the English, but also built to allow the Scottish monarchs to maintain a watchful eye on the warlike Armstrong, Elliot, Nixon, and Crosier families.

The "riding families" and the reiving culture remained unchanged because both governments found it advantageous to leave the borders as they were, as buffers against the opposing kingdom. It was good policy to keep your enemies on the other side of this lawless no-man's land off balance. Good money was available to fighting men, so the borderlands came to be populated by far more fighting men than the area could have supported through legitimate work. Both governments used their borderers to augment their armies; the Armstrong family alone could field 3,000 fighting men. Complaints were made (as might be expected of irregular troops) that the borderers were ill-disciplined and prone to distraction when plunder was available. However, their unmatched skill as "prickers" (scouts) and light horsemen meant the services of the borderers were frequently in demand. Their military functions were an extension of their daily life: scouting, ambushing enemy patrols, rustling livestock, stealing supplies, plundering towns, and harassing defeated armies. Henry VIII employed the Border Horse in his French campaigns, as well as in Ireland suppressing rebellions.[12]

A poor man called to service depended upon a wooden shield for defense and fought with a long spear, perhaps a battle-axe, a small sword, and a knife. If he went to battle with a horse he guided it with a thong or rope with one hand, using the other to wield the spear. Men carried a metal plate beneath the flap of their saddle, oatmeal in a bag stowed behind, and lived on simple oatmeal cakes cooked on the metal plate, augmented by beef acquired in the field.[13] Eventually the Scottish government specified what weapons and equipment men called to service must bring, and poorer men were expected to wear at least a steel skullcap under their customary headgear. The wealthier reivers wore helmets called "steel bonnets," many of them finely wrought by craftsmen in Spain or Italy.

The reiving ended abruptly when James VI of Scotland, nephew of Elizabeth I, ascended the throne of England as James I. Embarrassed by an extraordinarily violent raid led by the Graham family, James became determined to unify his Kingdoms. Harsh measures were taken against reiving families: mass hangings, forfeiture of land, and forced relocation as soldiers to other countries. Surviving members of the reiving families were forbidden ownership of horses and weapons. Farming life on the border became even more insupportable with rack-rents* and disinterested English absentee land owners.

In 1610 James I decided to plant a colony in Ulster, on land seized from Irish Catholic noblemen. He was delighted to send the violent and troublesome Lowland Scots and reiving families across the Irish Sea. He reasoned that he could save money since the transplanted settlers would require no army to protect them against the displaced and resentful Irish. They would be planted in sufficient numbers so that they could defend themselves.[14]

THE ULSTER PLANTATION
In Ulster the immigrants created a prosperous colony, the one fly in the ointment being the understandable enmity of the dispossessed native Irish, which often expressed itself in attacks by "wood kern," Irish bandits (or freedom fighters, depending upon your point of view). The land seizures ensured hostility from the native Irish, and "the new plantation towns of

---

*The practice of arbitrarily raising the rent on a leased parcel, in contravention of traditional practices of the era.

Ulster were walled and fortified. Each undertaker was expected to build within three years, a fortified estate house and *bawn* (fortified courtyard)."[15] Ill feeling between the settlers and the natives came to a head in 1641 when the British Civil War led to English disinterest in Irish affairs. The native Irish seized the opportunity to try and drive the Protestant colonists out. Savage fighting continued until Oliver Cromwell, who cared for neither Catholics nor Presbyterians, laid waste to all of Ireland in 1652. Researchers estimate the number of Protestant deaths to be 12,000 out of a total Ulster Protestant population of about 40,000. It was a massacre by any measure, regardless of whether the deaths occurred in combat or resulted from the murder of undefended families.[16]

War found the Protestants in Ulster again in 1695 when James II, deposed by British Protestants, invaded Ireland with French aid. The native Irish rallied to the Catholic monarch but he needed the northern port of Londonderry to launch an invasion of Scotland. The Protestants of Ulster received a warning, probably false, to expect James and his Catholic forces to massacre them. Given previous experience, this seemed plausible to the Protestants and they embarked upon a scorched-earth campaign, burning their crops and homes as they withdrew toward Londonderry. The horrific siege of Londonderry lasted 210 days before the forces of England's new king, William, relieved the city. The next year Ulster light horsemen played a significant role in James II's ultimate defeat at the Battle of the Boyne.[17]

English gratitude for the loyalty of the Ulstermen didn't last long. In 1710 high party Anglicans close to Queen Ann managed to pass The Test Act that barred Presbyterians from any government or militia position, voided Presbyterian marriages, and led to prosecution of long-married and respectable men for the crime of "fornication" with their wives. Their offspring became bastards overnight. Presbyterian ministers were expelled from their pulpits and forbidden to teach (Presbyterian ministers are "teaching elders"). Funerals could not be held unless an Anglican minister presided.

In response the first of the great Presbyterian migrations from Ulster began in 1717. This first wave of migration was followed by migrations to the American continent in 1725–1729, 1740–1741, 1754–1755, and 1771–1775. These latter migrations were primarily economic in nature, related to onerous taxation of Irish products (primarily wool) and rack-renting.

The Scots-Irish generally entered the American colonies through Delaware River ports and Philadelphia. The Quaker-dominated government encouraged them to move west, where they would find abundant land and could practice their religion freely. This also removed the fractious newcomers from the sight of Quaker sensibilities, and they served as a buffer against the native tribes. From western Pennsylvania the Scots-Irish began to move down the Appalachians to become a numerical majority and a dominant cultural force throughout modern-day western North Carolina, western South Carolina, Tennessee, and Kentucky.[18]

Other displaced ethnic groups, including Roman Catholic Highland Scots, French Protestant Huguenots, Lutheran Germans, and Welshmen also settled in the "back-country." To add to the volatile mix, new religions such as Methodism and the "New Light" movement further divided communities. The region became a patchwork of ethnic and religious communities, some living in harmony, others barely tolerated by their neighbors.

The least tolerated religion was the Church of England (Anglicans), the official religion of the Crown and the colony. By official policy only Anglican marital unions were legally recognized, and taxes were used to support the church as an involuntary tithe, further alienating the majority of the back country populace.

By the opening of the American Revolution the entire western frontier of the southern colonies was culturally dominated by the aggressive Scots-Irish, a people who had rejected outside rule from the days of William Wallace and Robert the Bruce, rejected the social hierarchy of Great Britain, remained fiercely independent and reliant only upon their families, and thrived in the most chaotic environments. Perhaps most significantly, these were a people who knew that it was possible to depose a King. Their ancestors had done it in Ulster; they were unafraid to attempt it here. Many of them fervently believed that God intended this land to be their own. They knew their own history of exile and forced removals, but this time, in this land that some believed God had chosen for them, they would not be moved. Improbably, the Scots-Irish had come home.

CHAPTER 3

THE BACK COUNTRY AND THE FIRST CHEROKEE WAR

*Wars are fought to see who owns the land, but
in the end it possesses man. Who dares say he
owns it—is he not buried beneath it?*
—COCHISE

SOME SCOTS-IRISH FAMILIES MIGRATED FROM PENN-
sylvania into South Carolina through the Shenandoah Valley. Others migrated slowly over generations, settling first in Virginia. Others came later
through the port of Charlestown,* then by pack-horse or on foot to their
destination.[1]

At no time was the western frontier a safe place. Scots-Irishmen from
the western Pennsylvania settlements hoped that good land and safety lay
south of them in the Carolinas.[2] The British and French had conducted a
covert war along the frontier throughout the War of the Austrian Succes-
sion (1740–1748), but the frontier remained unsettled as the French, Spanish, and British maneuvered against each other using native populations
of Creek, Cherokee, and Iroquois as pawns. The fragile peace of 1748 was
soon followed by the French and Indian War, the North American theater
of the global Seven Years War (1756–1763), and known as the First Cherokee War in the South.

---

*Originally founded as Charles Town, by the time of the Revolution the spelling had
evolved to Charlestown, and by the early 19th century to the modern spelling of
Charleston. By the time some veterans filed pension claims, the Charleston spelling
was in common use. Hereafter the modern spelling is used except in direct quotation
of period documents.

On 9 July 1755 Major General Edward Braddock was ambushed by the French and their Indian allies as he marched toward the Ohio Valley to attack Fort Duquesne; only the heroic efforts of Colonel George Washington saved a remnant of his force. One of the most significant defeats experienced by the British in the 18th century, its immediate consequence was a loss of western frontier land. Aware of British weakness, the Lenni Lanape and Shawnee began an extraordinarily savage series of raids on settlements in Pennsylvania, Maryland and western Virginia. Many families abandoned their land and fled east or south.

The McJunkin, Brandon, Bogan, Young, Kennedy, Cunningham, Savage, Hughes, Vance, and Wilson families, all from the same Pennsylvania Presbyterian congregation, were among those who fled south and settled in modern day Union County, South Carolina in about 1755.[3] Living first in tents, they soon built cabins, but the war followed them south. One notable event was an attack by the Overhill Cherokee of Settico on settlers along the Yadkin and Catawba Rivers in 1755. At about the same time Cherokees from Estatoe of the Lower Towns scalped three settlers on the Broad River. The new settlers were forced to "fort" for mutual protection.[4] Scots-Irish settlements routinely included at least one fortified home reminiscent of the *bastles* of the Anglo-Scottish border, and families moved to the nearest fortified home when danger threatened.

When fears of Indian attack subsided, the frontiersmen set to work. Trees were girdled and felled, the best logs saved for building a cabin, the rest split for fence rails. "The first planting done by the emigrants was invariably corn and flax. The product of the one was needed for bread, and that of the other for wearing apparel. No matter how small was the spot of ground reclaimed from the forest, a patch of flax was regarded as one of its necessary features. Upon the women of the family usually devolved the labor of securing this crop and preparing the lint for its destined uses. Cotton and hemp were cultivated at a later day, each family raising a sufficiency of both for its own needs."[5] Along with the cotton and hemp, frontier families would add crops of rye, wheat, and barley as they cleared more land.

Settlers usually kept chickens, occasionally ducks and geese. Hogs were a mainstay, kept in common pastures or allowed to roam the woods near individual farms. Pork was the primary meat for settlers, eaten fresh or cured. Cattle were cash crops, as farmers could exchange hides and butter for cash. A settler "usually grew peas, beans, collards, turnips, potatoes and pumpkins. Besides these vegetables he usually ate biscuits, cornbread, hominy, and rice with beef, pork or bacon. His meal was frequently supplemented by a wild turkey or goose, a haunch of venison or a fresh bear steak."[6]

Although the list sounds idyllic, the Reverend Charles Woodmason, an itinerant Anglican minister who lived in the back country in the mid-1760's, described the food differently: he noted that "standing and speaking 6 Hours together and nothing to refresh me, but Water—and their Provisions I could not touch—All the Cookery of these People being exceeding filthy, and most execrable." On another occasion, he complained that he went to bed at night having consumed nothing but "fat rusty Bacon, and fair Water, with Indian Corn Bread, Viands I had never before seen or tasted." On yet another occasion he complained of "Nothing but Indian Corn Meal to be had Bacon and Eggs in some Places—No Butter, Rice, or Milk—As for Tea and Coffee they know it not. These people are all from Ireland, and live wholly on Butter, Milk, Clabber, and what in England is given to the Hogs and Dogs."[7]

The settlers generally dressed in homespun linsey-woolsey, and in the simplest garments. Again, Reverend Woodmason was a keen, if not kind, observer: "How would the Polite People of London stare, to see the Females (many very pretty) come to Service in their Shifts and a short petticoat only, barefooted and Bare legged—Without Caps or Handkerchiefs—dress'd only in their Hair, Quite in a State of Nature for Nakedness is counted as Nothing . . . The Men appear in Frocks or Shirts and long Trousers—No Shoes or Stockings"[8] Although wealthier settlers could afford the occasional extravagance of purchases of hats and manufactured fabrics at stores, the majority remained dependent upon the women of their families to grow flax, cotton, and hemp, to create thread, weave cloth, sew clothing, and knit woolen socks. This dependence on home manufacture of clothing would continue throughout the American Revolution, and sometimes impacted the routine activities of militiamen who had no other resources for clothing.

THE FIRST CHEROKEE WAR, 1760

The back country settlers were a hardened people, but much of the savagery that marked the Revolution could be traced back to a more proximal cause, two decades of almost continuous warfare with the Cherokee.

The Cherokee were caught between covertly warring colonial powers, and attempts to expand the colonies westward brought settlers into conflict with them. The new settlers were pushing the envelope, as it were, encroaching upon Cherokee territory guaranteed by treaties with the Crown.

In 1758 the Cherokee helped the British take Fort Duquesne from the French, but quickly took offense over their treatment by the British. Following a miscommunication about where to acquire promised supplies, a party of Virginians whose horses had been taken killed and scalped thirty or more of their Cherokee allies. The Cherokee believed in a concept of "balance" similar to the Biblical injunction "an eye for an eye." As the Cherokee tell it, they achieved balance by killing white settlers on the Yadkin and Catawba because, if white people had no tribes, vengeance might legitimately be sought against any whites.[9]

The settlers responded with predictable Scots-Irish fury. Governor James Glen of South Carolina, adept at dealing with the Indians, was recalled and replaced by a new governor, William Henry Lyttelton. "Lawyer, politician, and fool, Lyttelton reversed the wise policies of Governor Glen."[10] He embargoed shipments of gunpowder, and when the Cherokee—desperate for powder for the fall hunts—sent a delegation of moderate leaders to negotiate, he imprisoned them. Lyttleton returned to Charleston, leaving the frontier to suffer the consequences.

Outraged at the imprisonment of their leaders, the Cherokee murdered 24 traders on 19 January 1760, but a hastily mounted attempt to free their leaders from Fort Prince George by force failed. On 1 February 1760 the Cherokee attacked the Long Canes settlers. The establishment of the Calhoun family settlement on Long Canes Creek had infuriated the Cherokee because the Indian Line as established by treaty ran along Long Canes Creek. Patrick Calhoun,* whether accidentally or deliberately, incorrectly surveyed his land, and placed his settlement partially on Cherokee land. Aware that they were too isolated to withstand an attack, the Long Canes settlers moved out, but their decision came too late.

An account of the attack appeared in *The South Carolina Gazette*, pub-

---

*Ancestor of the advocate of nullification and secession, John C. Calhoun.

lished in Charleston, 9 February 1760: "Yesterday night the whole of the Long Cane settlers, to the number of 150 moved off with most of their effects in wagons to go towards Augusta in Georgia and in a few hours after their setting off, were surprised and attacked by about 100 Cherokees on horseback, while they were getting their wagons out of a boggy place.

"They had amongst them 40 gunmen who might have made very good defense, but unfortunately their guns were in the wagons; the few that recovered theirs fought the Indians half an hour, and were at last obliged to fly. In the action they lost 7 wagons and 40 of their people killed or taken—including women and children the rest got safe to Augusta whence an express arrived here with the same account on Tues. morning."[11]

Nine year old Rebecca Calhoun was among the survivors. Hidden deep in a canebrake, she watched her grandmother be tomahawked to death and scalped. Days later, some of the settlers returned and found nine children wandering in the woods, dazed. A number of them had been scalped and left for dead, but others like Rebecca, had found hiding places.

On 16 February the Cherokee headman *Oconostota* (groundhog sausage) lured the commander of Fort Prince George out for a parley. As he turned away from Lieutenant Cotymore and his aides, he gave a signal to hidden men who opened fire and killed the whites. Soldiers inside the fort decided to chain their Cherokee hostages, and discovered that somehow they had obtained weapons. In a rage, they shot all the hostages. Following this affair the Cherokee began a full-scale offensive against all back country settlements, attempting to push white settlers back beyond the Congaree River.

In reaction to news of the Calhoun massacre communities built more elaborate forts. Some were simply strongly built houses surrounded by palisades. Others included a palisade with banquette and abatis, and a few built blockhouses with firing ports. Holding the backcountry forts, however, was a chancy business.

On the Enoree River settlers built a palisade around the home of Samuel Aubrey, but abandoned it for a stronger fort at Musgrove's Mill. There were other forts at Gordon's plantation on the Enoree, at James Otterson's home on the Tyger River, Lyles' Fort on the Broad River, Wofford's Fort on Fair Forest Creek, and Fort Thicketty near the mouth of Thicketty Creek. A dozen or more additional forts were built by individuals living in what would later become known as the Ninety Six District.[12]

Some forts could not be held. The Pennsylvania immigrants first moved to James Otterson's Fort, but they were driven from there to Pennington's Fort. There the women and children waited out the war, suffering considerable privation, while many men joined local militia units.

Edward Musgrove's fort was renamed Fort William Henry Lyttleton. An attack near fort "William Henry" occurred on 18 February 1760. A report in the *The South Carolina Gazette* described:

"That an officer and 6 men who had been sent out from Fort William Henry at Enoree cattle hunting, were on the 18th at midnight, surprised by a gang of 14 Indians, who at the first fire, killed the officer, Ensign William Gordon, and one Augustine Brown, and wounded two others Thomas Gordon and Gabriel Brown; then rushed upon to tomahawk them; but our people being resolute had a smart skirmish with the enemy killed one of them, wounded another, and drove off the rest, who left some match coats, guns, etc. behind.

"The action was so close that Thomas Gordon, the officer's brother, going to shoot one of the Indians, was seized by him and would have been killed had not another of the party come up, while Gordon threw his adversary, and tomahawked him; another Indian was knocked down with the butt end of a gun, which breaking in the hand of him who held it, he was pursued and obliged to fly, when another took up the Indian's gun and wounded the pursuer.

"Lt. Aubrey who commands the fort at Enoree brought down the scalp of the dead Indian last Monday, and confirms the above account. . . ."[13]

Edward Musgrove commanded a militia company, and a partial roster included Brandons, Bogans, Youngs, Gordons, McJunkins, Pennys, and Andersons. Christopher Brandon noted that his father, John Brandon, and his uncle, Thomas Brandon, later commander of the Second Spartan Militia Regiment, fought in (James) Grant's Campaign.[14]

Grant's Campaign, organized in 1761, followed a partially successful campaign led by Sir Archibald Montgomerie in 1760. Montgomerie, leading 1,200 Highlanders and Royal Scots, joined Richard Richardson and 350 Provincial troops and marched into Cherokee territory. The expedition destroyed a number of Lower Cherokee towns, and then moved up the path to War Woman Creek. At Rabun Gap they turned north into the valley of the Little Tennessee River, but were ambushed at the Narrows, about five miles from Echoe, the lowest of the Valley Towns. Montgomerie continued to fight in platoons although the Indians fired from cover. He pressed the attack, but the Cherokee flanked his force and attacked his pack animals. Burdened with a large number of wounded, and with his supply trains destroyed, Montgomerie pushed on to Echoe, but then retreated to the fortified settlement at Ninety Six. He afterward abandoned the colony, despite entreaties from the South Carolinians. Lieutenant Colonel James Grant served as adjutant general to Montgomerie, and his report implied cowardice on the part of the militiamen because they fired their rifles from cover instead of standing in formation like the Provincials. The Cherokee were apparently much amused by the Provincial tactics and compared fighting them to shooting turkeys.[15]

Montgomerie's withdrawal doomed Fort Loudon, the only frontier fort built amid the Overhill Towns. Captain Paul Demere's command held out until August 1760, but the isolated garrison faced starvation and surrendered. Promised safe passage, Demere's men were attacked the morning after they left the fort. "After the garrison of Fort Loudon had marched 16 miles and encamped, the Indians gradually withdrew in the evening; at dusk there was not one of them with our people; but on the 10th of August in the morning, a serjeant and 12 men were beginning to march and the rest were packing up their bundles to follow, a soldier from the advance guard discovered many Indians and gave the alarm; upon this Capt. Stuart ran towards the river or brook, and called to men to stand to their arms; the Indians in the grass immediately fired within 60 yards, and put our men, who were unprepared for such a piece of treachery, into the utmost confusion. Capt. Demere received two wounds the first volley, was directly scalped, and the Indians made him dance about for their diversion some time, after which they chopped off one hand or arm, then the other, and so his legs, using the most shocking barbarities on the bodies of others of our people."[16]

Although the total number of men killed more or less equaled the number of hostages killed at Fort Prince George, Demere's death by torture gave greater impetus to the government of South Carolina's determination to drive the Cherokee back. Among the survivors of the attack was Captain John Stuart, who was saved by the personal intervention of Little Carpenter

(*Attakullakulla*), who purchased his safety from the other Cherokee with his personal belongings.

Colonel James Grant succeeded Montgomerie in 1761. Assembling an enormous army and supply train, Grant succeeded in passing the Narrows and overcoming the Cherokee of the Middle Towns. Grant's force included men who would play major roles in the coming American Revolution: Henry Laurens, William Moultrie, Thomas Sumter, and Andrew Pickens. The Aubreys, Brandons, Gordons, Ottersons, and Browns would play their own parts as members of the Second Spartan Militia Regiment.

The Treaty of Charles Town in 1762 ended the conflict on terms favorable to the Cherokee of the Lower Towns, but small-scale raids and atrocities continued. The settlers soon faced yet another challenge, this one of their own making.

THE REGULATOR WAR, 1766–1768

"The end of the Cherokee War had rent the fragile fabric of society and attracted lawless individuals from other colonies."[17] A flood of immigrants to the western Carolinas followed The Bounty Act of 1761 which offered money to anyone bringing immigrants into the upcountry, on the theory that a larger white population would deter another war with the Cherokee. The territory was deemed safe, but many of the immigrants were penniless. Others were criminals, often operating in extended gangs, and the region became a criminal's paradise.

The wealthy elites of the coastal regions dominated colonial government. South Carolina was fabulously wealthy from an economy based on slave labor and plantation farming of rice and indigo, but the ruling class cared little about what went on in the interior so long as the lower classes held the Cherokee at bay. Efforts to obtain courts in the back country began in 1721, but by the 1760's none had been established. The people of the back country were taxed, but with few magistrates, and no courts, judges, sheriffs, or jails, criminals operated openly, terrorizing small farmers and merchants. Those who resisted were singled out for retribution. In short, ". . . political power and the benefits of government were confined to the older and more prosperous coastal strip, while little more than the obligations of government had been extended to the people of the Back-country. Westerners helped to bear the burdens of government, but they received few of the rewards."[18] The back country people had no means to protest. Although they were technically located in political parishes and extended the right to vote for members of the South Carolina Assembly, most were not allowed to vote because parish boundaries had never been surveyed. Settlers fortunate enough to know their parishes faced a long trip (perhaps a week or more on horseback) to polling places near the coast.

The Reverend Charles Woodmason, the opinionated missionary, became embroiled in the controversy. His 14 December 1766 journal entry mentioned efforts of the Chief Justice to suppress gangs of horse thieves, and noted that the "low People" in the neighborhood were connected to the thieves and that "'The Robbers gather'd in a Body and stood on their defence."[19] On 26 December he elaborated that the Chief Justice was unable to raise the local militia to attack the gang of thieves. In February of 1767 his travelling companions' horses were stolen, and Woodmason noted that the same gang of thieves was responsible. In the Savannah River Valley one John Scott was attacked and burned repeatedly with a red hot poker to make him confess where his money was hidden. John Huggins of the Waxhaws challenged four men approaching his house, and was shot in the neck.[20] Protecting themselves and their property, and establishing courts, churches, and schools became overarching concerns of the people in the back country.

The controversial Stamp Act of 1765 roiled the coastal communities, but made little impact on frontiersmen. They were accustomed to being taxed for no benefit, and their problems were far more immediate.

Six outlaws were finally captured by local men and taken to Charleston for trial. Five were convicted, but the newly appointed governor, Lord Charles Greville Montagu, was eager to demonstrate his benevolence. He pardoned the criminals. It was the straw that broke the camel's back.

Men in the back country began to organize to protect their families and communities. Pitched battles with the criminal gangs followed. Thieves were rounded up, horse-whipped, and driven away. These extralegal efforts met with success, but Governor Montagu concluded that the vigilantes were the problem and ordered them to disperse. Instead, the locals banded together in a single organization, calling themselves Regulators. An unlikely advocate for the back country settlers, the Reverend Woodmason—who had experience dealing with the colonial government—graphically laid out their grievances in *The Remonstrance,* read aloud in Charleston on 7 April 1767.

"Our large Stocks of Cattel are either stollen and destroyed—Our Cow Pens are broke up—and All our valuable Horses are carried off—Houses have been burn'd by these Rogues, and families stripp'd and turn'd naked into the Woods–Stores have been broken open and rifled by them (from wherefrom several Traders are absolutely ruin'd) Private Houses have been plunder'd; and the Inhabitants wantonly tortured in the Indian manner for to be made confess where they secreted their Effects from Plunder. Married women have been Ravished——Virgins deflowered, and other unheard of Cruelties committed by these barbarous Ruffians."[21]

The Remonstrance went on to rudely disparage lawyers and governmental incompetence, and it infuriated the legislators in Charleston. The most pressing demands of the Regulators were just: for courts, sheriffs, and jails; for churches and schools; and for an extended survey of the parish boundaries to make representation in the colony's government a reality. Their hopes for an amicable solution were soon dashed. When representatives arrived in Charleston with a petition, penned by Woodmason and signed by four prominent citizens on behalf of the thousands in the back country, civic leaders in the city demanded that they be arrested and their petition publicly burned. The threat was not carried out, but battle lines were drawn.

The Regulators met in June of 1768 and drafted the Plan of Regulation. They would no longer accept the authority of Charleston's courts, as the good folk of Charleston seemed more intent on arresting Regulators than common thieves. The ongoing struggle for courts and voting rights became violent. Deputy Sheriff John Wood ventured into the back country with writs from the Court of Common Pleas, including arrest warrants for Moses Kirkland and Thomas Sumter. On his way home he was attacked by Regulators dressed as Indians, tied to his saddle and whipped, and confined at a home on the Broad River. In August a constable and thirteen deputies ventured into the back country to seize property belonging to known Regulators. Met by a larger group of Regulators, members of the constable's party were whipped and some killed. A punitive expedition under Provost Marshal Roger Pinckney and Colonel G. G. Powell's militia ended in humiliation when 300 militiamen refused to cooperate in an effort to arrest Gideon Gibson. A mortified Colonel Powell offered to resign his position but consoled himself that the men's respect for him had, at least, prevented them from doing violence to Pinckney. The men of the back country now refused to pay taxes.

Although anxiety about the Regulators' intent pervaded Charleston, their next action was supremely practical: they were surveying the parish boundaries themselves in preparation to come east to vote in the October elections. When they met with some electoral success, the Governor suspended and then dissolved the Assembly.

As reports of Regulator excesses filtered into Charleston the Governor determined to activate a unit of back countrymen to oppose them. Commissioning a Colonel Joseph Coffell[22] to serve warrants against 25 Regulators, the Governor hoped to provide a counterbalance. Coffell traveled through the back country calling upon the King's loyal citizens to join his militia, but he was a man of ill repute in the back country. While he attracted decent citizens to his banner, he also attracted a great many of the very ruffians the Regulators wanted to be rid of. Unfortunately Coffell's progression through the back country occurred as a new election was being held. Hearing of looting and robbery at home, some back countrymen turned away from the polls to protect their families. Certain that Coffell's expedition was a conspiracy to stop them from voting, seven hundred Regulators marched to oppose Coffell. Fortunately three highly respected men—Colonel Richard Richardson, Lieutenant Colonel William Thomson, and Daniel McGirth—intervened, and both sides stood down. Civil war had been narrowly averted.

In the coming months, a circuit court bill was finally passed. By 1772 courts opened across the back country. But lingering bitterness remained. Soon the people of the back country would have to decide who they disliked the least: the government in Charleston or the government in London. Almost to a man, the Regulators would become Whigs or Patriots, their opponents Loyalists or Scoffolites.

CHAPTER 4

POLITICAL
MANEUVERING,
1769–1775

Three millions of people, armed in the holy cause
of liberty, and in such a country as that which
we possess, are invincible by any force which our
enemy can send against us. Beside, sir, we shall
not fight our battles alone. There is a just God who
presides over the destinies of Nations, and who will
raise up friends to fight our battles for us.
—PATRICK HENRY

FRONTIER RESIDENTS NOW HAD LIMITED REPRESENTA-
tion in the Assembly of South Carolina, but by and large remained preoccupied with their farms and families. Meantime, the political storm
brewing in Charleston "would threaten their homesteads and their very
lives."[1] While the people of the back country had been fighting Charleston's elite and the British government for basic legal infrastructure and voting rights, the British had repeatedly outraged the coastal dwellers with a
series of unwelcome laws. An old statute was revived mandating that trials
for treason be held only in England, while another required that colonies
assume responsibility for quartering Royal troops. The Townshend Acts
continued or added new import duties on items including "tea, wine,
molasses, sirup, paneles, coffee, sugar, pimiento, indigo, foreign paper, glass
and painter's colours."[2] These taxes had minimal impact on small-scale
farms and self-sufficient communities, but a huge impact on city dwellers.

The "Rice Kings" and other members of the wealthy low country elites generally reacted aggressively to any British moves that diminished their own ability to manage South Carolina's internal and economic affairs. In 1770–1771 they became embroiled in a bitter battle with the British government over the prerogatives of the Commons House of Assembly, South Carolinians' primary tool for self-government. The issue was whether the Commons House could appropriate money for use outside South Carolina. The British position was that they could not unless the Governor and Royal Council approved. Government ground to a halt. The Royal government functioned in the background, but the members of the Commons House more or less ignored it; the Commons refused to meet, while the wily men of Charleston began to create a number of extralegal organizations to circumvent British colonial government.

In December 1773, following a successful fight against importation of tea, the General Committee was formed to provide a framework for development of an independent government. The General Committee called a meeting for the following summer, inviting delegates from the entire colony to attend. First they lodged a protest against the Intolerable Acts. These, referred to as the Coercive Acts in England, were passed in 1774 in response to the Boston Tea Party of December 1773. Four of the five measures abrogated the rights of Massachusetts to self-government. The British believed that making an example of Massachusetts would force the other colonies into compliance; its effects were quite the opposite. The idea that the British could arbitrarily nullify any colony's constitution and close its ports infuriated rather than frightened the rebellious colonists. South Carolina's delegates to the First Continental Congress were elected. In another move designed to further development of self-government, the delegates created the Council of Ninety-Nine, a group that would become the actual governing body of South Carolina. Without Royal permission the Commons House met early one morning and awarded expense money for delegates to the First Continental Congress.

Within six months the Council of Ninety-Nine took the colony another step toward independence by creating a Provincial Congress. Although sixty percent of the non-slave population of South Carolina lived in the back country, those citizens were allotted only thirty percent of the delegates. From the perspective of the people of the back country, it must have been difficult to determine who was more highhanded, the British or the people of the low country. Very real discrimination by the low country leaders contributed considerably to problems with getting the back country settlers to follow Charleston's lead as the colony moved toward revolution.

In 1775 the smaller Council of Safety was created to more efficiently regulate affairs. On 14 April news arrived from London that the House of Commons had received a number of petitions from the American colonies, but refused them a hearing. Lord North "minutely discussed the same, describing the characters of the provinces and pointing out such as he declared were in rebellion. . . . He stated the supremacy of parliament over America, and the American measures of resistance." He concluded by moving "that an address be presented to His Majesty, to thank him for the information laid before the House; and, that he would be pleased to take such measures, as might be suitable to his wisdom, for enforcing the laws against America, and promising him to support him in a full and vigorous execution thereof, at the hazard of their lives and fortunes."[3] The King requested that an additional regiment of foot and horse as well additional ships be sent to control the colonies.

It was clear to the rebels that action must be taken, but what? A number of people on the committee held out hope for reconciliation. Nonetheless, a secret Council of Five was created to make military decisions. On 20 April "unknown" individuals (actually William Henry Drayton and others) raided the royal powder magazines outside Charleston and obtained 1,600 pounds of powder. The next night the armory beneath the statehouse was robbed, netting 800 muskets and 200 cutlasses.

Although things were going well for the radicals in Charleston, there were still major concerns. Drayton's mind may have been set on revolution, but he wanted to suppress public outbursts from those who disagreed. In May a rumor circulated that the British intended to use slaves and Indians to suppress the South Carolinians. Although the rumor was unfounded, it roiled the low country. With a population of 80,000 slaves and 20,000 whites, the specter of a slave revolt remained a nagging concern. And there was concern about the back country. Would the back country people follow the lead of the Council of Safety?

When new British troops and news of the fighting at Lexington and Concord arrived in Charleston on 8 May, the Council of Safety decided that "association" must be addressed, and it was far and away the most divisive measure to come before the Provincial Congress when it met in June. Hotly debated by the delegates, many feared it would do more harm than good, and future events proved them prescient. Every free male citizen of the state would be asked to provide his signature on a pledge of loyalty, not to England, but to revolutionary South Carolina. Other colonies had used this device as a litmus test of loyalty, and penalties for refusal to sign were uniformly harsh.[4] A refusal to sign the Oath of Fidelity to Maryland, for example, resulted in triple taxation of land and real property for life, and proscription from practicing as a merchant, lawyer, physician or surgeon, apothecary, minister of the gospel, or teacher. Those who refused to sign the oath were excluded from any office of trust, whether civil or military. In Virginia recusants were disarmed by local militia officers, and prohibited from holding public office, serving on juries, suing for debts, voting, running for any office, and buying land or buildings.

Revolutionaries in Charleston took it to another level. The Association provided that the signees agreed to sacrifice their lives and fortunes on command of the Continental Congress or the Provincial Congress. Anyone who refused to sign would be considered "inimical to the liberty of the colonies."[5] It was decided that "the non-subscribers to The Association were made amenable to the General Committee, and by them punishable, according to *sound policy.*"[6] In rebel controlled Charleston "retaliation against resistance, even speech, was swift and harsh."[7] Soon after passage of the Association, two men were charged with favoring arms distribution to "Negroes, Indians, and Catholics." Another was charged with making a toast derogatory to the Council of Safety and Provisional Congress. They were seized, stripped, tarred and feathered, and publicly exhibited about Charleston. Later one of the men was allowed to apologize for his behavior and return home. The other was deported to England as an example to other non-subscribers. A free man of color who pronounced his loyalty to the King was summarily executed.[8]

Following Charleston's lead, The Committee of Surveillance in Augusta Georgia decided to mete out similar punishment to Thomas Brown. Brown was scalped, tarred and feathered, but still seemed unrepentant, so the mob held his feet over live coals. Brown took refuge with Colonel Thomas Fletchall, one of the most influential men in South Carolina's back country. Drayton, who apparently authorized the tarring and featherings in Charles-

Both Whig and Tory political tactics were often savage. This period cartoon, "Bostonians paying the exciseman," depicts Whigs pouring boiling tea down the throat of a Crown tax collector who has been tarred and feathered.—NARA

ton, would come to rue the day an injured and humiliated Thomas Brown retreated to the interior of South Carolina for safety.

In what should have been a straightforward act, the Provincial Congress raised three new militia regiments. The first and second regiments were infantry and staffed by officers selected from the low country. The third, a Ranger unit, was staffed with officers from the back country.

The respected William Thomson was named Lieutenant Colonel of the Rangers. Three candidates contended for the position of Major: Robert Cunningham, Moses Kirkland, and James Mayson, and the commission was ultimately awarded to Mayson. Although Kirkland was offended, he accepted a captain's commission. Robert Cunningham, his pride injured, refused a commission. The influential Cunningham family's opinions mattered. Andrew Pickens: "Mayson got the Commission, which so exasperated the others that they immediately took the other side of the question. . . . They both were men of influence, but particularly Cunningham who lived on the east side of Saluda River and had considerable connections in that part of the Country. If Cunningham had been appointed Colonel at that time, we would not have had so violent an opposition to our cause in this part of the country." Long after the war, Pickens added "I never had a doubt but that he would have made the best officer."[9]

Unknown to the Provincial Congress, the unintended consequences of officer selections for the Ranger regiment, combined with the new law requiring "Association," would be the equivalent of lighting the fuse of a political bomb and tossing it into the back country.

Lord William Campbell, destined to be the last Royal Governor of South Carolina, arrived on 17 June but the colonial government's control was already tenuous. Although the Provincial Congress was disbanded in August, the Council of Safety, headed by Henry Laurens, remained in place to interfere with the Governor's activities. When Campbell dispatched gunpowder to the Royal Governor of Georgia, the Council of Safety sent Captains John Barnwell and John Joyner to seize the powder. To the Council of Safety, it was imperative to stop the British from arming the Creeks and Cherokee.

Having accomplished this first feat, on 26 June Henry Laurens directed Major Mayson's Rangers to seize the gunpowder stored at Fort Charlotte on the Savannah River before Campbell could send it to the Cherokee.* Mayson surprised the fort on 12 July and seized 1,750 pounds of gunpowder. Leaving some of his Rangers in charge of Fort Charlotte, he ordered Captain Moses Kirkland to convey the powder to safety at Ninety Six. Kirkland, smarting over Mayson's elevation to Major, instead sent a message to Colonel Thomas Fletchall asking him to take control of the powder. Fletchall refused, so Major Joseph Robinson of the New Acquisition Militia called out the companies of Robert and Patrick Cunningham, who pretended to take the powder from Kirkland by force. The Cunninghams took revenge on Mayson, arresting him on charges of theft and imprisoning him at Ninety Six. Kirkland resigned his commission, disbanded his company, and left for Charleston to acquire a separate commission from Governor Campbell.

---

*The Cherokee needed the munitions in part for subsistence hunting and generating trade items like hides.

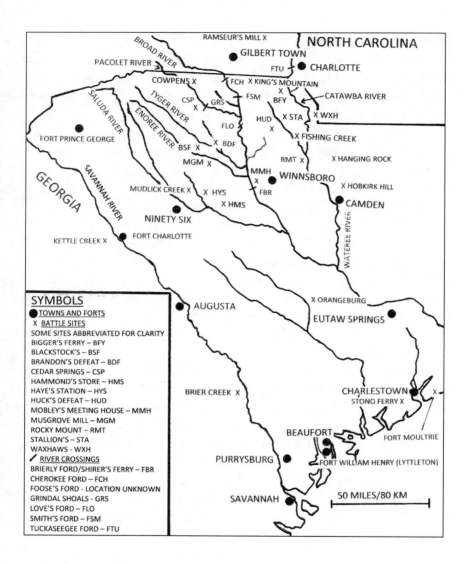

In the meantime, rumors concerning the loyalty of German settlers in the back country led Henry Laurens to authorize a mission to those settlers by some of their fellow immigrants. The men returned disheartened, admitting to failure in changing the sentiments of the Germans. John Drayton noted that "It was now further ascertained the spirit of disaffection daily spread itself in some back parts of the Colony; and particularly in the fork of the Broad and Saluda Rivers. In this section of the Colony

Thomas Fletchall, residing at Fair Forest, was Colonel of the regiment of the militia, which, of course, gave him great influence in that part of the country; and his conduct of late had been such as to give great uneasiness to the Council of Safety.

"At length they determined, if it were possible, to induce him to join the common cause; or to make known his sentiments on the situation of affairs. Accordingly, on the 14th of July, a suitable letter was ordered to be written to him." On 24 July Fletchall replied that he had—at the request of Assembly members James Williams, John Williams, and John Caldwell—mustered his men for a reading of the Resolution of Association. No one, he reported, signed. Instead Fletchall assigned Major Joseph Robinson of the New Acquisition Militia to draw up a local resolution of association; it stated that they would fight Great Britain only if forces were sent directly against them. This local resolution was signed by Fletchall's adherents, and Fletchall added that it "had generally been signed from Broad to Saluda Rivers." Fletchall reiterated that his conduct should be of no concern to anyone else, and made a vague reference to "Highland gentlemen" who might spread lies about him. He added "that he utterly refused to take up arms against his King." However unwillingly, Fletchall had drawn a line in the sand. Loyalists would not concede control of the back country.[10]

Simple arithmetic made the Council of Safety's abandonment of western South Carolina impossible. The odds that the low country could successfully wage both a civil war against their fellow citizens and war against the British were poor. It was decided to send an official mission to the back country to explain the Council of Safety's position. William Henry Drayton and the Reverend William Tennent, a Presbyterian minister and native of Northern Ireland, were joined by the Reverend Oliver Hart, a well-known Baptist preacher, and two members of the Provincial Congress from the back country, Colonel Richard Richardson (a planter and militia leader) and Joseph Kershaw (a prominent merchant from Camden). It is impossible to fathom how much autonomy these revolutionary committees gave individual members. As a member of the Council of Safety, Drayton carried with him a letter from Henry Laurens that essentially gave him *carte blanche* to call up militia or Ranger forces needed for his personal protection. As a member of the secret Committee of Five, Drayton technically held ultimate authority over provincial troops.

The committee's representatives rapidly discovered that German settlers of the Orangeburg and Saxe-Gotha districts demonstrated a distinct lack of sympathy to the Whig cause. "That resistance to royal authority could be reconciled with protestations of loyalty was a distinction that was lost on the people at large, especially those in the backcountry."[11] Terrified of losing their British land grants, the German settlers simply wanted to be left alone. The commission members were dogged through the back country settlements by the Cunningham brothers, Thomas "Burnfoot" Brown, Moses Kirkland, and Joseph Robinson, who ridiculed the members of the commission at every opportunity. Drayton discovered that an article of faith among those he hoped to convert was that "gentlemen" from Charleston were inherently untrustworthy. Years of neglect for the back country's basic needs had left its mark. The opinions of prominent local men who settlers knew and trusted frequently trumped Drayton's fiery oratory.

After a particularly exhausting encounter at King's Creek, where early success had been negated by the influence of persuasive local Tory leaders, Drayton left for the home of Fletchall, still one of the back country's most influential citizens. Fletchall lived near modern day Union, South Carolina on a large estate. A local magistrate and coroner, his militia regiment numbered perhaps 2,000 men. By 17 August, when Drayton and Joseph Kershaw arrived, they were dismayed to find Brown, Cunningham, and Robinson waiting, flushed with excitement over their most recent disruptions of Drayton's tour. William Tennent and Richard Richardson had arrived the night before.

Tennent described Fletchall as "the great and mighty nabob." Had Drayton and Tennent been able to persuade Fletchall to their position, they might have succeeded in their mission, but hours of argument, cajoling, and discussion failed to sway Fletchall. In a letter to the Council of Safety Drayton reported that Fletchall said he "would never take up arms against the King, or his countrymen; and that the proceedings of the Congress at Philadelphia were impolitic, disrespectful and irritating to the King."[12] A drunken Burnfoot Brown and Drayton almost came to blows after dinner, and only Fletchall's intervention prevented a fight. The only small success resulting from this visit was that Colonel Fletchall agreed to muster his militia on 23 August so that the committee members might speak to the assembly.

In the next few days Tennent visited Camden District, where he met with little success, and then moved on to the New Acquisition District (modern day York County, SC). There and in the Thicketty Creek area (between modern Gaffney and Spartanburg) he finally entered welcoming Scots-Irish strongholds. Joseph McJunkin, later an officer in the Spartans and Second Spartans, accompanied the Committeemen through Union, Spartanburg, Laurens, and Chester, and left an account of a stump meeting at Dining Creek Meeting House. There the Loyalists were taken aback by McJunkin's father, Samuel's, response. "The assemblage was larger than could be accommodated in the building. Robinson therefore took his stand upon a rock in the woods, read one of the cutters [pamphlets from the colonial government] and was commenting on its contents. He alluded to the case of Saul and David to show the miseries which result from rebellion. He heaped abusive epithets upon the Continental Congress, George Washington, and the principles they advocated. He stated that when the rascals had involved the people in inextricable difficulties they would run away to the Indians, Spaniards, and Islands. When this last sentence was uttered Samuel McJunkin remarked: 'I wonder where Preachers Joe Robinson and Cotton will then be.'" Robinson was later heard to say, "I would have carried my point if it had not been for that old Scotch-Irish Presbyterian."[13]

Here the settlers were eager to sign the Association. McJunkin recalled that Captain (later Lieutenant Colonel) James Steen of Thicketty Creek could hardly wait to add his signature to the Association. Baptist preacher Oliver Hart's travels led him from Fletchall's home to the Lawson's Fork area, modern Spartanburg, where he and Drayton were welcomed into the home of Captain Joseph Wofford, one of Drayton's business associates. They met with Colonel John Thomas, Sr. who was raising a new regiment, the Spartans, from the Spartanburg and Union areas. Drayton wrote from Lawson's Fork on 21 August 1775: "Every person received satisfaction and departed with pleasure. I finished the day with a barbecued beef. I have also ordered matters here, that this whole will be formed into volunteer companies, but as they are present under Fletchall's command, they insist upon being formed into a regiment independent of him; and I flatter myself you will think this method of weakening Fletchall to be considered sound policy. These people are active and spirited; they are staunch in our favor; are capable of forming a good barrier against the Indians, and of being a severe check upon Fletchall's people, on whom they border. . . . I shall take the liberty of supplying them with a small quantity of ammunition; for they have not one ounce, when they shall be formed into regular companies."[14]

Drayton returned to Fletchall's home for the militia muster, but wrote the Council of Safety that he expected no good to come from the muster. When he arrived at the meeting place with Hart and Tennent, where 1,000 men usually appeared for musters, less than 300 were present. A full contingent of Tory leaders appeared: Robert and Patrick Cunningham, Moses Kirkland, and Thomas Brown, all armed. Drayton must have expected no less; he was armed as well. The meeting nearly degenerated into a riot, but cooler heads prevailed and the meeting was dissolved without bloodshed.

Drayton and Tennent moved on to Ninety Six District and had an enthusiastic rally. Tennent was particularly successful in the Long Canes Scots-Irish community where Andrew Pickens had become a prominent leader after marrying Rebecca Calhoun, survivor of the Cherokee attacks of 1760. Three militia companies were organized, with Andrew Pickens, Champness Terry, and James McCall as captains. Here the travelers heard more rumors: Kirkland was embodying men, the Loyalists intended to attack Fort Charlotte, and rumblings of alliances between the Loyalists and the Cherokee.

It was increasingly clear that talking was insufficient. "William Henry Drayton now proved his mettle. A majority of the Council of Safety was appalled at the thought of civil war. Drayton, however, was a true revolutionary, a man prepared to take the struggle to the bitter end. If he could not persuade, he would force compliance, and one way would be to deprive the Tories of their leaders."[15] Using his broad but ill-defined authority from the Council of Safety, he seized command of all the troops of the Provincial Congress. He ordered Major Andrew Williamson to increase his regiment to 300 men and march to Hardin's Ferry on the Savannah River to guard Fort Charlotte. He ordered Lieutenant Colonel William Thomson to leave Amelia with his Rangers and 300 militiamen from Orangeburgh, and post himself halfway between Augusta and the Congarees region. Richard Richardson was to embody 300 militiamen from Camden and encamp below the mouth of the Enoree River to watch Fletchall and the Loyalists of Dutch Fork. He publicly proscribed Moses Kirkland, offering a large reward for his capture.

Drayton himself took command of 120 militiamen from Fort Charlotte and tried to capture Robert Cunningham at his home. He failed, but seized Cunningham's correspondence and sent it to Charleston for analysis. Moses Kirkland panicked and escaped to Charleston where Lord William Campbell gave him protection. Now Drayton would face Thomas Fletchall, Thomas Brown, and the Cunninghams. Each group mustered their own militiamen. Drayton invited his foes to negotiate because his own support in the Council of Safety was too shaky to risk a defeat; Brown and the Cunninghams refused, but Fletchall agreed. Fletchall had about 1,200 men compared to Drayton's 1,000, but neither wanted to risk a fight. Fletchall and Drayton concluded the Treaty of Ninety Six on 16 September 1775. The Loyalists agreed not to assist the King's troops, while the rebels agreed to punish any of their people who harmed Loyalists. Matthew Patton went to Ninety Six with Captain John Blassingame, and later recalled that "after being in this service a short time Col. Drayton and Col. Fletcher who had command of the Royalists, made a treaty, truce or some agreement, in consequence of which their services were no longer wanted and they then returned home at the end of six days."[16]

Drayton did not deceive himself that he had resolved his problems. Other Loyalist leaders promptly denounced Fletchall in letters to Lord William Campbell. But therein lay a problem. Lord William had dissolved the Assembly on 15 September and fled to safety aboard the 16-gun sloop HMS *Tamar*. With him went the last vestige of British colonial government. The Provincial Congress immediately assumed both executive and legislative power. William Henry Drayton was now arguably the most powerful man in South Carolina, and he would tolerate no more Loyalist dissent.

CHAPTER 5

WAR COMES TO THE SOUTH

We began a contest for liberty ill provided
with the means for the war, relying on our
patriotism to supply the deficiency.
—GEORGE WASHINGTON

CHARLESTON, 28 JUNE 1776

IN 1775 THE BRITISH HAD BEEN PREOCCUPIED WITH
the siege of Boston and defending against an attack on Quebec. The primary 1776 strategic aim would be the isolation of the New England colonies. An attack on New York City would gain control of the mouth of the Hudson River, while a second force would drive the rebels from Canada and move southward via Lake Champlain. The two forces would meet in the Hudson River Valley to complete the encirclement of New England. Since this must of necessity be a summer campaign, the ministers at Whitehall felt the Royal Navy and Army might have time to first go south, mobilize Loyalists, and establish strong bases. Their initial target was Cape Fear but Sir Henry Clinton, commander in the Southern Provinces, and Lord William Campbell, Royal Governor of South Carolina, suggested a change in plan. Clinton had arrived in North Carolina in March, ready to unite his forces with the Scottish Loyalists of North Carolina, Commodore Peter Parker's naval squadron, and General Cornwallis with 2,000 Irish soldiers. Unfortunately the Scots had risen prematurely and been crushed by Patriot militia at Moore's Creek Bridge. Parker's squadron was nowhere in sight, having set sail two months late. News of Charleston's unfinished defenses was persuasive enough to make the city the target of a new strategy.

While the British belatedly set sail for Charleston, the Patriots bickered over its defense. At Sullivan's Island, a barrier island that dominated the mouth of Charleston Harbor, William Moultrie was building a fort of palmetto logs banked with sand. General Charles Lee, sent south to command the defense of Charleston, pronounced the fort a death trap, and ordered it abandoned. Moultrie continued work with the tacit support of President John Rutledge, while Rutledge distracted Lee with designing fortifications for Hadrell's Point. Rutledge's machinations gave Moultrie *de facto* command of the defenses of Sullivan's Island, and placed Lee in charge of the defenses of Charleston proper. At Hadrell's Point were around 3,000 men from the Carolinas and Virginia as a reserve in case Sullivan's Island should fall. Lee reinforced the back side of the unfinished fort with Colonel Thompson's Rangers and Lieutenant Colonel Sumter's regiment of riflemen. Lee attempted to build a pontoon bridge across the harbor in case it became necessary to evacuate Moultrie's men, but the British arrived too soon. Moultrie's final orders were to hold Sullivan Island, prevent Clinton's troops from crossing over from neighboring Long Island, and repel any landing parties. Private William Kenedy: ". . . from hier they were marched to Charlestown to the Barracks. and from then to Hadleys point [Hadrell's Point] was there when fort Moultrie was attacked."[1]

The first British step was to cross the Charleston bar into the harbor south of Sullivan's Island, an operation that required lightening the two larger ships. Soon Commodore Parker's squadron was anchored in Five Fathom Hole, in position for an attack when wind and tides permitted. The squadron consisted of two fifty-gun ships of the line (*Bristol* and *Experiment*), four 28 gun frigates (*Soleby*, *Acteon*, *Syren*, and *Sphinx*), and half a dozen other warships; counting the transports—fifty sail in all. Among the miscellaneous vessels was a sloop with 20 guns, and the bomb ketch *Thunder* used to fire heavy mortar shells. There were 2,500 soldiers and British Marines. The British were considered experts at joint naval and military operations, but the assault on Charleston's defenses went badly from the beginning.[2]

Winds blew in the wrong direction for two weeks so the British could not maneuver ships into the harbor, and Charleston's defenses were more challenging than anticipated. The harbor was protected by low-lying Sullivan's Island, now fortified at one end with Moultrie's fort, and at the other end with artillery and back country riflemen commanded by Colonel William Thomson. The main channel was narrow, shallow, and required a harbor pilot with firsthand knowledge; Parker failed to request that Lord William Campbell, who knew the harbor well, guide the British ships. Campbell instead requested a dangerous position of honor aboard the *Bristol*.

Sir Henry Clinton landed on Long Island just north of Sullivan's Island, and began searching for Breach Inlet where his men might ford at low tide. He had been told that the channel was no more than 18 inches deep, but it was seven feet deep. Thomson moved into position to repel Clinton's expected attack, and used the delay to build trenches and a redoubt.

At 0930hours on 28 June 1776, Parker signaled the attack. Moultrie, who was consulting with Colonel John Thomson at the other end of Sullivan's Island, raced back and warned his gunners to fire slowly and steadily as they had a limited supply of ammunition. They were directed to target the *Bristol* and *Experiment*. "Moultrie had a total of 31 guns available, a mix of British 18-pounders and French 26-pounders (captured by the British from a French warship nearly two decades before, and sent for the defense of the colony). By juggling ammunition, he had a total of 28 rounds (some accounts give a lower figure) apiece for the guns positioned on the critical channel ramparts and its bastion."[3] *Bristol* and *Experiment* took position, affixing spring cables to their anchor lines to allow them to shift firing positions. *Thunder* was the first ship to open fire, and by 1100hours both sides were firing.

Parker intended for three of his frigates to move into the harbor but two of them ran afoul of each other and all three stranded on the same shoal. *Acteon* could not be saved; her crew set her afire and the ship exploded. Parker declined to send any other ships into the harbor. *Thunder* developed a malfunction and ceased firing, but Parker was still confident that his ships could destroy the incomplete Fort Moultrie. The fort's blue Palmetto flag (designed by Moultrie) was sheared off its pole, but William Jasper leapt from an embrasure and seized it. Jasper was helped back over the wall and soon the flag, attached to a makeshift staff, again flew over the fort.

Clinton's attack on the other end of Sullivan's Island degenerated into a debacle. Clinton and Cornwallis assembled as many boats as possible and tried to ferry their men over Breach Inlet. The marshes, shoals and the sea itself seemed to be against them, funneling their boats into one narrow approach, which made them vulnerable to William Thomson's riflemen; losses were heavy, and the attack stalled. Meanwhile Fort Moultrie's sand and spongy palmetto logs continued to absorb the worst of the British bombardment. The fort had done considerable damage to *Bristol* and *Experiment*; shot severed *Bristol*'s springline and made it even more vulnerable to Moultrie's guns. Parker was wounded, Lord William Campbell and two of his captains mortally wounded, and at least seventy men were dead. As night fell, Commodore Parker broke off the action, retrieved Clinton, Cornwallis, and their men, and sailed north.

A letter from a Will Falconer to his brother in Scotland was found on the shore after the British evacuation. "We have been encamped on this island, for this month past. We sleep upon the seashore, nothing to shelter us from the rains, but our coats, or a miserable paltry blanket. There is nothing that, grows upon the island, it being a mere sand-bank, and a few bushes, which harbour millions of musquetoes—a greater plague than there can be in hell itself. By this sloop of war, you will have an account of the action which happened on the 28th June between the ships, and the fort on Sullivan's Island. The cannonade continued for about nine hours; and was, perhaps, one of the briskest, known in the annals of war. We had two 50 gun ships, five frigates from 24 to 30 guns playing upon the fort, I may say without success; for they did the battery no manner of damage: they killed only about fifteen, and wounded between forty and fifty. Our ships, are in the most mangled situation, you can possibly imagine. The Acteon, a 30 gun frigate run aground during the action; and, as it was impossible to get her off, we were obliged to burn and blow her up. Our killed and wounded amounts to between two and three hundred. Numbers, died daily of their wounds. The Commodore, is wounded in two different places; his Captain lost his left arm and right hand, and was wounded in different parts of the body; he lived but two days after the action. Captain Scott of the Experiment died of his wounds; and, a number of officers. If the ships could have silenced the battery the army was to have made an attack on the back of the island; where, they had about one thousand men, entrenched up to the eyes—besides a small battery of four guns, one 18, and three 4-pounders; all loaded with grape-shot. So, that they would have killed half of us, before we could make our landing good. We are now expecting to embark for New-York, to join General Howe with the grand army."[4]

A lucid account from the Patriot perspective is found in the pension application of Charles Brandon. "During this enlistment he was at the battle of Fort Moultrie which was attacked by Lord Parker. . . . The Americans in the fort were commanded by Colonel Rhea, and Francis Marion who had some commission, but he is not positive what was then his rank. The regiment to which he belonged under the command of Col Sumpter was stationed some distance from the fort to watch & count the movement of the British forces under Gen. Clinton who it was expected would land his forces at Bolton Landing on Sullivan's Island to assist the forces who made the attack upon the fort. He however did not land his forces as was expected. During the engagement at the fort which lasted about ten hours the British commander, Parker, was wounded, and his vessel, a fifty gun frigate, was shattered and much injured by the shot from the cannon in the fort. One of the enemys Vessels called the Acteon was abandoned by them & burned the next morning after the engagement."[5]

The second prong of the regional offensive would not falter so easily. Charles Brandon was finished defending Charleston, but would soon be on the march as Sumter's riflemen were ordered to the frontiers to join Colonel Andrew Williamson in the second phase of his fight against the Cherokee.

THE SECOND CHEROKEE WAR, 20 JUNE 1776–MAY 1777

In 1774, after Creek land was taken in exchange for debt incurred by trade, Creek and Cherokee warriors had struck white settlers, and the beleaguered Georgia militia attempted to take revenge. A militia lieutenant named Grant led his men on a raid, and was unhorsed. His men, taking him for dead, left him behind. When the militia party found his body, the *Carolina Gazette* reported that the Indians had tied him to a tree and spent a long afternoon torturing him. Thirty arrows were shot into his body, his genitals cut off, tomahawks struck into his head and body, and finally he was burned to death. The Creeks had ripped his scalp off as a token. The Cherokee were much amused by his wig, and enjoyed displaying it when the story was retold to others.

A second version of Grant's death, published in the *Carolina Gazette* four weeks later, added different details. His body was found tied to a tree, a red hot gun barrel had been rammed into his torso, his scalp and ears removed, a painted hatched left in his skull, twelve arrows in his breast, and a war club left on his body. The *Carolina Gazette* was widely read throughout the back country of South Carolina, and regardless of the truth of the details as news of Cherokee attacks spread, people remembered Grant.

The first rule of Indian warfare was never let them take you alive. The real problem was that no one could predict what the Cherokee would do with prisoners. Some they killed immediately, others were tortured, some made slaves, and still others adopted into families. It was a die no one wanted to cast.[6]

The actual events of the Second Cherokee War of 1776 have long ago passed into legend. Story after story differs in details, but one thing is clear. The settlers on the Carolina frontier were absolutely convinced that the new wave of Cherokee attacks was a second prong of a British attack on South Carolina. Modern historians may differ as to whether it was separate war altogether, but the fact remains that the Cherokees were supplied by the British Indian Agent, John Stuart (saved long ago by *Attakullakulla* and married into a Cherokee family) and his deputy, Alexander Cameron, who lived with his Cherokee wife on the Reedy River in western South Carolina. Both were objects of suspicion to the rebels of Charleston, and Stuart, in fact, had been forced to run away from Charleston's mob and relocate to Florida.

The British arrived in North Carolina in March, 1776, but the tribes did not attack Georgia, Virginia and the Carolinas until the British attacked Charleston, increasing suspicions of British manipulation of the Cherokee. Indian warfare usually consisted of quick raids, ambushes, and avoidance of major battles, and their elusiveness and knowledge of the area gave them an advantage over white settlers. The settlers had greater firepower, operated more efficiently in large units, and preferred to force battles only when conditions were to their advantage; they preferred a reconnaissance-in–force approach that forced the Indians to either stand and fight or abandon their homes and supplies.[7]

The Cherokee and settlers had fought a bitter war in 1760, and each side still nursed grievances, but life after the first war had regained a familiar rhythm. This war would put an end to any semblance of a 'live and let live' attitude. In a brutal, no holds barred conflict nothing and no one were off limits: neither people, livestocks, nor farms or villages were to be spared. The entire frontier became one enormous battlefield.

The settlers viewed the new attacks as proof that the Cherokee were utterly faithless and perfidious. There was a peace treaty in place, and the settlers, at considerable sacrifice, had retrieved munitions destined for the Cherokee from the Loyalists in the summer of 1775. Now the Cherokee were firing on their families with the powder given to them to show the Patriots' good faith.

Loyalist families (apparently at the direction of Alexander Cameron) were directed to mark their homes so that they would not be attacked by the Cherokee. "The Tories set up peeled poles at their houses, around which white cloth was wrapped. These were called Passovers. On June 20, in accordance with some previous arrangements, the Indians commenced the work of death among the Whigs, but the Tories sat under their passovers in safety. To this, however, there was one exception. Capt. James Ford, who resided on Enoree River at a place called the Canebrake, was killed while sitting under his Passover. His wife was also killed and his two daughters taken captives."[8]

As in 1760 the Cherokee first took aim at those settled near or sometimes over the line dividing Indian lands from that of the colonists. An early target was the Hannon family in Cherokee territory (now Polk County, NC). Mrs. Hannon was deceased, and ten-year-old Edwin and his younger sister, Winnie, were minding their two younger brothers, a toddler and an infant. The Cherokee killed their father and five older siblings working in the fields, scalped them, stripped their bodies of clothing and any belongings, and left their nude bodies where they fell. Edwin and Winnie went to investigate the noise from the field. The horrified children tried to slip away quietly when they saw the Indians, but the three-year-old broke free and ran into the open. Edwin followed, picked him up, and ran with the struggling child as the attackers gave chase. Exhausted, Edwin eventually dropped his brother and rolled into a hollow in a nearby riverbank, but not before he heard a tomahawk crunch into his brother's skull, a sound that haunted him the rest of his life. Winnie took the baby deep into a cane brake, and desperately tried to keep him quiet. After the Cherokee left, having plundered the cabin and burned it, Edwin found Winnie, and the children began looking for help. They took turns carrying their infant brother, and near nightfall chanced upon the home of Colonel John Earle, who took them in and later adopted them.[9] The attack led to swift retribution from a local militia group who tracked the war party and killed them.

Traders in Virginia and the Carolinas were also early targets. In South Carolina, Indian trader Jacob Hite, who lived on the Enoree River, thought himself on good terms with the Cherokee, but his home was attacked, and he was dismembered, apparently one joint at a time. His wife, Frances Madison Hite (aunt of future President James Madison), and their two daughters were kidnapped. One girl apparently died in captivity. The other may have been ransomed by a British officer, but later died en route to Pensacola.[10]

The Hampton family settled at the headwaters of the Tyger River— holy ground to the Cherokee. Two of the Hampton sons, Preston and Edward, had been robbed and forced to escape on their last peace mission to the Cherokee. When Preston Hampton saw Cherokees coming toward their home, he sent some children to warn the neighbors before they arrived at the Hampton's home. "As they [the Cherokee] approached Mr. Hampton's house, some of their men recognized the face of Preston Hampton, whom, as we have already stated, had just returned from the Indian towns and had given warning of their intended rising. Some of the children of Mr. Hampton were sent to give warning to the neighbors. Mr. and Mrs. Harrison were, at the time, absent for a short distance. Old Mr. Hampton, it is said, met the Indians cordially. He gave the chief a friendly grasp of the hand, but had not more than done this when he saw his son, Preston, fall from the fire of a gun. The same hand which he had grasped a moment before sent a tomahawk through his skull. In the same way his wife was killed. An infant son of Mr. and Mrs. Harrison was dashed against the wall of the house, which was spattered with its blood and brains. The Indians then set fire to the house of Mr. Hampton. Mrs. Harrison, on coming up, seeing her father's house in flames, came very near rushing into the midst of the savages. Her husband, anticipating what the trouble was, held her back until the savages were gone. Edward Hampton was, at the time, at the house of his father-in-law, Baylis Earle, on the North Pacolet."[11] Another grandson, John Bynum, aged eight, was saved from death by a Cherokee warrior and taken to live with him, and not returned until after the war when the peace treaty specified return of hostages.[12] Preston Hampton's wife was found days later, wandering with her clothing in rags. The Indians had raided her home as well, killing her two children; she never recovered her mental faculties.[13]

Any stragglers not safely in a fort became fair game. James Reed, a traveler from North Carolina, was attacked at a ford on the North Tyger River. He took two bullets but wrestled the tomahawk from the hands of an attacking Indian, at which the Indian ran away. Another traveler, Mr. Miller was attacked at Buffalo Bridge on the same river and killed. His two companions, Orr and Leach, ran up the south side of the river in an attempt to escape. Indians hiding beneath the bridge fired at the men, who then ran headlong into a marsh. Orr leapt over part of the marsh and continued running. Leach fell into the marsh and lay still, apparently saved by his lack of athletic prowess. The Indians thought him dead, and pursued Orr, who they scalped and killed.[14]

A war party again attacked Long Canes, killing most of the members of Aaron Smith's family: parents, at least four children, and five slaves. Young John fled to the home of Francis Salvador, who wrote William Henry Drayton on 18 July: "Dear Sir, You would have been surprised to have seen the change in the country, two days after you left me. On Monday morning, one of Captain Smith's sons came to my house with two of his fingers shot off; and gave an account of the shocking catastrophe at his father's. I immediately galloped to Major Williamson's to inform him; but found another of Smith's sons there, who had made his escape, and alarmed the settlement.

"The whole country was flying; some, to make forts—others, as low as Orangeburgh. Williamson was employed night and day, sending expresses to raise the militia; but, the panic was so great, that the Wednesday following, the Major and myself marched to late Captain Smith's, with only forty men. Then next day, we were joined by forty more; and, have been gradually increasing ever since; tho' all the men in the country were loath to turn out, till they had procured some kind of fancied security for their families. We had, last night, five hundred men, but have not been joined by any from the other side of the river [Saluda.][15]

Williamson had called up the militia, but the men of Ninety Six District were busy moving their families to forts and stockades or toward the low country. Militia duty had to wait. Williamson was also unaware that his own emissary to the Cherokee, Captain James McCall, had been ambushed and captured on 26 June. Some of McCall's men straggled back into Ninety Six by mid-July. The Cherokee thought McCall too important to kill, but they forced him to watch the execution of others while they pondered his fate. McCall later recalled the death of a twelve year old boy. "Warriors suspended the boy off the ground between two poles while they tossed burning darts into his body. Whenever one succeeded in sticking a dart without extinguishing the fire, the whole crowd shouted and clapped. This terrible scene went on over a two hour period before the boy died."[16]

Salvador's letter to Drayton alluded to another attack by Cherokees and Loyalists on Lindley's (Lyndley's) Fort in modern day Laurens County on 15 July. The fort was filled with local families and about 150 militiamen including James Williams and part of the Little River Regiment. The commander, Major Jonathan Downs, was able not only to defend the fort, but brought his men out to chase down some of the Loyalists. Painted with vermilion and dressed Indian style, "white Indians" are treated as mythical by some sources, but are mentioned repeatedly in contemporary letters and pension applications. Patriot militiamen attributed this to an effort to hide their identities, but it seems equally likely that they were ensuring their Cherokee allies could distinguish them from the Patriots.

Major Williamson had called out the Regiment of Ninety Six immediately after the Smith family massacre. When only forty men responded, he moved to a plantation a few miles below De Witt's Corner (modern day Due West), and camped on Hogskin Creek. By 8 July he had 222 men, and by 16 July, 450 militiamen.[17] On 19 July Williamson wrote to Drayton: "I am now, encamped here, with about seven hundred effective men, from this regiment; which with 130 who do duty in the different fort, you'll perceive, have turned out pretty well. My numbers would soon increase, if I had arms.

"Captain Tutt's and Princes' companies of riflemen, have just now joined me; they consist of ninety-three effective men: and to-morrow, Col. Williams (who has been at least fourteen days contriving a mode to cross Saluda River) will also join me, with about two hundred men. Captain Hammond marched off with a detachment of one hundred picked men, on Friday morning, for Pearis's house where I am informed, a party of the enemy has been skulking about some days past. I expect, hourly, to hear from him, and some agreeable news. He has my orders, if he can conveniently join Colonels Thomas and Neel, to act in concert with them, and proceed directly into the nation by Estatoe; while I penetrated by way of Seneca, and the Sugar Town. Thomas, has acted in every respect, agreeable to his declaration when at his house—I have wrote and sent him express upon express, to no purpose; it is really disagrreable to have any connection with such men; he has not wrote me a line since the Indians first commenced hostilities. Lieutenant-Colonel Polk, of Neel's regiment, with three hundred men well armed, has joined Thomas; . . . [18]

Crown Indian agent John Stuart had warned that a Cherokee attack on the frontiers would be disastrous for the tribe, and in fact Loyalists began to join (or sometimes be impressed into) Patriot militia companies. A common need for defense among the Patriots and Loyalists led to this alliance of erstwhile enemies. Two unwelcome Loyalists offered their aid: Richard Pearis rode down from his plantation on the Reedy River, while Robert Cunningham, recently released from prison, asked Williamson for permission to raise his old company. Williamson sent both men packing. He had good reason to distrust Pearis, but he wrote the Council of Safety that although he believed Robert Cunningham's intentions to be good, it seemed unwise to place him in a position of trust. Williamson's distrust of Pearis seems warranted. "It is interesting that while Pearis accompanied Cunningham to visit Williamson, several Tories who had attacked Lindley's Fort were sheltered at his property near the eastern boundary of the Cherokee Nation (proximate to what is now the outskirts of Greenville, South Carolina). Those Tories were the 'party of the enemy' Williamson referred to in his letter [to Charleston], and they used Pearis' place as a base camp while they continued to attack Whig settlers around the area."[19] In a letter to William Henry Drayton on 22 July, Williamson noted: "Pearis' house having been a rendezvous for Indians and Scopholites, Colonel Thomas intended to attack it on Monday . . . one of our spies was there on Tuesday . . . and all the buildings in ashes."[20]

By the end of July Williamson had over 1,150 men and marched a few miles to DeWitt's Corner to meet more. Colonel Thomas and Colonel Neel's regiments were instructed to go straight to the Indian Nation by way of Estatoe while he led a force to Esseneca. Samuel Otterson recalled

". . . that under said Captain MacKee as First Lieutenant he went on an expedition against the Cherokee Nation of Indians the Regiment to which his company belonged was commanded by Colonel John Thomas and that regiment and a regiment commanded by Colonel Neille left Prince's Fort as well as he recollects sometime in July or August"[21] Williamson's men began their march toward the Cherokee Nation, but received word from spies that Indian Agent Alexander Cameron was camped on the Keowee River, and Williamson took a detachment of 330 well-mounted men in an attempt to surprise Cameron. Moving directly up the Keowee Path, Williamson camped on the Keowee River that night and attempted to ford the river before dawn.

Williamson was ambushed by a large force of Indians and Loyalists, led by Cameron himself, according to some accounts, and positioned in the fortified village of Esseneca on the east bank. The Indians and Loyalists had daubed the openings between the rails with dirt and plant matter to camouflage the pickets. Williamson's smaller force, confused and outnumbered, was saved by the prompt action of Captain Le Roy Hammond, who with twenty men rushed the palisades, firing point blank at the defenders and employing their bayonets. The rest of Williamson's men re-formed, and were relieved by Andrew Pickens who raced up with the rest of their party. From high ground Pickens' men fired down upon the defenders. In the initial melee Francis Salvador was shot and unhorsed; he was scalped and left for dead by the Cherokee. The Indians fell back after dawn, and Williamson's men cautiously advanced toward the river and found Salvador still living. He died soon after, the first Jewish Patriot to die in South Carolina's Revolution. Finding the east bank village deserted, Williamson's men torched it. Le Roy Hammond crossed the river alone, as another ambush was a real possibility, and ensured that the west bank village was empty; it was destroyed as well.

Williamson then led another force of 640 men in burning the Lower Towns. The main town of Keowee was put to the torch, as well as groves of peach and apple trees and cornfields, and all livestock were slaughtered. Obliteration of the other Lower Towns—Chehohee, Estatoe, Eustash, and Tugaloo—followed. John Hall: ". . . we marched from Col. Thomas' Mill the place of Rendezvous and where we were encamped about one month— to the Cherokee Nation—before we got to the nation we were joined by

Col. Neill off of the Catawba—we destroyed a great many Towns by burning, cut down their corn and did them all the damage we could—one of the Towns was named Eastatoa where we were stationed."[22] In this expedition Joseph McJunkin ". . . served under Capt. Joseph Holly [Jolly] in Col. Thomas' regiment. Williamson's command first met the Indians at Parris'; they, and a few tories with them, fled. They were pursued to their towns on Seneca and Tugaloe rivers. Many skirmishes and battles ensued, in one of which, . . . they came up with a party of Indians who had with them as a prisoner, an old lady of the name of Hite, . . . when they found they would be overpowered, they stripped and killed her. Her naked body was recognized by her nephew, Edward Hampton, and covered with his hunting shirt."[23]

On 10 August Williamson's advance force had begun to ford the Tugaloo River, when a party of Indians and white men opened fire on them. The Patriots rapidly retreated to the South Carolina side of the river where they and their comrades kept up a brisk fire on their opponents. Under cover of that fire Williamson sent other men across the river in canoes he found nearby. When he had about 220 men across the river, they attacked the enemy party, driving them from the river. No bodies were found, and the Indians made their escape.[24]

On 12 August Andrew Pickens and a picked group of 25–35 men set out on a reconnaissance. No more than two miles from Williamson's camp they were ambushed at Tamassee (Tamassy, or Timmosa Old Town) a village within sight of Tamassee Knob (Oconee County, SC). As they made their way through a cornfield a party of nearly 200 Cherokee opened fire. The Cherokee ran forward to encircle the militiamen, and Pickens yelled for his men to form a circle. Pickens divided his men into a double ring. The men on the inside would fire, fall to the ground and reload, while the men in the outer circle stood and fired. They fell down in turn to let the inner circle fire. Fighting on both sides was fierce, as the encircled men desperately fought for survival. Fighting became hand to hand. One Indian attacked a white man, and as they fell to the ground struggling, the Indian said, "Brother, enough,":—but his antagonist answered him, "You will never have enough while you are alive," and in his own defence, put him to instant death."[25] The previous version of this fight was published in 1821, but a subsequent version seen first circa 1850, included considerably more egregious violence including the Patriot cursing while gouging out his opponent's eyes and bashing in his brains.[26] Whatever, the truth of these stories, Pickens' response to the attack bought the trapped men time enough for his brother, Joseph Pickens, to hear the gunfire and rush to their aid. The Cherokee exchanged fire with Joseph Pickens' men, and then retreated into the woods, but Pickens lost six men and five more died of their injuries. The Cherokee lost 65 men, and left 14 wounded men behind. Pickens' buried his dead in the abandoned houses of the village, and then set the village on fire.[27]

From Tamassee, Williamson's force marched toward the Blue Ridge, mercilessly slaughtering livestock and burning fields and towns. Having destroyed all the Lower Towns that regularly threatened Ninety Six District, Williamson turned his men back toward Esseneca. The Cherokee of the Lower Towns had sustained crippling losses of fighting men, had been deprived of an effective base for mounting raids against the settlers, and faced the oncoming winter without food or shelter.

Williamson apparently felt that he and his men were finished. It is a terrible irony that these farmers' own fields lay neglected while they destroyed the work of other men, and it certainly wasn't the Cherokee who were the only people facing starvation. James Caswell of Ninety Six District had written William Henry Draper in July: "Ninety Six is now a frontier. Plantations lie desolate and hopeful crops are going to ruin. In short, Dear Sir, unless we get some relief, famine will overspread our beautiful country."[28] Nonetheless, Governor John Rutledge ordered Williamson to remain in place and coordinate with General Rutherford of North Carolina, as the Continental Congress had ordered the Indians utterly destroyed. North Carolina, Georgia, and Virginia militia had been mustered to cooperate with the South Carolinians. Colonel Jacks of Georgia marched south down the Chattahoochee River. Rutherford with some 1,900 militiamen had orders to destroy the Middle Settlements, while the Virginians were told to assemble at Fort Patrick Henry on the Holston River and attack the Over Hill Towns.

At Esseneca Williamson began building Fort Rutledge, and in mid-August sent men home to acquire winter clothing, provisions, and to gather more recruits. Samuel Otterson: ". . . we moved down the river to Seneca on the Seneca River and remained there some Time preparing to take a tour to the middle settlements and valleys. . . ."[29] Captain William Young recalled that, "He was marched under the same Captain Lewis [Bobo] to Ellis Fort where they met Colonel Brandon [Major Thomas Brandon] and two other companies one commanded by Captain Gordon, the other by Captain Lisle—That they marched from there to the Cherokee Nation to a place called Keewee—there we joined our General Andrew Williamson's Brigade"[30] In later years the formidable Lieutenant Colonel Joseph Hughes could not recall his exact age at the time of his first campaign: "He entered the service in the militia of South Carolina at the commencement of the war between fourteen and fifteen years of age attached himself to and was enrolled in Captain Joseph Jolly's company roll at the Seneca towns on the Seneca River . . ."[31]

The impatient Williamson was told to remain in place until Sumter's riflemen could march back from Charleston, and on 12 September Sumter and 270 riflemen finally reached Esseneca. The next morning Williamson's men marched through the burned out Lower Towns to the foot of Oconee Mountain, stopping at Estatoe Old Town. Williamson formed his troops into three columns, the left wing assigned to Le Roy Hammond, the center to Colonel Thomas Neil, and the right wing to Lt. Col. Thomas Sumter. By 17 September they were at the Narrows, the spot where Montgomerie and Grant had been ambushed in 1760 and 1761. This time there was no ambush, and they moved on to the Connutee River where they hoped to meet General Rutherford. William Young: "We were to have met at or near where we had the skirmish with the Indians Col Rutherford and his troops but did not meet him . . ."[32] Andrew Pickens was dispatched to find Rutherford, and Williamson moved his force cautiously along the Little Tennessee River, and then down the Coweetchee into a narrow gorge called the "Black Hole."[33]

Joseph McJunkin: "After passing through several deserted Indian towns, Williamson's command passed a part of the North-Carolina army encamped, who reported that their main body had marched against the valley towns. Soon after passing them, on the 22nd of September, the advance of Williamson's army fell into an ambuscade prepared for the North-Carolina army. The Indians were posted on the crest and sides of a mountain, in the form of a horseshoe. Williamson's advance defiled through the gorge, which might be called the heel, and were suffered to approach that part which may be called the toe."[34] Williamson sent Sumter's wing to the right, in charge of the baggage train, and to act as a reserve. He sent Hammond to the left toward the base of the mountains with orders to swing back toward the middle. Williamson moved through the middle with Colonel Neil of the New Acquisition District militia. When Colonel Neil's force neared the mountains, Colonel Edward Hampton apparently saw the Cherokees first. Terrified of being surrounded and then cut off in the gorge, Williamson sent men to bolster the baggage guard, as loss of provisions in this situation meant certain disaster, while his second in command, Le Roy Hammond, sent detachments to climb the mountains, gain elevation on the Indians, and attempt to turn their flanks. Edward Hampton, with twenty men, advanced directly on the enemy, and passed the main advance guard of one hundred men. The advance guard, panic stricken, was rapidly retreating. "Hampton, however, clambered up the assent, with a manly presence of mind; which much encouraged all his followers, calling out 'Loaded guns advance, empty guns fall down and load: 'and being joined by thirty men, fell desperately on their foe. The Indians now gave way; and a panic passing among them from right to left, the troops rallied and pressed them with such energy, as induced a general flight; and the army was thereby rescued from a total defeat and massacre."[35]

The battle raged on for two hours, but the terrain left no option except moving straight ahead up the mountainside, often fighting hand to hand. Hampton's furious charge and the efforts of Hammond's men slowly turned the tide of battle. As the flankers gained elevation, and Hampton's furious direct attack forced the Indians to give way, the Cherokee faded back into the mountains, leaving most of their own baggage behind. It is said that among the Cherokee Edward Hampton killed that day was one wearing his brother Preston's coat. Alexander Cameron escaped and was thought to be on his way to Mobile. His race was not run, and the Patriots would meet him again.

Descriptions of this desperate action by the participants are somewhat laconic. Joshua Palmer: "In May 1776 I was drafted and joined the Company Commanded by Captain Jolly in Colonel Thomas' Regiment, and marched to Prince's Fort and thence pursued the Indians to the neighboring towns, and having destroyed them returned to the Seneca Fort, and after joining with other forces crossed the mountains and had an engagement with the Indians . . ." William Young recalled "That they marched from there to the Cherokee Nation to a place called Keewee—there we joined our General Andrew Williamson's Brigade—from there marched up into the nation, met the Indians and defeated them." Samuel Otterson succinctly described the engagement as "severe"; Joseph Hughes simply noted that he was in only one engagement after joining Williamson's brigade at Seneca.[36]

Williamson moved up to the Hiwassee River where his men visited destruction on all the Valley Towns, and then turned south down the Nacoochee Valley. Sumter was ordered to burn Frog Town. Joseph McJunkin: "We then joined General Rutherford about the first of October, a detachment of which was commanded by Colonel Thomas Sumpter was sent to a place called Frog Town where we burnt and destroyed the Indian towns . . ."[37] They then destroyed all the fields in Frog Town Valley and the next day, burned Chotee, the old Cherokee capital on the headwaters of the Chattahoochee.

Andrew Williamson and his men began their march toward home. They had defeated the Cherokee in at least five pitched battles and burned 35 towns. Their victory had been overwhelming, and that winter an unknown number of Cherokee men, women, and children perished from starvation and exposure.

As the South Carolinians made their way home, the Virginians were on their way to the Overhill Towns (Overhill referred to towns west of the Appalachians) to destroy Tellico, Settico, Chilhowee and Big Island Town. With them was Williamson's missing envoy, James McCall, who had been hidden in the Overhill Towns by his captors. Having escaped on horseback without a saddle, a nine day ride led him toward Virginia and William Christian's troops. He would serve as a guide on their mission to the Overhill towns.[38]

In May of 1777 William H. Drayton, Andrew Williamson and a number of other officials from Georgia and South Carolina met with Cherokee officials at DeWitt's Corner and negotiated a treaty. The Cherokee ceded essentially all their ancestral lands south and east of the Blue Ridge Mountains. "At this treaty they gave up their prisoners, and amongst them the daughters of Capt. Ford, who said that their treatment among the Indians, after their first initiation, *by washing and whipping*, was very kind. These young ladies were very remarkable for their beauty; they were afterwards the wives of William Ford and William Mitchusson. The murder of their father and mother, and their captivity, carried many a tory into the ranks of Williamson's army, and probably made some of them staunch defenders of their country's rights. Their brother, James Ford, and the husband of one of them, William Mitchusson, are still well remembered as determined whigs in the darkest period of the night of the British domination in South-Carolina."[39]

Although a frontier war with the Cherokee and Creeks might seem of small moment in the greater picture of the American War of Independence, it caused previously unallied back country settlers to question the wisdom of entrusting their lives to the British government. The short term consequences for the Cherokee were terrible, but the long term consequences would ultimately be far worse. Indian depredations reported in newspapers were seen throughout the colonies, and certainly contributed long term toward a negative view of not just Cherokee, but all Native American tribes.

THE FLORIDA FOLLIES, AUGUST 1776–AUGUST 1779

In the aftermath of the Second Cherokee War many of South Carolina's Tories fled to East Florida, where Alexander Cameron joined his superintendent, John Stuart, in Pensacola. Stuart organized a militia regiment called the West Florida Rangers, and Cameron and Richard Pearis were named as captains. Thomas "Burnfoot" Brown, in St. Augustine, recruited a militia regiment from refugees, the Florida Rangers. Generally known as Brown's Rangers, Governor Patrick Tonyn placed them under the command of General Augustine Prevost who employed them for scouting, raiding, and building strongpoints.

Following the British attack on Charleston, Jonathan Bryan, a Patriot leader from Savannah, came to see General Charles Lee to make the case for a campaign against the Tories of East Florida. Lee agreed, and on 8 August set off for Florida with troops from North Carolina and Virginia. President Rutledge of South Carolina ordered Colonel Moultrie to take his men southward to support Lee. At Savannah Lee received word that he had been recalled to Philadelphia, so he marched his troops back to Charleston, where he was replaced by General Robert Howe. Moultrie and the South Carolinians were left behind in Savannah. While the Cherokee campaign and this campaign were going forward, the Continental Congress established a national army, and on 20 September the General Assembly of South Carolina attached its six regiments to the Continental Army. This change caught Francis Marion and his 2nd Regiment—in Sunbury with Colonel Moultrie—and Thomas Sumter's 6th Regiment unawares.

Marion returned to Savannah, and General Howe left Captain Richard Winn and his company of Thomson's Rangers to hold Fort McIntosh on the Saltilla River. On 23 February 1777 a courier reached Savannah with the news that Winn was under attack by Brown's Rangers. Before Marion could relieve Fort McIntosh, General Prevost sped to the aid of Brown, and Winn was forced to surrender. An infuriated Francis Marion returned to Savannah, then to Charleston on 18 March 1777.

Sumter continued campaigning in Florida, moving down to Sunbury and garrisoning the fort. He pursued Colonel Fuser to Fort Howe and from there to Fort McIntosh on the Saltilla. He went no further when Georgia politics became too Machiavellian for the South Carolinians to bear. Button Gwinnet of Georgia and Brigadier General Lachlan McIntosh, commander of the Continental Line of Georgia, engaged in a power struggle that climaxed with a duel in which McIntosh killed Gwinnet. Revolted by the whole affair, General Howe ordered Sumter's 6th Regiment back to South Carolina in early May of 1777.

In 1778 John Rutledge was succeeded as President of South Carolina by Rawlins Lowndes. Rutledge had always hoped for reconciliation with Britain, and he resigned after a revised constitution made it clear that the state no longer sought reconciliation. Lowndes reorganized the militia under three new commanders, Stephen Bull, Richard Richardson, and Andrew Williamson. Williamson's orders were to guard the frontiers against the Indians and to cooperate with Patriot forces in Georgia.

In the spring of 1778 General Howe, with the enthusiastic support of President Lowndes, decided to again campaign against the Loyalists of Florida. On 19 April he ordered Colonel Charles Cotesworth Pinckney and the 1st Regiment to Savannah, followed by Thomas Sumter and his 6th Regiment. On 13 May Howe arrived at Fort Howe on the Altamaha River. The remnant of Fort Howe was too small to serve effectively as a base of operations so Howe moved his men to an open field above Reid's Bluff. There was insufficient food, few kettles for boiling water and cooking, and a scarcity of tents. John McCracken recalled that ". . . his father often talked of the scarcity of provisions in the Florida expedition."[40] Illness rapidly followed the inadequate hygiene and lack of proper cooking facilities: the troops came down with dysentery, and that misery was followed by epidemics of malaria and yellow fever. Healthy men began deserting, and were chased down by officers and returned to camp.

Despite it all, General Howe continued moving southward, and on 14 June reached Old Town on the Saltilla River. He moved down the St. Mary's River toward Fort Tonyn, but "Burnfoot" Brown and his Rangers set the fort afire and rejoined General Prevost. Howe waited at Fort Tonyn for the militia. When they arrived General John Houston of Georgia refused to put his men under Howe's command. Brigadier General Andrew Williamson arrived on 8 July, and took the same stance as Houston. The campaign fell apart from bickering among the commanders.[41]

Joseph Hughes: "Soon after his return [from the Cherokee campaign] he was sometime in the service in Georgia without being in any engagement when General Williamson commanded an expedition to Florida. He thinks in that expedition Major Brandon commanded Col. Thomas' regiment & is not positive whether Captain Jolly or Captain Palmer commanded the company that he went in. In that expedition tho he believes that Palmer did. In passing Georgia her militia joined Williamson. The only Georgia officer he recollects was Col. Twigg who commanded in some way & this expedition was as well as he recollects in 1778 and started from early in the spring until late in the fall. The army suffered much from heat, hunger, and thirst, and had no general engagement except for one skirmish on the River Santilles with an infamous Tory (commonly known by the name of) Burnfoot Brown & his party."[42]

Robert Long of the Little River Regiment recalled that "The object of this campaign was to take St. Augustine. We crossed Ogeechee, at Gov. Wright's plantation, and he forded at the precise time of the notable eclipse of the sun, 24th June. July 4th over Cat Head Swamp had 13 guns fired there for independence; 2 or 3 days after, crossed the Altamaha river, then Little Satilla and Great Satilla, then St. Mary's. Gen'l Robert Howe, of the Continentals, with 3 or 4 regiments of South Carolina regulars were there, as also Gov. John Houston, Georgia. His army was composed of regulars, minute men and militia.

"Gen'l. Williamson's army consisted of Col. Hammond's regiment commanded by himself and Major Pickens; Col. [John] Winn's, commanded by himself; Col. Goodwin's, the same; Col. Thomas' regiment commanded by Maj. Thomas Brandon; Col. Lyle's by himself, and Williams as above, amounting, as was said, to 1,200 men. Had no fighting except that Col. Clarke did at Brown's Battery on Alligator Creek. Major Pickens was sent there with 500 men. Brown was gone. A council of war was called, and they determined to return home, where we arrived 14th August, being about four months out."[43]

William Beard: "I then went home and shortly afterwards volunteered with our whole company under Captain Irwin a second time and went to Whitehall, at which place half of Captain Irwin's and half of Captain Logan's companies were joined together and made one Company, I fell to Logan and went to Florida under him and remained there three to five months. I cannot recollect the precise time and fought the British Tories and Indians between St John's and St Mary's Rivers; we lost a great many men (one thousand I think). We were commanded by Generals Williamson and Pickens, Col. Brandon and Major Purbas [Purvis]—Major Purbas never showed himself;—Williamson was highest in command but Col Brandon had the honor of the battle. The enemy was under Colonel Brown I think. After the battle at St. John's I returned to 96."[44]

The three-year-long Florida Follies were finally finished. Sir Henry Clinton was set to launch his Southern Campaign, and soon Florida and Georgia would be reclaimed by the British. Now the local militias would have to shift gears. Offensive campaigns against Florida were pointless; all they could do was try to stop South Carolina Tories from joining the British in Georgia and Florida.

Samuel Otterson noted ". . . after the division of Col Thomas' Regiment which was as well as I recollect in the latter part of the Year 1778 [Marked out] or early in 1779 I was frequently under Col. Thom. Brandon To whose regiment I then belonged in scouting parties. During one of these scouting parties, we intercepted & took 20 or upwards Torys who were on their way to St. Augustine to join the British Army. These we took to General Williamson's camp on Savannah River opposite to Augusta & he sent them to the Jail at Ninety Six."[45]

As Otterson indicated, in 1778 the Spartan Regiment was divided into

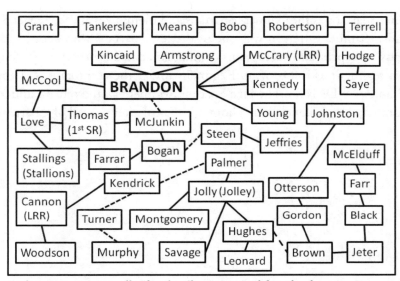

Militia units were usually "family affairs" recruited from local communities which often consisted of families who had intermarried for generations. This chart depicts some of the established and probable (dashed) family relationships within the Second Spartans and the closely-aligned First Spartans (1stSR) and Little River (LRR) Regiments. Most families had numerous members serving in the regiment.

the First and Second Spartan Regiments, but the precise date of the division is unknown. Samuel Otterson recalled it as "late in 1778." In one memoir Joseph McJunkin placed the division prior to the end of the Florida Campaign: "About this time the Spartan Regiment was divided and the Regiment under the command of Colonel Thomas Brandon was called the Second Spartan Regiment to which I was attached. I was again called out under the command of Colonel Thomas Brandon on a Tour of two months and was ordered to Stono and marched as far as Bacon's Bridge and was dismissed by the last of June 1778."[46] But in an affidavit related to John Jolly's pension application, McJunkin states that "the next tour of service done by John Jolly was in the Florida campaign. Deponent was not with him but knows John Jolly was out four months in Captain Joseph Jolly's company of Col Thomas' regiment."[47]

There are no records suggesting discord over command, and the division seems to have been geographical, as soldiers frequently referred to the

First Spartans as the "Upper" Spartans and themselves as the "Lower Spartans." Samuel Otterson was one of the few Spartans who kept his commission papers, and his captain's commission dated February 1780 denotes his regiment as the Spartan Regiment under the command of Thomas Brandon, 2 Division. The First Spartan Regiment would remain under the command of Colonel John Thomas, Sr. until after the fall of Charleston.

CHAPTER 6

THE GEORGIA CAMPAIGN, 1779

It is far better to be alone, than to be in bad company.
—GEORGE WASHINGTON

FOR THE BRITISH, THE WAR IN THE NORTHERN AND central colonies was not going nearly so well. In New Jersey George Washington's army was proving to be an elusive foe, and in the autumn of 1777 Crown forces suffered a stunning defeat in upstate New York. A British army under General John Burgoyne, moving south from Canada to sever the troublesome New England colonies from the rest, was soundly defeated near Saratoga, in part because of poor coordination with British forces in southern New York.

Burgoyne narrowly prevailed in the first battle at Saratoga (Battle of Freeman's Farm on 19 September), but the two armies remained in close proximity. The overall American commander, Horatio Gates, played only a limited role in the actual conduct of the battle. When Gates—whose interests lay more in political intrigue than military service—claimed sole credit for the unexpectedly good performance of the American forces, it infuriated his senior aide, Benedict Arnold, who was considered one of the most promising officers in the Continental Army. Growing acrimony between Gates and Arnold ultimately resulted in Arnold's dismissal.

On 7 October the two armies clashed again at Bemis Heights, where Arnold unexpectedly appeared and though wounded, distinguished himself on the battlefield. Another Patriot leader of distinction was Daniel Morgan. Bemis Heights was a dreadful defeat for the British. On 17 October Burgoyne surrendered some 5700 men, and the fragments of his shattered army limped back to Canada.

The Saratoga episode would have far reaching consequences in many different ways. Gates' continuing intrigues led to Benedict Arnold's ultimate treason, his offer to betray the defense of the crucial Hudson River defenses at West Point to the British. The very talented Daniel Morgan quit the army in disgust, depriving Washington of two of his ablest officers.

Gates claimed full credit for the victory, and would be rewarded by Congress with higher command. Sensing an advantage, Gates—with the collusion of influential New England members of Congress—began plotting to supplant Washington.

The French, ever on the alert for a British fumble, recognized American independence on 9 February 1778. The entry of France, with its large army and powerful fleet, changed the entire balance of power. Thwarted at every turn, now locked into a war with France that threatened the lucrative British West Indies colonies, Parliament and the King's advisors groped for a new strategy to end the stalemate.

Loyalist exiles in London convinced influential members of Parliament that Crown sentiment in the South was overwhelming, and a new Southern Strategy gradually took shape. The primary British effort would now be directed against the wealthy southern colonies, drying up rebel funds from the rice and indigo trade. Loyalist militias would flock to the King's banner to subdue the rebels and secure the southern colonies, freeing the regular army to sweep northward and "roll up" the rebellious colonies from Georgia to Virginia. Deprived of foreign revenue and food resources from Virginia, the rebellion would quickly collapse.

In December 1778, execution of the new British strategy began auspiciously. Forces were sent south by sea, and marching north from Florida. This resulted in the easy recapture of Savannah with minimal losses, and the following month Augusta was retaken. The British were confident that Georgia would remain within their grasp so long as they held these two cities—Savannah because it was the most populous and a port, and Augusta because of its location on the Savannah River as a gateway to Cherokee and Creek territories. With Georgia secure, South Carolina lay before them, ripe to roll up as the next step in the subjugation of the southern colonies. Lieutenant Colonel Alexander Innes, aide to Sir Henry Clinton and previously secretary to the deposed Provincial Governor, Lord William Campbell, was appointed to govern Georgia. All colonists were to gather ". . . guns, ammunition and other military accoutrements and surrender them to a commissary. He also enjoined the inhabitants to reveal where arms or military stores were hidden."[1] Colonel Archibald Campbell and Commodore Peter Parker extended a proclamation of protection on 4 January 1779; those who wished protection were to swear an oath of loyalty. To help govern Savannah and administer the oaths, additional troops would be required. Loyalist companies were formed into a new regiment, the South Carolina Royalists. The British also sent Loyalist John Boyd on a successful mission to recruit Loyalist militiamen from Georgia and North Carolina.

Andrew Pickens was besieging Fort Carr in Georgia when he received word from his brother, Joseph, that Colonel John Boyd was marching through Ninety Six District with 800 Loyalists recruited in North Carolina, and that they were laying waste to the property of Patriots as they came. More important to the Pickens family, they were headed for Long Canes Settlement, home of the extended Calhoun and Pickens clans. Robert Long: "Having heard of a refractory spirit North (of) Enoree river, in now Spartanburg. Maj. [Colonel] Brandon and Captain Palmer had been sent with 30 men to allay it, but the Tories were then too numerous for them. Capt. Greer, having notice, raised 30 men to reinforce them, of whom he was one, when there was found that they amounted to about 500. We got reinforced to about 250 in two or three days, and pursued after them, crossing Saluda, Little River and Rocky river to Savannah river. Col. Pickens defeated them in Georgia. Set out about the 7th of January, 1779, and got home about the 13th February—37 days on horseback."[2]

KETTLE CREEK AND BRIER CREEK, 14 FEBRUARY–3 MARCH 1779
Pickens halted the siege of Fort Carr, and moved back across the Savannah River toward home. Receiving word that Boyd was moving toward the Cherokee Ford[3] on the upper Savannah River, he dispatched Captain Robert Anderson of the Upper Ninety Sixth Regiment to cross the river and harass Boyd as he attempted to cross into Georgia. Anderson complied, although the tall canes on the riverside saved Boyd's force from much injury; Anderson retreated and rejoined Pickens. On 10 February Pickens and Georgia Militia Colonel John Dooly crossed the Savannah River again

and met Colonel Elijah Clarke's mounted militia. On the morning of 14 February Pickens moved forward with Dooly on his right wing, Clarke on his left, and his Regiment of Ninety Six in the middle. A reconnaissance by James McCall reported that Boyd was camped in a field by Kettle Creek, horses loose and grazing, while the Loyalists killed beeves. Pickens attacked immediately. Boyd took advantage of fence rails and fallen wood for cover, so Pickens maneuvered his regiment right of the fence onto high ground, while Dooly and Clarke fought their way through a canebrake to join him. Fighting was vicious and hand to hand, but the Patriots overcame the Loyalists. At the height of the battle Boyd was felled by three rifle balls.

In a somewhat garbled narrative, Thomas Davis placed himself and several officers of the Second Spartans at the battle of Kettle Creek. "The year that the Tories broke out of North Carolina and passed through South Carolina . . . he volunteered into the Militia, as he believes, for a tour of three months. . . . His officers were, as well as he remembers, Captain William Grant, Lieutenant Colonel James Stein [Steen], and Colonel Brannum [Brandon], who were all volunteers. The company of volunteers marched into the state of Georgia to near Briar Creek. At Savannah River they overtook the Tories and had an engagement in which our men were [worsted]. Several of our men were wounded but none were killed. The next day we attacked them at Kettle Creek in the state of Georgia and routed them—killing about 15 of their number and among them Colonel Boyd who commanded them."[4]

The victory at Kettle Creek was followed by an equally devastating defeat on 3 March at Brier Creek. British General Archibald Campbell trapped John Ashe's North Carolinians on marshy ground at the confluence of Brier Creek and the Savannah River. Pickens and his Ninety Six Brigade were attached to Ashe. The humiliating defeat assuaged British pride and humbled the Patriots. Mayfield Crane: ". . . entered the service about . . . under Capt. Thomas Branon [Colonel Thomas Brandon], Col William Farr [not yet a colonel] and Lamuel Jackson Lieutenant—does not recollect the other officers names, says that he was [hired] or served as a substitute this Tour for another man & was about Twelve or fourteen years of age, & continued in service about Twelve months. Had one Skirmish during this tour in which our captain and forces were defeated & himself together with the rest of the men returned home, says this battle Took place on brier creek in Georgia, & that It was with a company which had detached Itself from the main body—says there was 3 or 4 killed & several wounded."[5] The result of this defeat "removed a corps from the American Army and it left north Georgia exposed to inroads of the Loyalists."[6]

Following the battle at Kettle Creek, Pickens' prisoners were marched back into South Carolina and jailed at Ninety Six. On their passage through South Carolina, Boyd and his men had looted and wrecked Patriot property, and the emotions of the moment demanded punishment. Governor John Rutledge ordered a special commission to try the prisoners on charges of treason instead of theft and mayhem. Seventy men were convicted and sentenced to hang. All the sentences were commuted except for seven whose crimes were judged most outrageous. The executions set a precedent in the increasingly violent struggle as South Carolina lurched toward civil war. The British and Tories would soon follow suit, executing Patriot prisoners.

Georgia settlers were increasingly concerned about Indian hostility, and on 21 March 1779, British Indian Agent John Stuart died. His department was divided between two agents: Alexander Cameron would supervise the western section (Choctaws, Chickasaws and neighboring tribes), and Thomas "Burnfoot" Brown would supervise the eastern section (Cherokees, Catawbas, and Creeks). Brown called for 800 Cherokee and Creeks to assemble at Augusta. Brown's deputy and Alexander McGillivray, the chief of the Creeks, began a march toward Savannah. Andrew Pickens, Colonels John Dooly, Benjamin Few, and Le Roy Hammond joined forces and went after the Indians. The first Indian camp they found was deserted, but the Patriots followed their trail and killed several; none made it to Brown's camp.

General Benjamin Lincoln was operating from a base in Purrysburg, South Carolina, and his Continental Army force was roughly the size of the British forces under General Prevost. Lincoln's army included militia from both Carolinas and Georgia, and he had his militiamen monitoring the Savannah River crossings between the coast and Augusta. This concentration of forces caused the British to abandon Augusta, so Lincoln now felt confident enough to tighten the cordon around Savannah. On 1 March his officers voted to leave a guard of 1,000 militiamen at Purrysburg, while Lincoln marched on Augusta to deprive the British in Savannah of supplies and contact with their Indian allies. Unknown to Lincoln, the British were already in desperate straits for supplies. Major General Augustine Prevost saw his opportunity when Lincoln moved toward Augusta, and moving 2,500 troops into South Carolina, he drove the militia commanded by William Moultrie to the gates of Charleston.

Matthew Patton: ". . . on or about 17th March 1779 he went out as a captain under Col. William Wofford; that they marched near Augusta and left their baggage wagons and crossed over into Georgia and scoured the country until about the first of May when they heard of Lincoln's approach. They were then ordered to recross the Savannah River and join Lincoln. They swam the River near the mouth of Briar Creek and passed through Ashes' Battle ground on the 1st of May 1779. They were ordered to scour the country between Saltcatcher and Savannah River and to be on the tract [track] of Provost. They left Purysburgh to the right and recaptured about a thousand Negroes which had been taken by the enemy; and near Edisto William Young or William Cunningham was made prisoner."[7]

On 10 May companies from the two forces skirmished at Ashley Ferry, seven miles from Charleston. On 11 May the British crossed the Ashley River, surrounded the forts guarding Charleston, and Prevost peremptorily demanded the surrender of the city. While General Moultrie and Governor Rutledge contemplated the humiliating terms, Prevost intercepted a message: Benjamin Lincoln was marching back from Augusta. Prevost retreated, leaving a rearguard of about 900 men commanded by Lieutenant Colonel John Maitland behind at Stono Ferry.

STONO FERRY, 20 JUNE 1779

Stono Ferry was an hour's march from an important bridge and the Charleston road, and was the ferry used to cross the Stono River from the mainland to John's Island. Some Second Spartans recalled leaving Union in the spring for service in Georgia as part of the force stationed on the South Carolina side of the Savannah River, and many of these men fought at the Battle of Stono Ferry. Aaron Guyton: "In March or April of 1779 he was drafted or called out under Captain James Steen under Col. Wofford [Wofford may actually have been Brandon's Lieutenant Colonel] marched to Augusta Garrison to Ogeechy: then returned into S.C. to join Genl. Lincoln. Meet Lincoln at Parkers Ferry on the Edisto, continued with him until after the Battle of Stono 20th June. At this tour Zac Bullock was

Major of the Battalion a few days after the Battle was discharged having served out the tour of three months."

Prevost had moved his men off the mainland onto James Island, and Maitland's position was "located on the mainland bank of the river and was approximately seven hundred yards [640m] long. It was perhaps 175 yards [160m] deep, and protected on its right side by marsh. Dense woods bordered the road coming from Rantowles Bridge."[8] Slaves impressed from neighboring plantations built an abatis around three strong redoubts. The defenders included Highlanders of the 71st Foot and Hessians of the Regiment Von Trumbach, along with Loyalists. On 20 June Lincoln attacked after an eight-mile night march from the Ashley Ferry (now Drayton Hall). He would advance from the mainland while Moultrie would cross the river and pen up Prevost's forces. Near dawn the British pickets were fired upon, and by dawn both sides were blazing away. Attacking on the left ". . . were light infantry, a large body of militia, and the mixed-forces, infantry-cavalry 'legion' commanded by the Polish officer Casimir Pulaski; attacking its right were the Continentals and light infantry, commanded by Brigadier General Isaac Huger of South Carolina. A force of Virginia militia made up the American reserve."[9]

As the day went on casualties from artillery fire mounted on both sides. Heat claimed even more victims, including Hugh Jackson, brother of future President Andrew Jackson. The Patriots fought their way to the abatis and engaged in fierce hand-to-hand combat, destroying two companies of Highlanders, but Maitland was able to bring his faltering Hessians back into the fight.

An elderly Simon Davis garbled some names of senior officers, but stated: "I am not able to give the date I served the tower [tour] under Captain William Grant and Major Joseph Jolly we was ordered on to Charleston so we passed on through Granby Orangeburg four holes* and Dorchester to the 10 Mile House above Charleston . . . from that place we was marched on to Stono where the battle was fought it was Close Cutting with me to see my comrades falling on both sides of me. I escaped without a wound from that place."[10]

---

*Four Hole Swamp is a tributary of the Edisto River, and a bridge across the stream was a well-known site.

Captain Matthew Patton: "Nothing more of importance occurred until they met Genl. Lincoln or his troops at Bacon Bridge in the Spring of 1779 when the enemy made an attack on their picket guard and then deponent first saw Count Pulaski. And on the 20th June 1779 he was at the Battle of Stono where deponent was engaged & acted in carrying off one field piece & Adjutant Davie who was wounded in the thigh. They and the enemy retired neither having obtained the victory; that he was out in this campaign about four months and returned home about the 16th of July 1779."[11]

William Moultrie had been unable to find enough boats to relieve Lincoln; low on ammunition, Lincoln withdrew. Maitland charged, but the militia of Virginia and the Ninety Six Regiment covered the Patriot withdrawal. Casualties were high on both sides.

Joseph Hughes, then a member of Palmer's company, may have summarized the action at Stono Ferry most aptly: "The next important service was under General Lincoln from the North who commanded the expedition against Stono in South Carolina. He was in that engagement a desperate conflict. It was his regiment commanded Brandon there as Colonel and his company by Captain Palmer. Many were killed in this engagement and neither side had the advantage. Not much good however was done for our cause."[12]

THE SIEGE OF SAVANNAH, 16 SEPTEMBER–20 OCTOBER 1779
Benjamin Lincoln's hopes for wresting Savannah back from the British now depended upon French cooperation. The commander of the French fleet in the Caribbean, Charles Hector Theodat le Comte d'Estaing, had risen rapidly through the ranks of the French army, and then switched to the navy, and at age forty-eight was made a vice-admiral in 1777. Assigned to aid the American rebels, he failed to capture Newport, Rhode Island when a gale disrupted his landing operations. True to the practices of the times he then concentrated on picking off the rich British West Indies colonies, capturing St. Vincent and Grenada in July 1779, and defeating a British fleet.[13]

Wary of the unpredictable hurricanes that wracked the coast in summer, d'Estaing had for most of the season kept his ships safely in harbor at Cape Francois in Hispaniola (modern day Cape Haitien, Haiti). Receiving plaintive letters from the Patriot leadership and Msr. Plombard, the French consul in Charleston, d'Estaing saw an opportunity to redeem his campaign. Braving the storm season he sailed from Haiti in late August, and the first of his ships arrived off Savannah on 4 September.

In an unaccustomed flurry of activity the South Carolina legislature dispatched liaison officers and boats to assist in landing operations. The British, caught completely by surprise, were granted a reprieve when storm winds temporarily scattered the French fleet. During the reprieve the British struggled to consolidate forces scattered about Georgia and South Carolina, without complete success.

Since December 1778 the British had neglected the defenses, but now frantically set a horde of slaves to work constructing a semicircular line of fortifications around the city. Bottled-up British ships were stripped of their guns to construct shore batteries, and several were scuttled in channels to prevent the French from bringing ships through the maze of waterways to bombard the town. Outlying buildings were torn down to clear fields of fire in the marshes south and west of the city.

The Americans were in no better condition, struggling to assemble Continentals from South Carolina and Georgia, State Troops, and militia. For the militia, fighting far from home was not an attractive proposition and apparently most were drafted. Samuel Mayes was a typical militia draftee, ". . . at that time about nineteen or twenty years of age, & was living with his father. . . ." With no formal military training, he was scooped up and marched south.[14]

Abel Kendrick: ". . . I was drafted for a three months tour as a private militiaman into Capt. William Grant's Company, marched to Fairforest and joined Col. Brannon's [Brandon's] Regiment. . . ." William Young said "That he was again ordered out & marched from the district on Ninety six to the siege of Savannah about the middle of Sep. 1779 under the command of Col. Thomas Brandon who was his Col. While he had the command of a captain in said Regiment. . . ."[15]

Impatient and worried about the exposure of his ships to storms and attack, on 16 September d'Estaing belatedly summoned General Augustine Prevost to surrender the city and its garrison of 1,700 troops. Indicative of the problems that would plague the operation, Patriot leader Thomas Pinckney advised d'Estaing that the British garrison at Beaufort SC could be readily cut off and prevented from reinforcing Savannah, but ". . . the Count was too great a man in court, in camp and at sea, to take advice from any one; he was too sure of success."[16]

Stalling for time to allow the 800 reinforcements from Beaufort under Lieutenant Colonel John Maitland to join him, Prevost engaged in a lengthy exchange of communiqués with d'Estaing. By mid-day on 17 September Maitland had crossed the Savannah River by boat and was safely inside the defenses. Prevost was at last confident of his ability to withstand an attack.

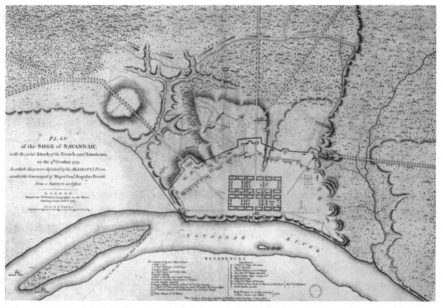

The siege of Savannah was the first experience of European-style warfare for most of the militia. The main militia attack was directed against the British position at the left of this map drawn by British Major General Augustin Prevost.—NARA

Admiral d'Estaing settled in for a siege. On 22 September the siege, with its formalities of bombardment by guns dismounted from the French ships and sorties by the defenders, commenced. The drier, more open ground to the east of the city was reserved for the French forces, while the western end of the line in more swampy ground was reserved for the Americans.

Brigadier General Andrew Williamson had brought 212 men of the

South Carolina militia, including five companies (Captains Robert Faris, William Grant, Nathaniel Jeffries, Robert Montgomery, and William Young) from the Second Spartan Regiment. Many of the South Carolina militiamen were assigned peripheral duties to support the siege. Lieutenant Colonel Charles Sims was sent ". . . with a hundred men to guard a pass on Steven's Creek, in Edgefield. The weather was hot, the place sickly . . . his men were all with himself soon down with the fever. He was afterward disposed to charge Gen. Pickens with a want of regard to the welfare of his men. Being relieved he made his way home. . . ."[17]

Aside from disease, even in the midst of the campaign the usual problems of turnover plagued the militia commanders. Shadrach Gibbs had enlisted in the militia in the Spring of 1776, and in March 1779 had entered a third term of service as a substitute for another man. ". . . in the fall of 1779, the detachment to which I belonged was ordered to Savannah he served this tour under Captain Jeffries, John Davidson, Lieutenant, Ensign not recollected. Brandon was our Col. and Grant our major." (Like many applicants Gibbs alternated between referring to himself in the first and third persons.) Gibbs' term of service expired while the regiment guarded Dawson's Ferry, a Savannah River crossing, but he again extended his service as a substitute.[18]

The expiration of so many enlistments required reorganization of companies, and Private Samuel Mayfield later recalled that ". . . he was one of the soldiers engaged in the courageous but unsuccessful attempt to recover it [Savannah] . . . the captain that commanded him at the battle was Gilky—(he thinks his first name was Jonathan)—this happened from several companies or parties it being drafted from headquarters to form a company for when he left home he was commanded by Captain Montgomery; who in detailing out the men lost his command & he returned home. . . ."[19]

Ten days of cannonades and muddy trenches was as alien to both the personal and cultural experiences of the militia as was possible. Interestingly, the militiamen who were at Savannah thought little of it compared to subsequent actions, and their comments on it tended to be terse.

Days of artillery exchanges resulted in limited damage to either sides' positions, though carcasses (incendiary shells) fired by the French artillery burned sections of the city. Admiral d'Estaing was increasingly apprehensive: his sailors were starving and scurvy-ridden aboard their poorly-provisioned ships, diseases ravaged the camps, and the fleet was under constant threat from storms and potential British naval attack with most of his ships' cannon ashore. With the concurrence of American Major General Benjamin Lincoln, d'Estaing organized a full-scale assault for 9 October.

The main attack would be executed by the French. Americans would form a second wave to support the French and Continentals. Five hundred militiamen under Isaac Huger would infiltrate the swamps along the river, and make a diversionary attack on the left, to be exploited only if successful.

The night before the attack an American deserter from the Charlestown Grenadiers betrayed the entire plan, in detail, to the British, who reinforced the threatened positions. The militia and other Patriot troops assembled at 0100hours, but the guides lost their way in darkness and dense fog. The militia waded through a half-mile (800 meters) of stinking muck in the rice fields, but still managed to attack on schedule.

Abel Kendrick was typical in that he did not think much of the battle; he ". . . attacked the British forces in the city, but were repulsed and compelled to retreat." Private Lewis Turner later recalled that "The fight commenced on Sunday morning about the break of day; the British were too hard for us we had to retreat" in the face of heavy musket and artillery fire. Samuel Mayfield said that "In this attack of Savannah he received no wounds but many of his comrades fell around him." Captain William Young recorded that the militia ". . . made a charge on the British redout after being exposed to the fire of the army for some time were repulsed with great loss. . . ." Huger's militia had lost 28 men and quickly recoiled from the attack.[20]

The carnage was vastly worse in the main attacks. The French and Patriot units lost cohesion struggling in the wet ground, became entangled in the defensive abatis, and were raked by musket fire and grapeshot. Units that gained the front slopes of the British positions were met by massed point-blank fire. Twice-wounded, d'Estaing still hoped to reorganize and press the attack, but the defensive fires were too much. After nearly an hour of brutal punishment, the senior Patriot officer forward, General Lachlan McIntosh, with two regiments of South Carolina Continentals, ordered a retreat. The mutilated bodies of French and Patriot troops were strewn over the defensive ditch and parapets of the defenses, and hanging from the sharpened stakes of the abatis.

This engraving from a painting by A.I. Keller accurately depicts both militia supporting an attack by French troops, and the clothing of the militia. The final assault at Savannah, the single bloodiest day of the war, does not figure prominently in the memoirs of the militiamen who were there.—NARA

John Jeffries related his involvement to James Saye. "I was at the Siege of Savannah. I knew Rhd. [Richard] Saye, of the Irish settlement on Fairforest, & went in the same battalion with him. He was shot when the assault was made on the British works & mortally wounded. When word came to the place where I was stationed that he was wounded & needed help taking him in, four of us went—Matthew Robinson was one, I another. When I first saw him, the holes in his breast & back were stopped with sassafras leaves. We carried him a mile on a blanket. James Lusk drew a will for him that night, and understood that he died that night at 10 o'clock. As far as I know of him, he was highly respected & did his duty well."[21]

Little-remembered today, it was the bloodiest single day of the entire war. Prevost recorded only 103 killed and wounded and 48 deserters. D'Estaing reported 760 French enlisted men and 61 French officers dead or wounded, and 312 American casualties. Many of the wounded, including Polish-born Count Casimir Pulaski, the "father of American cavalry," later died. Amid the carnage Pulaski's death was one of the few that left a lasting impression, as recorded by Mahlon Pierce: ". . . Count Paleski with his legion of horse was there & was killed . . . The American troops were repulsed with considerable loss." Over General Lincoln's objections d'Estaing broke off the siege, and on 1 November the last French ship sailed away. The Patriot forces withdrew into South Carolina.[22]

The end result of the disastrous battle was that the British were able to secure Georgia and reestablish Crown government, making Georgia the only independent state to revert to colony status. Despite the nominal protection of British troops, Loyalists burned and plundered the homes of Patriot families, and drove many from the state. The die-hard "Georgia refugees" retreated into South Carolina. The British would one day come to regret the alienation of these refugee militiamen.

In the chaos, men from far and wide entered militia service, or stayed in service for self preservation. John Jeffries ". . . did a tour of duty, & was stationed at Ten Mile House under [Lieutenant] Col. Steen."[23]

Henry Deshasure had enlisted as a Continental in Virginia, and marched south to Savannah where he was transferred to the 3rd Georgia Regiment. He retreated to the vicinity of Augusta, where after Savannah ". . . while making a bridge across Brier Creek the British troops got in our rear and we had to retreat and I had to swim Brier Creek and the Savannah River and we again rendevouzed at [illegible, probably Mulberry grove] in South Carolina and again retreated to Augusta where I was discharged at the expiration of my time and on my way home at Saluda River I was taken prisoner by the Tories who stripped me and took and destroyed my discharge. I was detained as a prisoner about one week when I made my escape and in the neighborhood of a Colonel Branham [Brandon], I volunteered in Captain Hughes' company of s[ai]d Brandon's Regiment of the South Carolina militia. . . ."[24]

CHAPTER 7

THE BRITISH ASCENDANCY

*Never were men or women less
dainty and more courageous.*
—BENJAMIN WEBB

THE FALL OF CHARLESTON, 12 MAY 1780

THE LESSONS OF THE FAILED ATTEMPT TO CAPTURE
Charleston were not lost on Lieutenant General Sir Henry Clinton, and
he arrived in Edisto Inlet on 11 February 1780 at the head of 14,000 troops
supported by a fleet of 90 ships. Moving slowly and systematically, Clinton
took seven weeks to close a ring around the city. On 3 April Clinton's engineers commenced the construction of siege works, and on 9 April favoring
winds allowed Admiral Mariot Arbuthnot's fleet to run past Fort Moultrie
and anchor in a position to bombard the city.[1]

For a time the British blockade remained porous, and some Patriot
reinforcements were able to slip through. Other units marching toward
Charleston arrived too late to penetrate the British lines, but fought vicious
small engagements on the periphery, so Clinton sent forces inland to cut
Patriot routes into the city. On 13 April Lieutenant Colonel Banastre Tarleton's British Legion captured a rebel slave courier and learned of a force
of local militia and cavalry encamped at Monck's Corner, under instructions to hold open a last potential route into or out of the city. In a pattern
that would become all too familiar, Tarleton roused his troops early, and
at about 0300hours on 14 April launched a surprise attack on the Patriot
camp. The ensuing rout was a minor skirmish, but it severed the Charleston garrison's last potential escape route.

The ruthless Lieutenant Colonel Banastre "Bloody Ban" Tarleton was a favorite of Cornwallis, and his brutal Green Dragoons were the bane of the militia. This 1782 portrait by Sir Joshua Reynolds, from a painting in the British Museum, is romanticized; fellow British officers described him as pudgy and somewhat homely. After his massacre of surrendered American Continentals at The Waxhaws, "Tarleton's Quarter" became a Patriot rallying cry.—NARA

Tarleton's Loyalist British Legion was destined to earn a controversial place in history. A composite of several older Loyalist units from New Jersey, New York, and Pennsylvania, it was a brigade, or "legion" in the vernacular of the era, that included cavalry, infantry, and a small contingent of light artillery suitable for fast-moving independent operations. Tarleton quickly earned a position as one of Cornwallis' most trusted subordinates, and his "Green Dragoons" (from the color of their uniforms) equally quickly earned a reputation for looting, rape, and indiscriminate murder.

In the end Charleston's defenders were simply outgunned. The British bombarded the city with incendiary carcasses around the clock. Fire from skilled artillerists targeted areas where firefighting crews were operating, and systematically wrecked the defenses. Supplies of beef and pork were found to be spoiled, and the garrison and civilians were reduced to a diet of rice and sugar.[2]

Unknown to the defenders, a large French fleet was en route to break the siege, and Clinton considered a retreat. However, after six weeks of relentless shelling Benjamin Lincoln surrendered the city on 12 May. Among those who escaped capture was Lieutenant Colonel Francis Marion. He had broken an ankle (the circumstances are unclear and romanticized), and had left the city to recuperate.

Many of the back country units were—fortunately—slow to arrive. Joseph Hughes ". . . was called out to defend Charleston. But by the Time Brandon's Regiment reached Congaree news came that Charleston was defeated this was in May 1780 about this time he received a commission signed by Governor J Rutledge of first Lieutenant in Captain Benjamin Jolly's company in Brandon's Regiment called the Spartan Regt–Second Division . . . then after the news of the fall of Charleston reached Col Brandon he marched to Camden for the purpose of securing ammunition. . . ."[3]

The consequences of the surrender were far-reaching, since it included many of George Washington's most experienced Continentals who had been dispatched south to counter Clinton. Lieutenant Governor Christopher Gadsden signed the articles of capitulation.

There are few drawings of the hunting clothing worn as the uniform of the militia, and many of the few that do exist are highly romanticized. This depiction of a Virginia militia rifleman drawn by a US Army artist in 1890 correctly depicts the clothing and equipment. Note the recognition marking on the hat, necessary since Patriot and Loyalist militias wore the same "uniform"—NARA

The surrender of Charleston and the fall of civil government threw the militia into disarray. Two companies of the Second Spartans were in the vicinity of Charleston, the rest still marching south. In February Matthew Patton had entered service as a captain in Major Zecheriah Bullock's battalion of Brandon's regiment. He was ". . . stationed about two miles below Augusta in Georgia until a few days before the surrender of Charleston S.C. on the 12th day of May 1780 when upon receiving the intelligence through [dispatch rider] Samuel Clowney that all communication with Charleston being cut off by the enemy, the companies stationed below Augusta were disbanded by General Williamson & remanded to their respective regiments. . . ."[4]

The destruction of Lincoln's army at Charleston boded well for British success in the South, but a series of fumbles derailed the plan. The enlistment of a sizeable force of Loyalist militia to both provide an army of occupation and assist in rolling up other rebellious colonies was essential to the Southern Strategy. The problem was that since the 1775 subjugation of the Tories the rebel militias had gained combat experience in the Florida campaigns and at Savannah while the Loyalists had lain low.[5]

On 22 May 1780 Major Patrick Ferguson was appointed Inspector General of Militia to raise and train Loyalist units in the back country. Ferguson was ahead of his time in understanding the uses and limitations of local troops in counterinsurgency warfare, and understood the culture of the militia. He advocated the traditional model of locally-recruited militia, election of officers by the men who knew them best, and advised to use "Great caution in disciplining these men." He gained little traction within his own command structure.

THE WAXHAWS MASSACRE, 29 MAY 1780

A small command of inexperienced Virginia Continentals and a small artillery contingent under Colonel Abraham Buford was tardy in reaching Charleston. After the surrender Buford's command, some North Carolina militia, some Virginia State dragoons, and Governor Rutledge began to retreat toward North Carolina. Rutledge went on ahead of the slow-moving column, as did the North Carolinians.

Clinton was determined to destroy the last remnants of the Patriot forces, and dispatched Charles Cornwallis for the task. Cornwallis in turn assigned Tarleton's Legion to pursue Buford. Unable to overtake the Patriot column with his full Legion, Tarleton formed a detachment of horsemen from the 17th Light Dragoons and mounted infantry from the Legion for a faster pursuit.

On 29 May an advance party of Tarleton's troops overtook Buford. Tarleton uncharacteristically parleyed for surrender, but stipulated that no further offers of surrender would be entertained. Buford declined, and resumed his march. In mid-afternoon Tarleton overtook and captured Buford's rearguard, and horribly butchered one Patriot officer. Tarleton overtook Buford's main force in mid-afternoon, and both sides deployed for battle.

The inexperienced Virginians got off one volley before Tarleton's dragoons rode them down. There are conflicting accounts of what transpired after most of the Patriots threw down their weapons in surrender. Tarleton himself, ever the master of self-justification, wrote that ". . . a report amongst the cavalry, that they had lost their commanding officer, which stimulated the soldiers to a vindictive asperity not easily restrained." At any rate, Tarleton's dragoons continued to hack at those attempting to surrender, and even the wounded on the ground.[6]

The lopsided toll was seventeen British casualties to 113 Patriots killed outright, 150 wounded (many later died), and only 53 taken prisoner. Tarleton has his apologists, but whatever the facts the news of the massacre sped through the colonies and as far as the over-mountain communities of present-day Tennessee. "Buford's Play" and "Tarleton's Quarter" became Patriot rallying cries in the savage partisan war that followed. It would not be the last incident of mindless savagery on the part of Tarleton's Legion.[7]

In the aftermath of the fall of Charleston and the rebel government, many rebel militia leaders accepted British parole, among them Thomas Sumter, Andrew Pickens, and John Thomas Senior of the First Spartans. Among those who refused parole were Colonel Thomas Brandon, Colonel James Williams of the Little River Regiment, John Thomas Junior (who had assumed command of his father's regiment), and the die-hard Georgia refugees.

On 5 June Sir Henry Clinton set sail back to more comfortable New York, but before he departed he created a perfect storm. By decree South Carolina was to be considered a conquered province subject to martial law.

Clinton reinterpreted the articles of capitulation as *not* including the residents of the back country. As of 20 June the paroles of Patriots not captured within Charleston were invalidated, and all male citizens were instead required to pledge to take "*an active part in forwarding military operations,* or be considered and treated as rebels against his majesty's government." A 25 July proclamation prohibited any who had not accepted these terms from selling property, practicing professions, or collecting debts. The requirement to fight on behalf of the occupiers drove many paroled Whigs back into active resistance.[8]

Charles Cornwallis was appointed commander upon Clinton's departure, and he was having none of Ferguson's plans for the militia, preferring "men of property and substance" as militia officers—regardless of competence or experience. Various Whig partisan commanders like Francis Marion immediately pounced upon these novices.

Atrocities committed by vengeful Loyalists and opportunistic bandits rampaging around the countryside turned even more Whig parolees into active partisans. Cornwallis was left in charge of an unfunded army that had to support itself on the backs of the citizenry, in a land wracked by plagues, runaway slaves, and banditry to which the British Army turned a blind eye.

BRANDON'S DEFEAT (8 OR 10 JUNE 1780)
AND THE PRESBYTERIAN WAR

The ascendancy of the British army pushed many Tories who had been cowed by the Whigs off the fence of convenient neutrality. As Patriot officer Joseph McJunkin described: "When the news of the fall of Charleston reached the up-country the Whig population was greatly alarmed. And their consternation was by no means abated by the accounts of ravages committed by the victorious troops of Britain and the insolence of the Loyalists who thought proper no longer to disguise their devotion to the royal cause. As a large number of these had hitherto maintained a strict neutrality under the pretense of being non-combatants and as they now entertained but little doubt of success on the part of the British, they must need display a great zeal for the party in power to cast the veil of oblivion over their past lukewarmness, and meet the agents of despotism as though they were and ever had been the very champions of England."[9]

It quickly turned out that British parole offered no actual protection. The British army would not stop the emboldened Tories from plunder and murder, and the British army was no better. Among many depredations, Tarleton did not even think burning Sumter's plantation worthy of mention in his diary. Pickens' home met the same fate, and John Thomas Senior was summarily clapped into prison. The British had an idea of exploiting victory that alienated the populace.

Not all the Whigs had abandoned the region west of the Broad River. In early June Brandon and about a hundred followers were engaged in a three-fold mission: secure their stocks of munitions, recruit new men, and try to subdue the local Tories to keep them from aiding the British.

Joseph McJunkin: "Cols. Thomas [Junior], Brandon and Lysle [James Lisles] met on June 4 to concert measures for mutual safety and for the protection of the country comprehended within their several commands. They agreed to concentrate their troops and form a camp near Fairforest Creek, about four miles from the present site of Union, on the road to Adam's Ford on Tyger River. . . . As the place was near the center of Brandon's command, his men first arrived on the ground.

"He [Brandon] had in his possession a part of the powder formerly intrusted to Col. Thomas, and as he considered its preservation of the greatest importance, he directed Joseph Hughes, William Sharp, John Savage, Aquilla Hollingsworth, Samuel Otterman [Otterson], Benjamin Jolley and Joseph McJunkin to conceal it with great care in the neighboring forests. They were engaged in this business and absent from the camp on the night on which Brandon's men were assembling at the place appointed." Brandon also had the additional munitions confiscated from Camden after Charleston fell.[10]

The second task was to recruit, and the site was near the center of Brandon's potential recruiting district, while still removed from the residences where Tories would first search for them. The usual practice was to assign subordinate officers to scour the countryside seeking out good Whigs for enlistment, and Thomas Young (who was not at the fight, and uncertain of some key details) said that ". . . Col. Brandon was encamped with a party of 70 or 80 whigs, about five miles below Union court-house, where Christopher Young now lives. Their object was to collect forces for the approaching campaign, and to keep a check upon the tories."[11]

The exact location of Brandon's camp is unclear. Given the physical description and the distance from Union, the likely site of the ford was where the marshy valley of Fairforest Creek narrows and the stream has a rocky bottom, slightly upstream of where Sardis Road (State Road 44-16) now crosses the stream. Both banks of the river are heavily dissected by ravines. Statements such as that of Aaron Guyton say that ". . . . we was about eighty or one hundred men of us. we was Between fair forest and tygar Rivers. . . ."[12]

Of those actually there, Samuel Otterson was the most specific about the date, placing it on ". . .the eighth or tenth of June. . . ." According to Aaron Guyton ". . . we was about eighty or one hundred men of us. . . ," but some sources say Brandon had only ten or twelve men (our accounting demonstrates at least thirteen) going about normal morning camp chores.[13] Guyton said that on the morning in question "Corl Brandon of our ragimt was our Commander, Moses Guyton leuetaenant of our Company. . . ." According to McJunkin, "Intelligence of the intended movements of the Whigs had been conveyed to the Little River Tories a few days previous by Col. Fletchall, and [William] Cuningham made immediate arrangements to meet them at that place."[14]

Brandon was holding a prisoner brought in by one of the recruiting parties. McJunkin: "Some one of the parties coming in arrested a Tory and brought him into camp. He was of the kind then denominated 'a pet Tory.' He was examined and presently let go or made his escape. He went immediately to the troop of Tories commanded by the famous William Cunningham, better known as 'Bloody Bill.' Cunningham immediately set out to surprise Brandon." Thomas Young later said of the captive, "They had taken prisoner one Adam Steedham, as vile a tory as ever lived. By some means Steedham escaped during the night, and notified the tories of Brandon's position."[15]

Bloody Bill struck with his usual violence, and in overwhelming force. McJunkin: "He made a charge upon [Brandon's] camp soon after sunrise, killed a few of his men, took some prisoners and dispersed the remainder." Guyton: " . . . a large Body of torys come on us commanded by Wilm Cunningham and defieted us with loss of some killed and some taken prisoners. . . ."[16]

The action probably lasted a matter of minutes. A few Patriots who managed to mount horses tried to distract Cunningham's men, but five were killed. The men on foot dove into the adjacent ravine, too densely wooded and with sides too steep for Cunningham's horsemen to follow. John Jeffries: "I was in Brandon's defeat, June, 1780, where several of our men were killed, & a number taken. I made my escape in company with a number of others."[17]

Joseph McJunkin: "Among the slain was a brother of Joseph McJunkin and a youth by the name of [John] Young. . . . Robert Lusk was taken prisoner on this occasion and compelled to disclose the place where the powder was concealed. But the work of hiding had been done so effectually that the Tories found very little of it. This powder was afterward carried off by stealth to the east side of Broad River and constituted the principal supply of Sumter's men at Huck's Defeat, Rocky Mount and Hanging Rock. The Tories pursued some of the fugitives to the distance of fifteen miles. Among them was Samuel Clowney, who subsequently distinguished himself as one of the bravest of the brave."[18]

Daniel McJunkin was wounded and left for dead. "In the rout, he was overtaken by a British officer, who ran his thrust sword through his body. The blade entered between his shoulders, and came out in the breast, and came so far through that McFunkin [this second-hand source consistently misspelled the name] caught it and held it tight in his agony. The officer said to him: 'My good fellow, if you will let go, I will draw it out, and give you as little pain as possible.' He did do and the officer putting his foot against McFunkin's shoulder, as he sat on his horse, extracted the sword upon which McFunkin fell to the ground."[19]

William Sims—a boy of nine or ten years at the time—said of his father, Charles Sims (paroled after the Georgia debacle) that "He was not at Brandon's defeat, but hearing of that affair, went up & buried the dead &c. My mother attended to these wounded at that time. I remember Danl. McJunkin was run through with a sword—he suffered a great deal, but recovered. I have always felt a great regard for him, having been a witness of his great sufferings." Despite paroles, men like Charles Sims were not safe from Tory depredations. "He returned home, but was obliged to be concealed in the woods to escape the vengeance of the Tories. He had been instrumental in the condemnation and execution of a notorious Tory of the Fair Forest region. It was on this occasion that he was taken in, out of the woods, and protected by a good Quaker, old Eli Cook, who lived near the old Quaker Church on Tinker's Creek – a kind and humane man."

The Sims family fared no better in his absence, as bands of Loyalist partisans scourged the countryside. The raiders arrived at the Sims home and "Mrs. Sims having come out, he ordered her to prepare to leave the premises; he wished to put in her home one of the King's Men. Besides her own children, she had then with her her daughter Mrs. McDaniels and her two children. 'How can you require this of me, sir? You have driven off my husband, you have taken my horses and negroes.' 'That is not my look-out, madam; I will give you a week to move, if at the end of that time I find you here, I'll lock you up in the house and burn you in it.'

"An old man named Freelove Gregory, a non-combatant, hearing of her situation, [later] came down with some slides [crude sleds] and moved her and her effects some 15 miles away to Brown's Creek. . . . Lee and his party now plundered the house and while in the act, Mrs. Sims remembered that the McJunkins and Hayes, who lived some six miles higher up the creek, had just come in from their hiding places to see their families; she knew that not a man of them would escape the merciless swords of the Tories if they were caught. She called her son, W^m. Sims, then a lad of 12 years, to her, and whispered 'My son the McJunkins and Jollys are all at home, and will be taken by Lee if not apprized in time of their danger: can't you very soon run there by the path a nearer way than the main road, and tell them of their danger.' William at once consented to go, though it was already nearly dark, and the way a wilderness, full of wolves and other beasts of prey. He set out at once in a full run. He said the wolves soon began to howl around him, but grasping an old jack-knife he had in his pocket he felt quite safe. When he arrived at McJunkins, the family had just sat down to supper, their arms were lying by them, and their horses saddled in the stables, ready for a surprise. He rushed in out of breath, and exclaimed 'men, the Tories are coming.' They were soon in the saddle and running for a shelter, but had hardly disappeared on one side of the house before Lee and his scout came in at the other. Young Sims had hurried on to tell the Jollys of the impending danger. They all escaped and doubtless owed their lives to the intrepidity of young William Sims, for the Tories thirsted for their blood.

"As soon as William Sims had set out for the McJunkins, Mrs. Sims had continued to reproach and remonstrate with Lee for his villainy, in order to detain them as long as possible from their attack on her friends higher up the creek. While this was going on, B. Musgroves, one of Lee's men, went up to the bed on which Mrs. McDaniel's children were sleeping, and took from it one of the two blankets that so covered them, it was an exceedingly cold evening and raining. As Musgrove went out of the door with the blanket, Mrs. McDaniel said to him, 'Beaks Musgrove, you will answer for that at the day of judgement.' 'By God, madam' he replied, 'if I am to have that to my credit, I'll take the other,' and returning to the bed, took that also.

"After Wm. Sims' efforts to save the McJunkins and Jollys he became so obnoxious to the Tories that it became necessary for his friends to conceal him the best way they could, and he actually lived for a long time in the family of the good Quaker, Eli Cook, dressed as a female and passing as a little girl."[20]

The militia was armed with a bewildering assortment of firearms; one source alone list over forty types, including shotguns. These are, from top to bottom: the British .79caliber Queen Anne naval musket; the .69caliber Charleville military musket, supplied in large numbers by the French; the American-made .75caliber Committee of Safety musket; and an American-made .40caliber rifle. The so-called "Kentucky rifles" were actually rare, and ill-suited for military use.—US MARINE CORPS

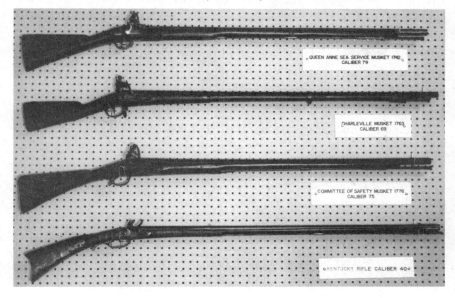

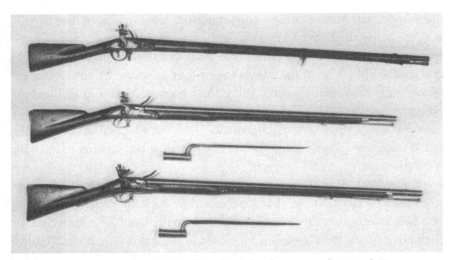

The most common weapons for British and Loyalist forces were the British Tower Musket, the famous .69caliber "Brown Bess" (top), and the Short Tower Musket variant (center). Patriot forces used captured British muskets and large numbers of the French Charleville musket (bottom).—US MARINE CORPS

The scattered survivors of Brandon's band of partisans included not only Clowney and Daniel McJunkin, but Moses Guyton, Edward Armstrong, Aaron Guyton, Joseph Hughes, William Giles, and John Jeffries. (Joseph McJunkin said that Hughes was away hiding powder, but his pension statement places him at the battle.)[21]

Cunningham had failed at one of his primary goals, however: retaking the store of powder. "Maj. Otterson's wife [Ruth Gordon Otterson]* knew where a keg of powder was hid, & learning that the Tories were coming to get it, went in the night and blew it up. In the morning the Tories came & demanded it. She told them what she had done. They did not believe her; cut her dress off at the waist, & drove her before them to show the powder. When they came to the place, the evidence was sufficient as to the fate of the powder." If the worst William Cunningham's men did was to just verbally abuse her and "cut off her dress," she was indeed fortunate.[22]

Colonel Brandon carried his nephew John Young's body back to his mother. Sixteen-year-old Thomas was John's brother. "On that occasion,

---

*Ruth Otterson's father Thomas Gordon built one of the early forts and was an officer in the First Spartans. She had two brothers in Brandon's regiment.

my brother, John Young, was murdered. I shall never forget my feelings when told of his death. I do not believe I had ever used an oath before that day, but then I tore open my bosom, and swore that I would never rest till I had avenged his death. Subsequently a hundred tories felt the weight of my arm for the deed, and around Steedham's neck I fastened the rope as a reward for his cruelties. On the next day I left home in my shirt sleeves, and joined Brandon's party. Christopher Brandon and I joined at the same time, and the first engagement we were in, was at Stallions' in York District." Thomas was enrolled in Captain Benjamin Jolly's company.[23]

Christopher "Kit" Brandon was the son of John Brandon, Colonel Brandon's brother and neighbor on Brown's Creek. "My father, and Col. Brandon, were engaged in the war with the Cherokees, in 1761, and belonged to the famous Grant's expedition. He was a Presbyterian, and in this faith brought up all his family. . . . It was the day after Brandon's defeat by the Tories in 1780, that I joined the little band of Whigs, which was then scattered over the Province. After that defeat, we carried Col. Brandon's children over to him, at Bell's, near Bullock's creek Meeting-house,* in York District where we joined the Colonel's force, then consisting of about thirty Whigs. On the next day we met Col. Neal's regiment, but could not induce him to cross the river into [western South] Carolina, and he returned to the Catawba, near Bethel."[24]

At about the same time the Patriots scored a small victory that helped lessen the sting. A small Patriot force congregated to break up a Tory gathering at Mobley's Meeting House, a tiny community with a church and forted house. The Patriots struck at dawn on 8 or 10 June (the date is again uncertain), driving the Tories out of the buildings and over a steep embankment; most of the Tory injuries were probably caused by the precipitate rush over the bluff. A considerable amount of plundered property was returned to its owners, and the prisoners marched to North Carolina.[25]

William Kenedy† recounted the general conditions and his participation: "the Tories then commenced doing much mischief in the country and all [near?]; every man who was friendly to his country was caled into

---

*Now simply a crossroads about 15 miles southwest of York SC.

†Neither the better known William Kennedy Senior or Junior, but a third "William Kenedy." The spelling is probably incorrect.

service an in fact and in that country at that, Time it was dangerious for a whig to remain at home and they were of more Service to the country when the[y] could act in a body—men being caled for he voluntiered under Capt John Steele in the State of South Carolina, for the purpose of breaking up a Body of Tories & was at the Battle at Maublys meeting house. To state all the points to & from which they marched would now from the nature of this Business Be out of his power. from the Battle of Maublys meeting house they went to North Carolina and rendevoused at Wasaw meeting House and was on several expeditions. cannot designate the points they were—they were then marched back to South Carolina and marched in various directions and many expeditions Guarding against the British Torris and Idians. . . ."[26]

After the setback at Brandon's Defeat the militiamen of Brandon, Lisles [Lyles], and John Thomas Junior, along with a few Georgia refugees, reassembled on June 12 at the Presbyterian meeting-house. Joseph McJunkin: "The men who had been engaged in hiding the powder, learning very soon what had occurred at Brandon's camp, collected as many of their friends as possible and retreated over Broad River." The Broad River, a significant geographic boundary, was also a sort of cultural divide. "Having appointed Bullock's Creek Church as a place of rendezvous, as many were directed thither as possible. The Rev. Joseph Alexander was at the time pastor of that church, and had been for a number of years past. He had, however, labored extensively as a supply* among the Presbyterian population on the west side of Broad River and had always taken a firm stand for liberty. So that now he had been compelled to escape for his life, as the Tories were determined on his destruction.

"Their situation is talked over. The British are victorious, the Tories rising in large numbers and asserting their zeal for the royal cause; not a single corps of Whigs is known to be embodied in the State; the cause of liberty is desperate. The offer of British protection is before them. What is to be done? What can they do? At length a young man calls his command together. He recites the facts connected with their present situation. He recounts their past toils, sufferings and dangers. He states at large the reasons for the contest in which they have been engaged, and the instances of

---

*In the Presbyterian Church a "supply" is an interim pastor who serves at need.

success and defeat which has attended their efforts in the cause of independence. He says: 'Our cause must now be determined. Shall we join the British or strive like men for the noble end for which we have done and spent so much? Shall we declare ourselves cowards and traitors, or shall we fight for liberty as long as we have life? As for me, 'give me liberty or give me death!' The speaker was John Thomas, son of the Colonel of the same name."[27]

After this meeting the Patriots retired to Tuckasegee Ford on the Catawba River in North Carolina. Joseph McJunkin: "The British and Tories having now overrun the country and from this date we were now what we call refugees not taking protection as many did but retreated from place to place and was continuously on the elert and having retreated over the Catawba River and there meeting General Rutherford and being determined to defend our country there we elected Colo. Thomas Sumter our General. . . ."[28]

Thomas Sumter thus became an unofficial brigadier to direct the actions of several militia regiments still active. This unofficial commission could of course not be confirmed by the governor-in-exile: in combination with Sumter's considerable ambition, it would be the source of much future internal jealousy and strife.

Brandon's men were now hunted prey, and according to Aaron Guyton ". . . at this time the torys over run our country a few of us and some refugees from Georgia got together and sometimes pursued our Enemy and sometimes they drove us. . . ."[29]

A few men simply left altogether, among them John Jeffries. "After that I went on to Virginia. I staid about home three weeks before starting. The Tories were so troublesome I thought I could not stand it—so I went on after my father."

For the Tories, it was time to settle scores. "Col. Patrick Moore (this I understand from others) a Tory colonel, built a fort on the waters of Thicketty Creek, after Brandon's Defeat, which was a place of resort and protection for Tory bands. From this place they went out & plundered Whig families in every direction, stole horses and everything else they could & desired. They plundered my father's house, stole his horses _ drove off his cattle, built up a fire on the floor, abused my mother as the meanest of all rebels. After my return from Virginia, I went out on tour with Capt.

[Matthew] Patton. I went afterwards to Edisto & Jacksonboro during the session of the Legislature there; we went there for ammunition for our army."[30]

Youthful Angelica Mitchell (married name Nott) had been sent to live with her aunt when her father moved to Tennessee, and described the life of civilians under the Tory yoke: "I recollect when Col Cunningham came to our house. He came after night with 250 men. They fed their horses with our roasting ears—burnt the rails to roast for themselves. . . . The (Lances), who lived on Pacolet, on land now owned by Wm. Norris, built a loom in the woods between four trees—wove in fair weather, & covered the loom in cow skins in wet. . . . We lived, at that time, generally without bread or meat or salt, on roasting ears. When we killed a beef, a pint of salt with hickory ashes preserved it. We went without shoes, & sewed woolen rags around our feet. I have done that many times." In one risky venture, "Aunt Beckham went to Granby with a guinea hidden on top of her head, a distance of 80 miles, bought a bushel of salt, & brought it home on her saddle."[31]

Others fared far worse. Samuel Hammond recounted a raid by Tories on an isolated Patriot household: "In his course he chanced to pass the residence of Capt. R., who was then from home on duty, and found Mrs. R. in great tribulation and [some?] distress. About 4 o'clock in the morning of the day on which Col. Hammond & party arrived, a considerable body of Tories had visited the place, and indulged in depredation and brutality to the fullest extent. Not an article of [illegible] Value or of use found on the plantation had been spared, the house alone was left standing; all else had been sent away or wantonly destroyed. Sparing the house, in this instance, was a mercy unknown to these [rascally?] redcoats. When left, however, it contained nothing beside the lady and her children. The furniture that could not be removed had been broken up and burned, and the clothing of every description appropriated to their own use, and packed off on horses and mules taken from the fields and stables—of all a goodly store. While engaged in removing the bed clothing from the last bed, the one from which Mrs. R. had risen at their approach, and where her infant still lay sleeping, the merciless wretches had in their haste and struggle for the booty, disregarded the child, which was thrown with much violence upon the floor, and its face and mouth mashed and otherwise seriously bruised.

"Not satisfied with the appropriation of all the goods and chattels appertaining to the premises, they began to look with covetous eyes upon the handsome new gown worn at the time by Mrs. R. Their avarice not restrained by common decency triumphed, and she was ordered to take it off and deliver it to them. Unfortunately the removal of the dress disclosed fine and costly dimity* and linen underclothes—not usual in this country at that time—which they must needs have also to correspond with the dress. This demand Mrs. R. positively and stoutly refused, and they were actively taken from her person by main force. Thus was this good Whig lady left with nothing in all the world but a single garment, and empty house, and her children. Mortified and chagrined beyond description, she was allowed to take from her floor her stunned and bleeding babe, amid the rude laugh and coarse jest of these monsters in human form, who told her that so far from feeling offended, or being grieved at the loss of her finery, she ought to thank them for their consideration in thus relieving her of it, and so placing her in a better condition to nurse her [illegible] Whig brat, who, they supposed would soon need and call for his breakfast.

"After this courteous manner of expressing themselves, they turned upon their heels and left her almost stupefied with vexation and shame. . . ."[32]

The deaths of his relatives and such Loyalist depredations were apparently taking a toll on Colonel Thomas Brandon, who acquired a reputation as an inveterate hater of Tories. Angelica Mitchell said that "I knew Col. Brandon—he was true and valiant, but overbearing and cruel."† For some undetermined period after the fall of Charleston a Captain Philemon Waters was temporarily under Brandon's command, and wrote that "He captured a man (a Tory) peculiarly obnoxious to the colonel. After this skirmish, when the prisoners were presented to the colonel, he, on seeing Waters' prisoner, drew his sword and was in the act of rushing upon him to slay him. Waters threw himself between them, and announced to his superior that the prisoner was under his protection, and '*should not be*

---

*A light-weight sheer cotton fabric. Prior to the invention of the Whitney's gin, cotton was an expensive fabric.

†In fairness the elderly Mrs. Nott did not like anybody very much; William Farr was "a great brag."

harmed.' The purpose of vengeance was not abandoned, and Capt. Waters most peremptorily ordered to stand out of the way. 'Africa,' said he to his servant, 'bring me my rifle'; no sooner said than done. With his rifle in his hand, and an eye that never quailed, he said to the colonel, 'Now strike the prisoner—the instant you do, I will shoot you dead.' The blow was not struck; the prisoner was saved."[33]

In his memoir, James Collins said that ". . . they commenced house burning and plundering. Among their leaders was one called Bill Cunningham, a man that will be execrated by some of the descendants of the sufferers, perhaps to generations yet unborn. Women were insulted,* and stripped of every article of bedding, clothing or furniture was taken—knives, forks, spoons, in fact everything that could be carried off. No piece of meat or a pint of salt was left. They even entered houses where men lay sick of the small-pox, that they knew were opposed to them, dragged them out of their sick beds into the yard and put them to death, in cold blood, in the presence of their wives and children, or relatives. We were too weak to repel them, and it seemed as though they had been let loose from the bottomless pit, to execute infernal vengeance on all that opposed the mandates of the British."[34]

The non-combatant father of one of Brandon's captains, Joseph Hughes, was murdered while out looking for his hogs, ". . . pierced by seven wounds. . . . Joseph after looking at the mangled corpse of his father, raised his gun, and swore he would kill every Tory he met."[35]

Another prominent Loyalist raider was Captain Christian Huck, a German-born Philadelphia lawyer and land speculator who after having his property seized by local Patriots, enlisted in the Loyalist cause. Later forming his own company of dragoons he came south with Clinton, and his company was stationed at Rocky Mount under the command of George Turnbull.[36]

From the very beginning King George III and many of his advisors considered the American rebellion a religious struggle, the "Presbyterian war," because so many of the Scots-Irish rebels belonged to that denomination. In 1776 King George III was told that "This has been a Presbyterian war from the beginning . . . the first firing against the King's troops

---

*One of several period euphemisms for rape.

was from a Massachuset meeting house." In truth, ". . . it was a stubborn fact that wherever a Presbyterian settlement was, the people were Whigs."[37]

In June and early July Huck launched a reign of terror, burning Presbyterian "sedition houses," cursing Presbyterians, burning Bibles, and ravaging the economic infrastructure. This of course had exactly the opposite of the desired effect, further hardening resistance. One of the most notorious episodes was Huck's 11 June raid on the Fishing Creek settlement. Huck's intent was to capture another Presbyterian firebrand, Reverend John Simpson, and capture or kill Whigs reported to be assembled there. Lieutenant Colonel George Turnbull later reported to Cornwallis that Huck's men surprised two men in "Rebell Uniforms" (whatever those might have been) in a field, killing one and wounding the other. Local lore, in part corroborated by later court testimony, described only wanton arson and murder.

The raiders arrived first at the home of the widow Janet Strong, who had two sons in the Patriot militia and a young teenager at home. The Tories plundered the house, taking all the food and dragging feather mattresses into the yard and shredding them. When a tame pigeon flew down to eat some spilled grain, Huck decapitated it with his sword, turned to Mrs. Strong, and said, "Madam, I have cut off the head of the Holy Ghost."

The widow gave Huck a piece of her mind, prophesying that "You will never die in your bed, nor will your death be that of the righteous." Then ". . . some of Huck's men went to the barn, where her son, William Strong, had gone shortly before their arrival. He had taken his Bible with him, and was engaged in reading the sacred volume. They shot him dead upon the spot, and dragged him out of the barn. The officers then began to cut and hack the dead body with their broadswords, when Mrs. Strong rushed from the house, pleading with all a mother's anguish, to the officers, that they would spare the corpse of her son. They heeded not her agonized entreaties, till she threw herself upon the bleeding and mangled body. . . ."

Finding neither Simpson nor rebels at the church, the raiders rode to the parsonage. Some of the Simpson family slaves who were at the church overheard the Tory plans and ran ahead to warn Mrs. Simpson of the plan to "burn the rascal out." Sighting Huck's men in the road, she and four small children fled out the back door and hid in an orchard, salvaging only a set of spoons, a gift from her mother. The raiders plundered the house and then set it ablaze. Noticing the outbuilding that housed Simpson's office and library, they torched that too before departing.

Mrs. Simpson saved two apron-loads of books, but was badly burned. After salvaging enough feathers from the yard to make a mattress, she and the children walked to a neighbor's house. There, four weeks later, she gave birth to another child.[38]

Huck capped off the day by burning the church. Almost single-handedly he had turned the conflict into a ruthless religious war like the ones so many settlers had left behind in the north of Ireland.

From Fishing Creek, Huck went toward William Hill's iron works. Scattering a disorganized contingent of local militia, Huck captured two of Hill's sons who tried to defend the works. Huck's men destroyed the furnaces and forge, grist mill, sawmill, store, and carried off everything portable including ninety slaves.[39]

RAMSEUR'S MILL, 20 JUNE 1780

The Tories in North Carolina were restive in anticipation of Cornwallis' advance into that state, but the general was wary of a premature uprising and sent Loyalist Lieutenant Colonel John Moore to try and calm the situation. Patriot bands were roving the area searching out Tories, and in contravention to his orders Moore instructed the men to disperse and reassemble a few days later at Ramseur's Mill on 13 June. Loyalist sentiment was strong, and by 18 June Moore had about 1,400 men, although only about a quarter were armed. In a protracted battle the Loyalists were routed, although many slipped away under cover of a truce.

Upon hearing of the plan to eliminate the Tories, according to Joseph Hughes ". . . from thence we marched to Ramseur's (a Tory) for the purpose of taking some Tories but before our arrival the Rowan Militia of N Carolina had defeated the Tories." Captain Samuel Otterson recalled the details that "On the day after the election [of Sumter as general] we Marched toward the house of a Celebrated Tory by the name of Ramsour for the purpose of Defeating some tories who had encamped at Ramsour's mill, but before we arrived the malitia from Rowan N. Carolina had defeated the tories & we Turned our horses loose into a large field of oats belonging to Ramsour & the oats were just ripening—from thence we retreated across the Catawba & went down into the old Catawba nation of Indians & encamped some days."[40]

REVENGE—STALLION'S PLANTATION, 12 JULY 1780
Fleeing east of the Broad River and into the territory of the Catawba Nation had provided little respite. Sumter and his larger band of followers for
the month of July concentrated on acquiring munitions and food needed
to continue the fight. Joseph McJunkin: "His men go out in quest of provisions, arms, and to rally their friends to take a stand under the standard of
liberty. Provisions were obtained with great difficulty, for the want of cur-
rent funds, so that their fare often consisted of barley meal without meat,
salt, or any other seasoning, and scarce at that. All the powder which could
be obtained was collected. The good ladies in the region round gave up
their pewter vessels to be moulded into bullets. Implements of husbandry
were converted into swords."

Smaller independent bands like Brandon's continued to plague the
now-dominant Tories in the region between the Broad and Catawba
Rivers, though ". . . under the necessity of maintaining the strictest vigi-
lance for the protection of their lives. The Tories watched their movements,
waylaid them and often fired upon them," and Private Thomas Young*
said that "For some time we dodged about in small squads."[41]

Kit Brandon left several statements covering his activities, differing in
small details, but his primary duty had been to escort Colonel Brandon's
children to safety. "Col. Brandon passed over Broad River with as many
men as he could gather. Thos. Young & myself took Brandon's children
& a negro fellow, & followed him. We found him & party at old Mr. Bell's
on Bullock's Creek. Thence we went on to [Rowan County] N.C.—Capt.
Reed† falling in the rear of the party was killed by two Tories" named
Robert Love and one Sadler.[42]

Thomas Young elaborated on the story. "While we were in North Carolina recruiting, an incident occurred which it may be well enough to relate. One Capt. Reid was at a neighbor's house, in York District, on a visit.

---

*In his elderly years Young was described as "of rather a thick make, broad shoulders
and brawny arms" with badly scarred head and arms from wounds suffered in the aftermath of Cowpens; Saye, Memoirs of Major Joseph McJunkin, p. 42.

†The name is also spelled Reid and Read in various sources, but a Captain James Reed
formerly of the New Acquisition District Militia was killed at this time. See Moss, Roster
of South Carolina Patriots, p. 803, 805, 807.

The landlady saw two men approaching the house whom she knew to be tories, and told Capt. Reid he had better escape, for they would kill him. He replied, no!—-they had been his neighbors; he had known Love and Sadler all his life, and had nothing to fear from them. He walked out into the yard, offered them his hand, and they killed him."[43]

McJunkin placed this murder near Bullock Creek, about three miles east of the Broad River, then in Tory-controlled ground.

According to Thomas Young, "His mother, a very old woman, came to where we were encamped in North Carolina. One morning we were called out on parade, and this old woman came before us, leaning upon the arms of two officers. She drew from her bosom the bloody pocket book of her son, and three times attempted to go to her knees, but was prevented by the officers who supported her.

"Col. Brandon stepped out and asked if there were any here willing to volunteer to avenge her wrongs. Twenty-five stepped out at once. I was one of the number. We started, rode all night, halted in the day, kept watch in the woods, but slept not; the next night we arrived at old Love's." Colonel Brandon, and Moses Cherry were among the party.[44]

"Twenty-five of us, under Col. Brandon turned out & rode all day & till midnight to the place where these Tories were." As was typical, the men concocted a hasty plan. "One part of our company was to attack the house, another the barn. The house was attacked, and the door broken down by a powerful man, by the name of Maddox, who was afterwards killed at King's Mountain. In staving open the door, he floored old Love and knocked some of his teeth out. At this moment a cry was raised that they were in the barn, and to the barn we all rushed. One of our men fired through the door and killed one of the murderers, the other was killed in the skirmish. What is most strange about the matter is, that another man was sleeping with them, and in the melee he escaped unhurt." Young and some of the party decided to return north, and "By the time we got back every man of us had two guns apiece."[45]

Christopher Brandon said only that "We did not long remain in Rowan, finding nothing to do, but returned to Crowder's creek, where Col. Brandon and Moses Cherry made up a party of ten or twelve to avenge Reid's death; they were successful, but were closely pursued by about thirty Tories, as far as Ross's Mill, and they went down Fishing creek."[46]

A pattern for an endless cycle of revenge killings was being set, and the Tories were not going to take such an affront lying down. "The Tories in the region collected to the number of 30 or 40 & followed Brandon as far as the widow Ross's; Brandon went into the Bethel Congregation (north of Yorkville) & he gathered as many men as he could & turned to meet the Tories."

Brandon turned the tables on his pursuers. Kit Brandon: "Our party being now all together, we set out in pursuit of them. I remember well meeting an old Mr. Love, who had been a prisoner of the Tories, and recollect his salutation—"'Fore God! you're a likely set of fellows, if you're good for anything!" He had just been discharged by the Tories,* and told us that they were then at Carroll's, and in what force. But as Carroll was a good Whig, we would not attack them at *his* house, for fear of killing some member of his family. We soon learned that they had removed their quarters to one Stallions, and we pushed on to attack them."[47]

The battle site has gone down in local history as Stallions, but the farm belonged to John Stallings (although yet other sources interpret the name as Stirling). Stallings was a staunch Tory, though his daughter-in-law, Sarah Love Stallings, was from a Presbyterian Whig family. She had two brothers active in Whig service, not uncommon in this "uncivil war."[48]

Kit Brandon: "From Carroll's they went to Stallion's, & took up to get dinner."[49]

There are several accounts of the fight at the Stallings plantation. Some accounts were written long after the fact, others by non-participants recounting family lore, and some are dubious fourth-hand accounts.[50]

Thomas Young's account is the most cogent, and the best known: "Before we arrived at the house in which they were fortified, we were divided into two parties. Capt. Love with a party of sixteen—of whom I was one—marched to attack the front, while Col. Brandon with the remainder, made a circuit to intercept those who should attempt to escape, and also to attack the rear."[51]

Christopher Brandon corroborated Young's account, with more detail.

---

*In another and contradictory account, elderly Kit Brandon said that "On the way the Tories pursued Col. A. Love into a briery old field, where he shot two of them and made his escape."

"When we got near the house, we tied out our horses, and Love took a party of fifteen under his command, of whom I recollect Wm. Kennedy, Thomas Young, John Brandon, my father, Richard Brandon and Nick Lazarus [in a later recounting he included Richard Hughes, John Jolly, William Giles, and William Sharp*]. . . . The Tories were fiddling and frolicking in high glee when we came up, and I presume the first intimation they had of our approach, was our fire.

"They returned our fire through the open door, all crowded together so closely, as to burn one another's faces [with the flash from their weapons' pans]."[52]

At some point Mrs. Stallings ran out of the house to try and end the fighting. Young: ". . . on the approach of her brother she ran out and begged him not to fire upon the house. He told her it was too late now, and that their only chance for safety was to surrender."

By some accounts she was ". . . wearing a sort of hat, as was the custom with her sex. . . ." which may have led some to mistake her for a man in the dim light.[53]

Young: "She ran back to the house and sprang upon the door step, which was pretty high. At this moment, the house was attacked in the rear by Col. Brandon's party, and Mrs. Stallions was killed by a ball shot through the opposite door."

Local lore had it that ". . . as she entered the door, probably mistaken for a man was shot through the head by some one on the opposite side [of the house] . . . she lived a couple of days."[54]

Thomas Young: "At the same moment with Brandon's attack, our party raised a shout and rushed forward. We fired several rounds which were briskly returned."

Some of the Loyalists attempted to flee, a risky venture. "He [William 'Squire' Kennedy Sr.] was regarded as the best shot with a rifle of any man in that section of the country, and whenever the well known report of his

---

*There are multiple accounts of the Stallions fight attributed to Brandon; see Scoggins, *The Battles of Stallions' Plantation and Bigger's Ferry*. We have included the additional names, but not Brandon's "more detailed" account recorded by Draper in 1871, since it was part of a hasty letter from David Wallace to historical fiction writer William Gilmore Simms listing potential plot devices and contains known factual errors; Sumter Manuscript Collection, 13VV, p. 178–200.

rifle was heard it was generally remarked, 'there is another tory less.'"[55]

Young: "While we were fighting a man was seen running through an open field near us. I raised my gun to shoot him, when some of our party exclaimed, 'Don't fire; he is one of our men.' I drew down my gun, and in a moment he halted, wheeled round, and fired at us. Old Squire Kennedy (who was an excellent marksman) raised his rifle and brought him down. We had but one wounded, William Kennedy [Junior], who was shot by my side. I was attempting to fire in at the door of the house, when I saw two of the tories in the act of shooting at myself and Kennedy. I sprang aside and escaped, calling at the same time to my companion, but he was shot (while moving) through the wrist and thigh."

All accounts agree that the trapped Tories surrendered after a heavy exchange of fire. Christopher Brandon remembered that finally ". . . the Tories ran up a flag and cried for quarter. Their loss was, I believe, two killed, four wounded, and twenty-eight prisoners, whom we sent to Charlotte, N.C."[56]

Another bit of local lore was that "The Tories were routed & one of them in fleeing to a thickly overgrown swamp near at hand, had the bottom of his powder horn shot up & lost his ammunition, & remained hid in the swamp with the wolves two days before he ventured out."[57]

Thomas Young: "After the fight, Love and Stallions met and shed bitter tears; Stallions was dismissed on parole to bury his wife and arrange his affairs."

After the fight "We took the prisoner's to Bigger's Ferry & shut them in the house of one Mr. Allen in N.C.—kept them there til morning, & went on to Charlotte," said Christopher Brandon.[58]

This was hardly the last incident in the spiraling cycle of reprisal raids. ". . . sometime after [Stallions], Richard (Joseph; Draper's annotation) Hughes, who feared to stay at home, for we had all to be out, went early one morning to his own house, to see his family on the Union side of Broad River, near where Pinckneyville now is. He approached his own house cautiously on horseback; when within a rod [16.5 feet/5m] of the door, three Tories stepped out of the door, and presenting their guns, said exultingly—'You damned Rebel; you are our prisoner.' 'You are damned liars,' said Hughes, and instantly spurred his horse to full speed. As he cleared the gate, all three fired and missed their mark. He escaped without injury.

The Tories had watched for him around the house all night, and just went in to get their breakfast."[59]

CHAPTER 8

THE IMPERCEPTIBLE
TURNING OF THE TIDE

Never give up, for that is just the place
and time that the tide will turn.
—HARRIET BEECHER STOWE

CEDAR SPRINGS, 12 JULY 1780

PATRICK FERGUSON HAD DISPATCHED HIS SECOND IN
command, Captain Abraham DePeyster, to help Tory partisans break up
the remaining Patriot bands in the Fairforest area, and DePeyster established two small garrisons there. From some source DePeyster learned that
the remnants of the First Spartans were encamped at Cedar Springs.

John Thomas Senior was incarcerated at Ninety Six, and his wife Jane
visited him on 11 July. Joseph McJunkin: "While there encamped, the wife
of Col. John Thomas, sen., and the mother of Col. John Thomas, jun.
Visited her sons William and Abram, who were prisoners at Ninety-Six.*
While there, she heard a woman tell some others, that the loyalists intended
to surprise the whig camp at the Cedar Spring, the night of the succeeding
day. This was to her interesting intelligence; for she had, at that post, two
sons in arms. She determined, if possible, to give the intelligence before
the blow was struck. She rode the whole intervening distance of about sixty
miles, the next day, and apprised her sons and friends of the impending
danger. A brief consultation ensued; they withdrew a short distance from
their camp fires. The enemy rushed upon the camp, in the confidence of
a surprise; but to their astonishment, they were assailed in the rear by the

---

*Sources differ; she was likely visiting her husband.

party they expected to strike unawares. Defeat, overwhelming defeat, was the consequence to the tories: they were about 150 strong; the whigs 60. Among the slain of the tories, was a man named John White, whom Major McJunkin says he claimed as his tory, inasmuch, as he lived in the limits of his command; and when the Indian massacre, called the Passover, took place, he was required to turn out by McJunkin, but declined, saying he was a non-combatant. But when Charleston fell, he joined the British, and at Cedar Spring met the just reward of his treason."[1]

It was one more indication that the rebellion was still alive and well in the back country.

HUCK'S DEFEAT (WILLIAMSON'S PLANTATION) 12 JULY 1780

Captain Christian Huck's earlier expeditions had done much to stir up trouble, but Colonel George Turnbull dispatched Huck again to recruit militia and "push the rebels." With a force of about a hundred men, Huck rode eagerly into the New Acquisition district.[2]

Thwarted in an earlier expedition to capture some of the Presbyterian clergymen, Huck compelled all the local men to attend meetings. His audiences included mostly men either too old or too young to fight, an indication of how things were headed. James Collins wrote that "He got up, harangued the people in a very rough and insulting manner and submitted his propositions for their acceptance." He sorely misjudged his audiences of hardened Presbyterians who even addressed God standing up. "Some bowed to his scepter, but far the greater part returned home without submitting." Many fled into solidly Presbyterian regions in adjacent North Carolina, or the valley of the Catawba River.[3]

Huck let his rhetoric get the best of common sense, telling his audiences that "God almighty had become a rebel, but if there were 20 gods on that side, they would all be conquered" and "if the Rebels were as thick as trees, and Jesus Christ himself were to command them he would defeat them." The soldiers also confiscated the horses of the attendees.[4]

After one of Huck's meetings James Collins' aged father walked home. Asked by his wife about what went on at the meeting he replied, "Nothing very pleasant. I have come home determined to take my gun and when I lay it down, I lay down my life with it." He went on to tell young James that "We must submit and become slaves, or fight."[5]

Huck was determined to capture several of the known rebel leaders, and singled their families out for special attention. His men looted homes of known Patriots and sympathizers, taking food, household goods, clothing, bedding, jewelry; anything that could not be carried away was destroyed. They manhandled the wives and daughters, whipped children, and recounted tales of the grisly fates that awaited their men.

"When his [Huck's] words and doings were reported in the Sumter's camp the Presbyterian Irish who rallied around his standard could stand it no longer. They demanded to be led against this vile man, Captain Huck."[6]

The atrocities committed by the likes of Huck and Bloody Bill Cunningham went on for years, and specific events in the local lore are impossible to precisely place in time. Ann Kennedy was left in charge of her father William Kennedy, Sr.'s farm in his absence. She had hired a young local to cut and stack ripe oats, and a few days later a party of Tory raiders appeared and scattered the grain, but were unable to find her absent father and brothers. Frustrated, ". . . they discovered two young men in the yard by the name of Watkins, whom they shot down and with their sabers hacked off their fingers and toes and mangled their bodies in a most shameful manner. After the Tories left she hired some Quakers of the neighborhood to bury their mutilated remains."[7]

Ann Kennedy would have to contend with other depredations in the course of the war. On one occasion the elder Kennedy ". . . while on a visit to his family, the tories attempted to capture him. He was at work in his shop when they approached and endeavored to surround him. They got his hat, but he successfully made a precipitous flight to the nearest thicket amid a shower of bullets, that whistled around his head. After the tories left he returned to view his pillaged house, and bid his family a hasty adieu and returned hatless to the army."[8]

On his next expedition Huck moved against the Brattonsville community, where one of his targets was Captain John McClure. The captain was away with Sumter, but on 11 July Huck's raiders called at his home. They surprised his son James and son-in-law Edward "Ned" Martin while casting musket balls from the family's pewter ware. The two men tried to hide, but were quickly winkled out by the looters and found in possession of bullet molds and a few balls. Huck summarily condemned both to death, and they were trussed-up to be carried along and hanged the next day.[9]

Huck demanded from Mrs. McClure to know the whereabouts of her other two sons, and then found several religious books, including the family Bible. Saying "It is these books that make you such d——d rebels," threw them into the fireplace. When Mary McClure salvaged the books, Huck struck her with the flat of his sword. "Sir, that will be a dear blow to you," she countered.

The raiders plundered and attempted unsuccessfully to burn the house. When they departed, daughter Mary saddled a horse and rode to Sumter's camp to advise her brothers Hugh and John what had happened. Huck moved on through the area, plundering and taking hostages.

At the home of Colonel William Bratton, Huck—with young John Bratton seated on his knee—first tried to cajole Martha Bratton into revealing her husband's whereabouts. When that failed he flung the child face-first onto the floor, and one of Huck's men ". . . seized a reaping-hook that hung near them in the piazza, and brought it to her throat with intention to kill her. Still she refused to give information that might endanger her husband's safety." A junior officer* intervened to prevent a murder, but Huck forced Martha to prepare a meal for his men. Gathering more hostages, Huck moved on, with the intimation that he would return the next day to burn Bratton's home.[10]

Huck finally ensconced himself in James Williamson's house, with seven hostages locked into the corncrib. His troops were outside, camped in the yard and adjacent fenced lane.

In the pre-dawn hours of 12 July about 130 men from William Bratton's Patriot regiment as well as volunteers from other units quietly approached. They captured a dozing sentry and crept into position, sheltering behind fences. The Patriots opened fire at short range, and then it became a slaughter as Loyalist bayonet charges failed because of the fences. Bratton's men kept firing into the milling mass of Loyalists.

James Collins was among those who had moved into an orchard behind the buildings. ". . . The sentinels discovered us—fired on us and fled." A detachment of the Green Dragoons were among the few who were able to form, Huck was in a white shirt, his jacket abandoned in the house. "The leader drew his sword, mounted his horse, and began to storm and

---

*Probably Lieutenant John Adamson.

rave. . . . When they had got pretty near the peach trees, their leader called out, 'disperse you d——d rebels, or I will put every man of you to the sword.' Our rifle balls began to whistle among them, and in a few minutes Lord Hook was shot off his horse and fell at full length; his sword flew out of his hand as he fell. . . ." The dragoons hesitated for a minute, and fled.[11]

With only three casualties, the Patriots had eliminated the despised Huck, dispersed his force, inflicted 85 casualties, and captured about thirty, including officers. Doubtless more Loyalist corpses lay hidden in the surrounding countryside where they had been hunted down. It was a small but vital victory.

ROCKY MOUNT AND HANGING ROCK, 28 JULY–8 AUGUST 1780
Leaders like Thomas Brandon and James Williams continued to operate as guerillas, skirmishing with and annoying the British and roving bands of Loyalists. Jacob Brown provided some indication of how nebulous the organizational structure was: "They then went down near the Catawba where they were stationed some time during which campaign this applicant belonged to the mounted infantry, and near the Indian land the troops joined General Sumpter still under the command of Col. Brandon and Capt. Gordon and had various skirmishes with the British and Tories but this applicant although in Sumter's army was not in them until Genl Sumpter attacked Rocky Mount. . . ."[12]

Brown's somewhat convoluted statement indicates that although he considered himself part of Sumter's troops, he was actually in Brandon's command that was operating autonomously inside South Carolina. This statement reveals one of the artifacts that cause considerable confusion. Sumter eventually gained such fame, and as a US Senator was so widely known, that many men mentioned being under his command to bolster their pension applications.

Cornwallis' strategy of holding a number of small garrisons to screen Camden and Charleston provided potentially lucrative small targets. The stubborn Sumter was not a man to be kept down for long. He had been rebuilding his force, and by late August had assembled a command of about 600 effectives. He decided to pluck some of the low-hanging fruit. Joseph McJunkin: "We then collected some Military Stores & marched again for So. Carolina & marched to Clems Branch, from there to Rocky Mount."[13]

McJunkin's description of the debates that preceded the assault on Rocky Mount provides an insight into how the fractious militia commands functioned. ". . . we camped one night, he [Sumter] summoned all his commissioners [officers] to attend his markee [marquee, an open-sided tent], which was composed of a wagon cloth & the broad canopy of heaven . . . " There ensued an argumentative conference, ". . . the subject of which was to fall on a method of the then opening campaign, the General being president."

Captain Samuel Otterson: ". . . from thence [Ramseur's Mill] we retreated across the Catawba & went down into the old Catawba nation of Indians & encamped some days. Thence we recrossed the Catawba & went to the British station at Rocky Mount & about the 28th July 1780 made an unsuccessful attempt to take the British & Tories. . . ."[14]

Sumter's plan was to attack the position at Rocky Mount while Major William R. Davie's mixed force of North and South Carolina militia made what amounted to a diversionary attack on Hanging Rock.* Davies' diversion went quite well; he was able to attack and scatter a force of Loyalists camped outside the defenses, capturing horses and weapons.[15]

Rocky Mount was a fortified farmhouse protected by an abatis. The attackers were under the impression that the position was a clapboard house, easily penetrable by small arms fire, but the industrious garrison had fortified the position by constructing log walls about a foot inside the exterior walls and packing the space between with earth. In the first rush Colonel Neil and seven privates were killed. The attackers retreated to a safe distance, and developed a plan out of a bad movie.[16]

William Hill and a private named Johnson would attempt to gain the protection of a rock outcrop, and toss burning torches onto a nearby outbuilding in hopes that the flames would spread to the main house. "Rich lightwood split & bound with cords to cover the most vital parts of our bodies, as well as a large bundle of the same wood to carry in our arms, being thus equipped we run the 100 yds. to the rock. . . ." Johnson was

---

*Among Davie's troops was a thirteen year-old scout and courier from the Waxhaws District, future Major General of Tennessee militia, and President of the United States, Andrew Jackson.

to light the fire while Hill kept watch, but a sally from the house drove them away.*

Covered by concentrated rifle fire, the two men raced back to the rock and succeeded in lighting a fire, ". . . & throwing fire brands on the roof of the little house & we staid until that roof was in flames & the heat of it had caused the wall of the great house to smoke—We then concluded the work was done, & undertook the 4th race, which was much more haz-ardous than the former ones, as the Enemy during the interval, had opened a great many more port-holes in that end of the building. . . . neither of us lost a drop of blood. . . ." although their clothing was riddled with holes and hair clipped from their heads.

No sooner had they reached a safe distance than ". . . to our great mor-tification, when the great house was beginning to flame—as heavy a storm of rain fell, as hath fallen from that time to the present, & which extin-guished the flames. . . ."

In a letter to General Gates' aide, Thomas Pinckney, Sumter reported that ". . . the action continued upwards of Eight hours; was offten within thirty feet of their works; but they were so constructed that I Coud by No means force them. I Made an attempt to fire them in the evening, and should have Succeeded, if the afternoon had Not proved excesively wet. My led being exhausted, I withdrew a small distance; I interrupted two parties going to Reenforse that post."[17]

Thwarted at Rocky Mount, Sumter shifted his attentions to a joint assault on Hanging Rock with Davie, reaching that post in the pre-dawn hours of 7 August after a night-long march. The troops apparently stopped to rest at some distance from Rocky Mount, since according to Joseph McJunkin ". . . at the order to rest on their arms, he and Mitchell High, of Fair Forest, sat down by a fire and slept a little; when they awoke, High said to McJunkin, 'this day I shall die'. . . ."[18]

In his pension statement Joseph McJunkin seriously overestimated the strength of the garrison at Hanging Rock: ". . . marched to Hanging Rock at which place there were 400 British regulars & 1400 Tories which we

---

*Hill's memoir preserved by Draper was chock-full of tales of Hill's heroics, so perhaps this account should be taken with a grain of salt.

attacked & defeated after marching all night when we were about 540 Strong." About 40 would serve as horse-holders, so the effective strength of the attackers was probably about 500.[19]

In McJunkin's memoir by O'Neall the enemy disposition and strength was described in more detail: "The detachment of British forces at this post consisted of the Prince of Wales regiment [about 278 men], and a large party of tories [probably 600–700] from North-Carolina, under the command of Col. Morgan Bryan. The latter were encamped south of Hanging Rock Creek, on a hill, something in the shape of a crescent; the regulars lay about two hundred yards from the tory camp on the Camden road."[20]

In McJunkin's memoir Sumter divided his force into three divisions. On the right Lieutenant Colonel Steen and the Second Spartans, including Captain McJunkin, were to push in between the two camps. On the center and left three regiments (Colonels Lyles, Watson, and Ervin) would isolate the more formidable redcoat regulars.

The plan miscarried in the darkness, and the entire Patriot force stumbled into contact with the North Carolina Loyalist militia under Colonel Bryan [Bryant in some accounts]. The attack was launched about dawn and the Second Spartans quickly severed the Tory militias from the redcoats.

McJunkin reported that ". . . when the former [regulars], led by Capt. McCullough, commenced, what was then called street-firing,* upon Stern's [a British officer] command. The right and left, led by Sumter, succeeded in turning their flank, and the whole of the Prince of Wales regiment were killed or taken except nine. McCullough fell wounded near the tory camp and surrendered. Simultaneous with Sumter's turning the flank of the regulars, the tory camp was attacked and carried, and the whole British force driven from the field. McCullough during the action, unable to move from his wounds, begged for water, which McJunkin gave him in a canteen procured from the tory camp." True to his premonition, Mitchell High was killed in the first exchange of fire.[21]

---

*This was a tactic for fighting on a confined front, like a street or bridge. The lead platoon or rank fired, peeled off to either side and passed down the flanks of the column to re-form in the rear. The second platoon advanced through, halted, presented and fired, and in turn retired back down the flanks of the column to be replaced by the third platoon, and so on. It was a complex drill quite beyond the capabilities of militia.

McCullough's plea for water is significant. The weather was hot, the fighting heavy and brutal, and the course of the battle not so simple. The Patriot pursuit of the fleeing Tory militia faltered when they ran headlong into the infantry of the British Legion and Brown's Rangers. Massed musket fire and a bayonet charge by the Prince of Wales Regiment drove the Patriots into a nearby tree line, and their sniping from that cover is actually what wrecked the Prince of Wales troops.

The British commander, Major John Carden, lost his nerve and turned command over to Captain John Rousselet of the Legion infantry. Rousselet retreated to high ground and formed a defensive square. Sumter reported that Rousselet's men ". . . were well posted, and had the advantage of a field-piece and open ground all around them. They had Detached a Colum to support Bryant, who, through a swamp, found means to turn my Right flank." Nothing could convince Sumter's weary troops to charge the British bayonets.[22]

In his memoir Tarleton served up scathing criticism of the Loyalist militia, and only faint praise to other units. He gave full credit for a victory to the British Legion, the infantry for repelling Sumter's attack, and described how a late-arriving detachment of forty mounted Legion infantry "deranged the American commander, and threw his corps into a state of confusion, which produced a general retreat."[23]

In reality the salvation of the British owed more to conditions than to any British feat of arms. Sumter reported that "They rallied again in Col. Robinson's encampment, and Notwithstanding their opposition was but feeble, and I in possession of two-thirds of their camp also for More than Half an hour, yet was obliged to leave them from Several Causes, the action having Continued without Interruption for three hours, men fainting with heat and Droughth, Numbers Kild and Wounded; but the true Cause of my not totally defeating them was the want of Led, having been obliged to make use of arms and ammunition taken from the enemy."[24]

Jacob Brown recalled ". . . the hanging rock where Col. Briant the Tory from the Yadkin was defeated which was a tough struggle." One North Carolina militiaman said, "This I believe was the hardest fought Battle during the war in the South."[25]

Unable to break the final defense, McJunkin remembered that ". . . Sumter took up his line of march toward Charlotte, N.C., until 2 o'clock, when the army stopped and took some refreshments, which was the first for twenty-four hours, although they had marched all of the previous night."[26]

After the battle at Hanging Rock the militia again demonstrated its organizational fluidity as men decided, individually, who they would follow next. Jacob Brown: "Then Genl. Sumpter and Col. [James] Williams separated and this applicant then went with Col. Williams [Little River] and then was attached to the company of his cousin Gabriel Brown [Second Spartans]."[27]

Within a matter of weeks Jacob had been under three commanders: Brandon (with Sumter as overall commander), Williams, then Brandon again. Brown later would switch regiments before the battle at King's Mountain to join John Sevier's Tennesseans

The affair at Hanging Rock was at best a draw, but held strategic significance. The war had not been going well for the Americans, and here at last was evidence of a senior militia leader—Sumter—who would fight on. It was also rumored that Congress was willing to cede Georgia and South Carolina in return for peace. This embarrassment prompted a Congressional resolution to fight for recovery of all lost colonies, and the dispatch of a new Southern Army to be commanded by no less than the victor at America's greatest triumph thus far, "the hero of Saratoga."[28]

A HERO MOVES SOUTH

The shift of a major British force to the south and the fall of Charleston prompted Congress to dispatch another army, of necessity marching slowly overland, to counter the move. To lead it they chose one of the most ambitious and controversial leaders in American military history, General Horatio Gates. Gates had proven an able military administrator during the French and Indian War, and Washington appointed him the adjutant general of the new Continental Army. He was promoted to Major General and given command of the Canadian Department in the aftermath of the disastrous Quebec expedition of 1776.

Gates was supremely ambitious and courted New England Congressmen who resented the appointment of a Virginian—Washington—to lead the Continental Army. Absenting himself from his command to lobby Congress to have him replace Washington as commander-in-chief, Gates missed the battle of Trenton and his ambitions were thwarted. Gates accepted credit—and a special gold medal—for the victory at Saratoga, although Gates himself proved timid and actual field command was exercised by a quartet of lesser officers including Benedict Arnold and Daniel Morgan. To capitalize on Saratoga, Gates began to bypass George Washington and report directly to Congress. His Congressional supporters appointed him head of the Board of War, strangely making him Washington's military subordinate but civilian superior. Washington's supporters in Congress finally broke up the "Conway cabal" (General Thomas Conway was one of Gates' co-conspirators); Gates apologized and was appointed to command the Eastern Department.[29]

For his Southern expedition Gates was given some of the best Continental regiments, one Delaware regiment and seven of Marylanders, under General "the Baron" Johann DeKalb. Militia and State troops added another 2,900 or so to his bloated force. Eager for further glory, he marched his army relentlessly through the late summer heat. To take the most direct route, he marched through regions of pine barrens, bypassing rich agricultural areas that could have fed his hungry army. He apparently scorned the services of Francis Marion and his superb scouts as being too ragged and unmilitary in appearance, and sent Marion away on a "make-work" mission.

Gates loaned two of his eight cannon and 100 of his Continentals to Thomas Sumter to break up British supply convoys. Sumter captured two convoys, but remained preoccupied with capturing yet more supplies. On 10 August Sumter wrote to Gates from the Wateree Ferry about five miles south of Camden, reporting "thirty prisoners, among Which Was Col. Cary, their Commander, together With thirty odd Waggons loaded with Corn Rum &c, also a Number of horses." In a dispatch dated two days later from "Lands Foard, Catauba River" some forty miles north of Camden, Sumter reported intelligence on British positions, and that "Our fieldpiece and houtozer are Now moving into the Neighbourhood of the Post; Camden altogether Defenseless, without the Troops have Retreat to it, Which I judge is Not the Case."* He went on to propose falling upon

---

*Gates' provision of a howitzer to Sumter is interesting. A field piece was a direct-fire weapon for solid balls and grapeshot. A howitzer lobbed a time-fuzed carcass (high-explosive shell) at a high angle, and would have been useful for plunging fire into fortified positions.

another supply column, and predicted the British would not defend Camden. From his reports Sumter was marching rapidly north up the west side of the Catawba-Wateree River (the river changes name at the confluence with Fishing Creek, which enters from the west), and away from Camden as Gates was marching south toward Camden on the eastern side.[30]

Other local militia units were also uncooperative, or perhaps scorned by Gates. At any rate the Second Spartans along with other regiments from the region turned west toward home, probably after reaching a consensus among the men. It turned out to be a wise decision. Brandon, and James Williams and his Little River Regiment, turned toward Ninety Six, the base from which Tory raiding parties were plaguing their home districts. Williams took up a position at Smith's Ford on the Broad River, a few miles from the camp occupied by McDowell. There the two developed a plan to attack the British garrison at Musgrove's Mill on the Enoree.[31]

MUSGROVE'S MILL, 18 AUGUST 1780

Also among those traveling west with the Little River and the Second Spartan Regiments was a detachment of the First Spartans, commanded by Major Benjamin Roebuck, Colonel William Bratton's regiment, and some of the "refugee" militiamen from the Ninety Six Brigade. Captain William Smith: ". . . I shortly afterwards returned to South Carolina under Sumter, and the troops, being divided, a part with my command, moved to the west, while Genl Sumter moved down the River."[32] Samuel Mayes: ". . . afterwards attached himself to the same Col. [Thomas Brandon], who had united his regiment with that of a Col. Williams of Ninety Six." Jacob Brown likewise recalled: "Then Gen Sumpter and Col. Williams separated and this applicant then went with Col. Williams."

Williams moved his men to Smith's Ford, on the Broad River, a few miles south of the Cherokee Ford, where McDowell's North Carolina militiamen were camped. It was a relatively normal divergence of militia units with differing priorities, and division of supplies was customary. Fractious Colonel William Hill thought otherwise: ". . . it was discovered that our commissary [Williams] and a col Brannon [Brandon] had eloped & had taken a great number of the public horses a considerable quantity of provisions with the camp equipage & and a number of men." In Williams' version of events, Colonel Edward Lacey was sent after Williams, but was unable to retrieve the "public property."[33] Research has failed to substantiate this charge, as it is unmentioned in any other memoirs, pension applications, or British letters regarding the activities of their enemies, nor is the incident is mentioned in the definitive biography of Lacey.[34]

In August of 1780 Elijah Clarke and Isaac Shelby brought a force over the Appalachians from what is now Tennessee into South Carolina. Samuel Hammond recalled that "Before this affair a few days, Colonels Williams and Bratton, of South-Carolina, Colonel Clark of Georgia, Colonel Isaac Shelby, of the Virginia or Holston settlement, McCall, Hammond, and Liddle of the Ninety-Six Brigade, formed a junction in the State of North-Carolina, near General McDowal's rendezvous, _____ county.[35]

"General McDowal was consulted on the propriety of making an excursion into South-Carolina, to look at the enemy, and to commence operations against their outposts, if they should be found assailable with our force."[36] McDowell's scouts reported a group of about 200 Loyalists at Musgrove's Mill on the Enoree River about 30 miles north of Ninety Six (modern day Cambridge, South Carolina). The Loyalists were camped near the mill to guard the ford, and although Major Patrick Ferguson was positioned within a few miles of Musgrove's Mill, his presence was not considered hazardous enough to prevent an attack. As historian John Buchanan has described: "The Rebels would not concede the upper Piedmont to Ferguson. He was an energetic soldier who had the reputation of being one of the few British officers who gave time and effort to sitting down and listening to the problems of the Back Country people instead of treating them as inferior colonials. A man like that had the potential of being a far more dangerous foe than Tarleton."[37]

The arrangement was typical of the often chaotic militia operations. Williams, Shelby, and Clarke agreed to share command, but afterward men who were there differed as to who actually excercised command. Bailey Anderson: "The head commander was General McDowell, but there were many other officers in the command. He recollects Colonel Clark of Georgia, Colonel Shelby of Holsten river, Colonel Williams of South Carolina . . . " Joseph Hughes recalled: "Col Clark of Georgia commanded at Musgroves" while soldiers like William Kenedy recalled only their own officers, noting that he was at Musgrove's Mill under the command of Captain Joseph Hughes and Colonel Thomas Brandon. Joseph McJunkin:

"I then fell under the command of Colonel Williams and hearing at Smith's Ford that the British and Tories was encamped at Musgrove's Mill on Enoree River marched 40 miles that night and attacked the Tories at daybrake and defeated them on 20th August 1780."[38]

The march would take them near Ferguson's camp, so they moved quickly and quietly, setting off about an hour before sundown on 17 August.[39] It seems most reasonable to assign the date of the battle as 18 August, as that matches James Williams' action report most closely. The column travelled through the woods until nightfall, when it became safer to use a road. Colonels Thomas Brandon and James Williams knew the area well enough to guide them, but it required fording numerous streams: Thicketty and Gilky Creeks, the Pacolet, the Tyger, and Fair Forest.

In the course of the night Colonel William Bratton and his command left the group with the intent of checking on his own neighborhood and rejoining them in the morning. Hammond complained: "This was injudicious in every point of view, for it afforded more than a double chance to the enemy of gaining intelligence of our approach, and a probability of our not falling in with them, or of their aiding us in this affair; and this proved to be the case, for they did not rejoin us until the affair was over."[40]

Arriving within a half mile of the enemy camp near daybreak, scouts were sent out to reconnoiter the enemy position. Crossing the Enoree well away from Musgrove's Mill, the Patriot patrol ran into an enemy patrol returning to camp, and in the ensuing melee, one Loyalist was killed and two wounded, leaving the survivors to race off to warn their camp. The Patriot scouts sped back to their party, who were waiting about a mile and a half away.

That morning a local man had arrived in the Patriot camp with grim news; the position at Musgrove's Mill had been reinforced the previous night with the arrival of Colonel Alexander Innes from Ninety Six with 200 Provincials from the New Jersey Volunteers, and DeLancey's New York Battalion with another 100 mounted South Carolina Royalists, all on their way to join Ferguson. The situation was critical: instead of 200 Patriots against 200 Loyalists, they now faced 500 men, 200 of whom were disciplined Provincials. The Patriots' horses were exhausted, rendering retreat impossible. They had to fight; the question was how.

Williams described their position: ". . . and being formed across the road, our line Extended at least 300 Yards in length, on a Timbered Ridge, and Twenty Horse was ordered on each flank, waiting the enemy approach." The traditional tale is that within half an hour the Patriots raised a breast-work of brush and fallen logs, but Williams' original report mentions no breastwork, simply stating "But Col. Williams gave orders that not a man should fire until (sic) the Enemy came within Point blank Shot, and every man take his Tree and not fire until (sic) Orders were given. . . ."[41] Shelby commanded the right, Williams the center, and Clarke the left. Behind Clarke was a reserve of forty men. The men were placed in a single line "in scattered or open order" and each group commanded by their own colonel. Sixteen men were detached to guard the horses in the rear.[42]

Captain Shadrack Inman of Georgia proposed to go forward and lure the enemy into an ambush; the commanders agreed, and Inman with twenty-five men crossed the Enoree. Inman skillfully engaged and ran, dropped back, engaged and ran at last three times. The Loyalists took the bait and chased Inman, halting about 150 yards from the Patriot position, due largely to the experienced Captain Abraham De Peyster's counsel. The Loyalists came on in three groups, with Major Fraser and his Provincials in the center, shouting and chasing the "fleeing" Inman and his men. The Provincials fired a volley at about 150 yards (45m) from the Patriot posi-tion. The Patriots patiently awaited a signal from their commanders, and fired at about 70 yards range.

The volley staggered the Provincials, but the well-trained infantry quickly recovered. Samuel Hammond: "On the second fire, they fell back in confusion. The fire then became brisk, and was kept up on our side. The tories saw the regulars fall back in disorder, and they also gave ground in confusion, and in fact without anything like pressure on our part."[43]

By this time Clarke had sent his reserve to bolster Shelby, and just as Clarke's men reached Shelby, the Loyalists' Commander Colonel Alexan-der Innes was shot by Wataugan William Smith. Within moments another Wataugan rifleman shot Major Fraser. "Our troops," said Hammond, "en-couraged by this disorder, rushed on with more boldness then prudence. The mounted riflemen on both flanks charged into the ranks of the retreating foe, and they fled and re-crossed the river in great disorder."[44] Men on foot ran forward with the mounted riflemen shouting the "Indian

This engraving of the Battle of Camden, from a painting by Alonzo Chapel, is fraught with symbolism. At far left militia flee in the face of British cavalry and bayonets, abandoning the Continentals to be overwhelmed by superior numbers (far right). At center Continental Major General Johann de Kalb is bayoneted; redcoats taunted the mortally-wounded de Kalb for hours.—NARA

halloo."[45] Abraham DePeyster would recall the eerie screeching sound of the battle cry at King's Mountain.

"The smoke, as well as the din and confusion, rose high above the exciting scene. The Tories ceased to make any show of defense when half way from the breast-works to the ford. The retreat then became a perfect rout." Loyalists and Provincials were shot down as they attempted to re-cross the rocky ford. One Loyalist stopped on the far bank of the Enoree to moon the victorious Patriots, and Thomas Brandon asked Golding Tinsley, the owner of an excellent rifle, "Can't you turn that arrogant braggart over?" Tinsley shot the fellow in the buttocks, and fellow Loyalists rushed out and dragged the injured man away.[46]

Onlookers watching from the roof of the Musgrove home cheered as they saw Inman chased across the river, but their shouts of joy ceased when they saw the battered Loyalist force struggling back across the Enoree. Edward Doyle, of Williams regiment: "They were entirely Defeated. I saw

52 Dead Bodies on the field of the Enemy and among them a British captain—it was said Captain Ennis was wounded in the neck but made his
escape. Our Troops was commanded by Col Williams Col Clark and Col
Shelby in all about Two hundred; in this Battle we had three men killed
and But few wounded."[47] On 5 September 1780, Colonel James Williams
filed a report, noting "We Kil'd dead on the field 60 of the Enemy the
greatest part British, and took 70 prisoners, among the Killed was a Major
Frazer of the British [Frazer was only wounded], one British Captain, and
Three Torie (sic) Captains. Col. Innis of the British by report mortally
Wounded by two balls one in the neck, the other broake his Thigh. Our
loss in this Action was Three killed on the field, Eight Wounded, one of
which is Mortal."[48] One of those killed was the brave Captain Shadrack
Inman, shot in the final chase of the broken Loyalists.

Following the rout, Samuel Hammond noted that the Patriot forces
were in such disarray that they needed to re-form their party and retrieve
their horses before crossing the river in pursuit of the fleeing Loyalists. The
pursuit never happened. The Patriots received word by express rider that
both General Gates and Colonel Sumter had been defeated, their armies
dispersed, and that Colonel Ferguson was in pursuit of them.[49] Samuel
Hammond: "Our retreat was hasty, and continued, without halting, day
or night, to feed or rest, for two days and nights" toward North Carolina.
Hammond added, "This little affair, trifling as it may seem, did much
good in the general depression of that period. Our numbers continued to
increase from that time, and all seemed to have more confidence in themselves."[50] The determined Patriots had proven that they could strike even
in the heart of Loyalist-held territory.

THE BATTLE OF CAMDEN, 16 AUGUST 1780

As Horatio Gates moved to threaten the strategic road nexus and British
base at Camden, Cornwallis marched from Charleston to reinforce Lord
Rawdon and the Camden garrison. Gates' force was twice that of Cornwallis, but half were suffering from heat exhaustion, dysentery, and other
maladies. Then, on the eve of battle, Gates finally fed his ravenous men a
hearty meal of corn meal and molasses, the latter a natural laxative.

On 16 August Gates and his debilitated men tried to face the redcoats
in formal battle. The bulk of the militia fled in the face of a bayonet charge,

most without firing a shot. Gates joined the militia in flight. The stampeding militia buffeted the Continentals, who somehow with a few North Carolina militiamen stood fast, but they were quickly overwhelmed; General DeKalb was killed.

The American Southern Army was utterly destroyed. The only remarkable achievement of sorts was that in his flight to Charlotte, Gates rode his powerful horse 170 miles in three days, something of an achievement for a man of his years and rotundity.

Gates had ruthlessly pursued charges against other officers, but despite this calamity his New England supporters in Congress quashed a board of inquiry. Gates eventually joined Washington's headquarters; although rumors implicated his staff in fomenting another mutiny in the army (the 1783 Newburgh Conspiracy), no charges were brought.

FISHING CREEK, 18 AUGUST 1780

Thomas Sumter had been advised of the British victory at Camden, but his militia force moved slowly, now encumbered with prisoners, two heavy cannon, and 80 wagonloads of captured supplies. On 17 August Cornwallis detached parties to hunt down the troublesome Gamecock. Banastre Tarleton, with about 350 men of the Loyalist British Legion, was soon hot on the trail, easily tracking Sumter but hampered by the Patriots' head start. Tarleton pared down his force to 100 dragoons, and mounted about 60 of his infantry.

Tarleton always roused his troops early, and on the morning of 18 August he surprised Sumter at a spot where several roads converged to cross Fishing Creek. James Collins and a small party of stragglers had joined up with Sumter for self-preservation. Collins said, ". . . there was a guard or picket posted at a short distance in the rear; the men were all fatigued; some had kindled fires and were cooking and eating; others tumbled down and were fast asleep, and all scattered in every direction. . . ."[51]

Collins: ". . . all at once the picket guards gave the alarm—they retreated on the main body with the enemy at their heels."

Most accounts say that Sumter slept through the first gunfire and barely escaped, half-dressed, into the surrounding woods; this seems to have originated with Tarleton. Wilson instead recalled that ". . . when wakened up by his men on the approach of the enemy, he rose up, rubbed his eyes—took in at a glance his situation, & exclaimed 'Let every man take care of himself.' . . . he sprang upon his horse, & jerked the bridle from the limb to which it was tied, & made his escape, with a couple of British troopers close on his heels, across the old Nation[?] Ford."[52]

Collins wrote that "Before Sumpter could wake up his men and form, the enemy were among them cutting down everything in their way. Sumpter, with all the men he had collected, retreated across the creek at the main road, leaving the remainder at the mercy of the enemy. It was a perfect rout, and an indiscriminate slaughter. No quarter was given. . . ."

Tarleton's dragoons easily routed Sumter's much larger force of 800 or more. With others Collins fled into the forest, where they slept uneasily, thinking the whole army dead or captive.

In the morning Collins and his comrades crept back. "The dead and wounded lay scattered in every direction over the field; numbers lay stretched cold and lifeless; some were as yet struggling in the agonies of death, while here and there, lay others, faint with the loss of blood, almost famished for water, and begging for assistance. The scene before me, I could not reconcile to my feelings, and I again began to repent that I had ever taken any part in the matter. . . ."

Collins and his companions scavenged the battlefield. "There was no time for choosing, and every man ate whatever he got hold of, asking no questions. . . ." Loose horses were wandering about. Someone found a fine rifle, complete with all accessories. "The gun was presented to the Colonel and after viewing her for some time, he observed 'Well, boys I have a use for this gun—I shall have to claim her as my part of the spoils.' Then calling me up, said, 'Well, James, you have been wanting a rifle for some time; here is one I think will suit you; she is light, and I think, a good one; she has an excellent lock; lay down your little shot-gun; take her, and take good care of her; I think you can do better with her than with your little shot-gun.'"

After hastily burying the dead ("poor fellows it was badly done") Collins and his comrades caught some horses and carried two wounded men to a nearby farmhouse. There they found an old cart, and carried the men onward to their homes ". . . where they both recovered, but not without being much disfigured by their wounds."

For minimal loss Tarleton killed over 150 Patriots, captured 300 or so including Continentals, the cannons, and all of Sumter's booty. His command completely shattered, Sumter rode into Charlotte alone two days later.

Within days the British had crushed a Patriot army, and eliminated the primary remaining militia force. South Carolina now seemed secure for the Crown. All that stood in the way of complete domination were the pesky Swamp Fox's guerillas, and a few disorganized rebels in the back country.

The rebel cause had now reached its nadir, with only scattered bands of hunted men. Collins went on to describe in detail how they kept a "flying camp"; never staying long in one place, avoiding roads, dividing into smaller parties. Sometimes dinners were served up by sympathizers. ". . . in these cases there was a long table, prepared of planks, set in an open place, at some distance from the house. Never stripping off saddles, and only unbitting our bridles, our horses were put to feed . . . each one sat down with his sword by his side; his gun lying across his lap, or under the seat on which he sat, and so eating his turn, until all were done. . . ."

But the stubbornness and resilience of the rebels in adversity would prove the stuff of legend.

THE FIRST SEIGE OF AUGUSTA, GEORGIA, 14–18 SEPTEMBER 1780

Atrocities committed beyond the borders of South Carolina would impact later events. Another important anchor of Cornwallis' screen of outposts was Augusta, Georgia, commanded by that staunchest of Loyalists, Colonel Thomas "Burnfoot "Brown.*

When Archibald Campbell landed in Georgia, Brown had joined forces with Campbell's redcoats to march on Augusta, participated in the British victory at Briar Creek, and helped to successfully defend Savannah. After the fall of Charleston he returned at the head of a powerful force of Loyalists to reclaim Augusta, and was named superintendent of the Creek and Cherokee.

Lieutenant Colonel Elijah Clarke of the Georgia Whig militia had

---

*Brown's name was also spelled Browne in various sources. It was not uncommon to see varied spellings of names, even in the person's own correspondence.

gained an increased following as the result of the victory at Musgrove Mill, but mostly because of his threats to kill any Whigs who did not join with him. On 14 September 1780, Clarke launched a failed surprise attack against the larger British and Indian garrison at Augusta. A brief siege ensued, and in broiling hot weather, conditions inside the position became desperate; cut off from their water source—the river—the garrison was reduced to drinking their collected urine. A Loyalist relief force from Ninety Six arrived on 18 September and the Whigs retreated, leaving behind those too badly wounded to move, one teenager who would not leave his wounded brother, and a Captain Asby.[53]

In accordance with Cornwallis' orders, Colonel John Cruger, the commander of the relief force, ordered one Whig who had violated parole hanged. In all thirteen Whigs were hanged from the outside staircase of the White-house, a large trading post building where "Burnfoot" Brown was lying wounded. Reportedly Brown had this done "… so that he might have the satisfaction of seeing the victims of his vengeance expire. Their bodies were delivered to the Indians, who scalped and otherwise mangled them and threw them in the river. . . . All this was merciful, when compared to the fate which awaited the other prisoners; they were delivered to the Indians to glut their vengeance for the loss they had sustained in the action and siege. The Indians formed a circle and placed the prisoners in the centre, and their eagerness to shed blood spared the victims from tedious torture: some were scalped before they sunk under the Indian weapons of war; others were thrown into fires and roasted to death."[54]

Many of the "Georgia refugees" again fled back into South Carolina, and their tales of British brutality would influence events in coming weeks.

BIGGER'S FERRY, 26 SEPTEMBER 1780

With the rebel forces apparently dispersed in South Carolina, Cornwallis was ready for an invasion of North Carolina. Marshalling numerous supply wagons, he began to move up the east side of the Catawba-Wateree River system, with Tarleton moving up the western side to forage and screen that flank. Both Sumter and Tarleton were stricken with fevers, Sumter in Charlotte, and Tarleton was left behind with a security detachment of the 71st Foot, so that their commands devolved upon Colonel Richard Winn and Major George Hanger respectively. Hanger shifted back east of the river.

Caught in Hanger's path on the eastern side of the Catawba, Winn gathered up all the supplies he had stripped from the countryside, and on 25 September crossed to the western side at Bigger's Ferry and a nearby ford.

The next morning Hanger's men tried to force a crossing back onto the western bank at Bigger's Ferry to deal with Winn's militia. The effort was unsuccessful, and the fighting devolved into a stalemate with both sides sniping at each other across the river. It was a small victory of sorts, and another badly-needed boost for Patriot morale.[55]

Other partisan bands plagued the British, conducting small raids and ambushes long since lost to history. In his autobiography James Collins described coordinated attacks on Loyalist posts at "Black Stock's" by local militia under Moffitt and at Musgrove's Mill by the Georgia refugees. Collins places these raids between Fishing Creek (August) and King's Mountain (October), but with no firm dates. Collins went on to describe in some detail carrying off the Patriot wounded from the Blackstock's raid, and convoying fifty or more Whig families to safety across the Broad River.[56]

CHAPTER 9

CHASING FERGUSON: THE POLITICS OF MILITIA COMMAND

Out of discord comes the fairest harmony.
—HERACLITUS

THE BATTLE OF KING'S MOUNTAIN WAS AT ONCE ONE of the pivotal battles of the war, and one of the least understood. The battle was a badly-needed victory at a time when the Patriot cause was at its lowest ebb, and it was lauded by George Washington and Thomas Jefferson. As late as the early twentieth century President Teddy Roosevelt, himself a student of history, wrote, "The victory was of far-reaching importance, and ranks among the decisive battles of the Revolution. It was the first great success of the Americans in the south, the turning point in the southern campaign, and it brought cheer to the patriots throughout the Union. The loyalists of the Carolinas were utterly cast down, and never recovered from the blow; and its immediate effect was to cause Cornwallis to retreat from North Carolina, abandoning his first invasion of that State."[1]

Today it is largely forgotten outside limited historical circles and some parts of the southern United States. King's Mountain had the misfortune to be fought in the backcountry with no major regular formations involved, so no Continental officers wrote detailed reports or memoirs. It was a violent but extremely brief and compartmentalized battle, fought in rugged terrain, with no central control by an overall leader. But worst of all was the myth-making that ensued over the following century.

Part of the mythology stems from the rivalry between the states of

South Carolina and Tennessee over whose troops contributed more to the victory. The story of the Tennessee "over mountain men" who made an epic march over the rugged terrain of the Appalachian Mountains to engage in the battle is an integral part of that state's identity. The Tennesseans played a significant role, but Carolinians often feel that Tennessee "hijacked" the story of the battle—mainly because several Tennesseans went on to become prominent politicians. The history was further muddied when two of these politicians—John Sevier, the first governor of Tennessee, and Isaac Shelby, the first governor of Kentucky—long after the fact, and for unknown motivations, accused the deceased William Campbell of Virginia of cowardice, triggering a long and bitter exchange of accusations.[2]

The worst fate to befall the battle was its most prominent historian. In 1881 Lyman C. Draper published *King's Mountain and Its Heroes*, and ever since, Draper's work has been considered the definitive study of the battle, and indeed much of the Southern Campaign. Unfortunately Draper must be read with a very critical eye, not a simple task for 593 pages of small print and no linear temporal narrative.

In details very relevant to our work Draper relied heavily upon a memoir of Colonel William Hill, who was not at the battle, written decades later. Hill hated James Williams, the senior Patriot officer present—killed at the close of the battle—with such an all-consuming passion that thirty-five years later he was still attacking the long-dead Williams. Hill's attitude was likely not improved by decades of listening to Williams being lauded in folk ballads like "Ferguson's Defeat":

> Brave Colonel Williams from Hillsboro came,
> The South Carolinians flocked to him amain,
> Four hundred and fifty, a jolly brisk crew,
> After old Ferguson we then did pursue. (verse 2)

Or "King's Mountain—1780":

> Up—up the steep together brave Williams led his troop,
> And join'd by Winston, bold and true, disturb'd the Tory coop.
> (verse 2)[3]

The Williams-Hill controversy and its complexities are the subject of a lengthy book,[4] and the Hill version of events was accepted by generations of historians as a "primary document." Despite the fact that Draper himself discounted Hill's story that Williams was shot down by Colonel William Lacey's men for his supposed cowardice, for a time the National Park Service interpretive placards at the King's Mountain National Battlefield implied that Williams had been so despised that he was "fragged"—killed by his own men. Draper followed Hill in attributing only a small group of miscreants to Williams' command, and the park placards even now attribute only "30 North Carolina militiamen" to Williams' command.[5]

Hill's unrelenting hatred of Williams and the subsequent errors it propagated are relevant here because in his efforts to denigrate Williams, Draper found it necessary to obliterate the role of Williams' Little River Regiment, as well as Thomas Brandon's Second Spartans and other militia units that had willingly subordinated themselves to Williams. Some subsequent authors have gone so far as to place Brandon's command under Isaac Shelby of Tennessee.

Draper often contradicted himself, for example citing a post-battle communiqué signed by Colonels William Campbell, Isaac Shelby, and Benjamin Cleveland that stated ". . . we were joined by Col. James Williams, with four hundred men, on the evening of the 6th of October. . . ." This indicates that these colonels considered that the South Carolinians at the battle were a sizeable force under Williams' command. This is also consistent with Williams' letter to General Horatio Gates (2 October 1780) giving his strength as about 450 men.[6]

Recent historians have been kinder to Williams: "His steadfast commitment to the Patriot cause exacted the severest sacrifices from him and his family. That commitment and those sacrifices entitle him to a much better treatment than he has enjoyed at the hands of historians."[7]

Rather than rely upon Draper or derivative accounts, we have examined the pension records and memoirs of men known to have fought at King's Mountain. An example is another case where Draper again contradicts himself, citing Thomas Young: "On the top of the mountain, in the thickest of the fight, I saw Col. Williams fall, and a braver or a better man never died upon the field of battle. I had seen him but once before [on] that day. It was in the beginning of the action, as he charged by me at full speed around the mountain. . . .

"The moment I heard the cry that Col. Williams was shot, I ran to his assistance, for I loved him as a father, he had ever been so kind to me...." This and other accounts hardly seem the description of a thief and coward scorned and ultimately assassinated.[8]

By the autumn of 1780 Cornwallis' mission in the Carolinas—to break organized resistance and recruit local militias—was foundering. South Carolina was proving a tough nut to crack, and he could no longer adequately supply even his weakened army from local resources. Shifting north out of necessity, he prepared to move into North Carolina.

Cornwallis summoned Major Patrick Ferguson to his headquarters near Camden and assigned him a new mission. By early September Ferguson had returned and informed his subordinates, including Lieutenant Anthony Allaire of the American Volunteers, that "... we were to be separated from the army, and act on the frontier with the militia."[9]

Ferguson's mission, eagerly accepted, was to sweep through the back country, screen the left (inland) flank of the main army, and recruit as many Loyalist militiamen as possible. Born in 1744 in Scotland, Ferguson had served since the age of sixteen, fought in Europe during the Seven Years War, designed a practical breech-loading rifle, and was a world-renowned marksman, staunch advocate of light infantry tactics, and was experienced in frontier warfare. Badly wounded at Brandywine (11 September 1777) his right arm was paralyzed. Ferguson was highly regarded by Sir Henry Clinton, who assigned him to a staff billet (intelligence) while he recuperated. Ferguson veered to and fro between suggesting tolerance and harshness in dealing with the rebels, and at one point advised wholesale destruction in Connecticut and Rhode Island. He was eventually returned to full duty, and having distinguished himself in the northern colonies in both field and staff positions, he came south with Clinton as a major in the 71st Regiment of Foot.[10]

In late May of 1780 Clinton promoted Ferguson to Inspector of Militia, an independent role he eagerly embraced. As a Clinton protégé Ferguson came under a cloud of suspicion from Cornwallis and his inner circle after Clinton departed. There was never any suggestion of disloyalty, but nevertheless members of Cornwallis' inner circle distrusted and undermined Ferguson at every turn.

Still, Ferguson threw himself into his assignment with his customary fervor, recruiting militia, clothing some in redcoat uniforms, and training them in musket drill and the use of the bayonet, even if most were equipped only with crude socket bayonets: butcher knives with the handles cut down to shove into the large bores of their muskets. Also these were men from the same culture as their Whig opponents: headstrong, argumentative, ill-disciplined, and prone to desertion. Most of the Loyalists were also cowed by the years of Whig domination, and Ferguson would have an uphill battle in trying to turn them into a determined, disciplined fighting force.

In some ways Ferguson may have been well ahead of his time in attempting to win "hearts and minds" in the partisan war, in an era when British officers were often arrogant and callous. "It would be hard to imagine a better partisan leader. . . . his courtesy stood him in good stead with the people of the country; he was always kind and civil, and would spend hours in talking affairs over with them and pointing out the mischief of rebelling against their lawful sovereign. He soon became a potent force in winning the doubtful to the British side. . . ." If true, it was a tactic well-suited to the local culture.[11]

Despite his problems Ferguson was eager to carry the war into the back country and invade North Carolina. Perhaps too eager. In an era when officers were expected to be ambitious and headstrong, Nisbet Balfour, the garrison commander at Ninety Six, repeatedly advised Cornwallis that he thought Ferguson too full of himself, and that "I find it impossible to trust him out of my sight." In reply Cornwallis wrote, "I am afraid of his getting to the frontier of N. Carolina and playing us some cussed [or cursed] trick."[12]

Cornwallis was rightfully pessimistic about Ferguson's militia, and wary of Ferguson's trust in his own abilities. He advised his own superior, Sir Henry Clinton, that "Ferguson is to move into Tryon County [NC] with some militia, whom he says he is sure he can depend upon for doing their duty and fighting well; but I am sorry to say that his own experience, as well as that of every other officer, is totally against him."[13]

Based in Gilbert Town, North Carolina, Ferguson prepared to move back into South Carolina on another recruiting sweep and a "search and destroy" mission to root out the last rebel resistance. It was a mission that would present him with a new and previously unrecognized threat.

The largely Scots-Irish settlers had long since breached the 1763 Proclamation Line that marked the westward boundary of legal white settlement and had settled along the Watauga, Nolachucky, and Holston Rivers in modern-day Tennessee. In 1772 these settlers declared the semi-autonomous—and quite illegal—Wautauga Association (sometimes called the Wautauga Republic) seen by some as the first independent and democratic American government. The Republic purchased large tracts of land that had previously been "leased" from the Cherokee. Dissident tribesman had never recognized the legal nicety of the lease, and by July 1776 fighting had again flared along the frontier. In November 1776 the newly declared State of North Carolina annexed the outlaw republic.

The residents of this new western province had already acquired several derisive names from the British. One was the back-water men, so named because the rivers flowed west. Another was the over-mountain men. Whatever they were called, they lived in an environment even harsher than those of the eastern piedmont. They were even more violent, ruthless, and independent-minded than their brethren east of the mountains, if that was at all possible.

Colonel Isaac Shelby had anticipated the eventual threat from Cornwallis and his operations east of the mountains, but with the exception of Shelby's small band at Musgrove's Mill, the over-mountain communities had largely sat out the conflict.[14]

Stung by the presence of Shelby at Musgrove's Mill, at this juncture Ferguson's benevolence—and his common sense—both seem to have deserted him. On 10 September 1780 he paroled Samuel Philips, a kinsman of Shelby, to deliver an ultimatum to the over-mountain communities: ". . . if they did not desist from their opposition to the British arms, he would march his army over the mountains, hang their leaders, and lay their country waste with fire and sword."[15]

It was a catastrophic error in judgment. With their own communities already threatened by British-sponsored Cherokee raids, the over-mountain men had the same visceral reaction to Ferguson: a desire for utter annihilation. Lord Rawdon in Camden would eventually record that, "A numerous army now appeared on the frontier drawn from Nolachucky and other settlements whose very existence had been unknown to us."[16]

Philips made haste to report the threat to Shelby, and a few days later

Shelby interrupted Colonel John Sevier's autumnal celebration for an urgent conference. Roosevelt described the celebration as ". . . feasting and merry-making, for he had given a barbecue [in the vernacular of that time and place, roasting a whole hog], and a great horse race was to be run, while the backwoods champions tried their skill as marksmen and wrestlers. . . ."; Buchanan described it simply as a horse race.[17] It was more likely a typical frontier post-harvest bacchanalia, with eating, alcoholic excesses, contests of various sorts, fighting, gambling, courting, and general carousing.

Quickly agreeing to a 25 September assembly at Sycamore Shoals on the Wautauga River, Sevier in turn contacted Colonel William Campbell of Virginia, since sufficient men had to be left behind to defend against the Cherokee. The rendezvous assembled about 1,040 men (estimates vary slightly) including Campbell's Virginians, and Charles McDowell's North Carolinians who had taken refuge at Sycamore Shoals. The Presbyterian Reverend Samuel Doaks concluded a rousing sermon with a battle cry: "The sword of the Lord and of Gideon!" and the assembled force set off on an epic march.[18]

On the march two men deserted from Sevier's command; it was suspected that they had ridden to warn Ferguson, so the route of the march was changed. The over-mountain men arrived at Quaker Meadows (present town of Morganton NC), the family seat of the McDowells, on 30 September.

The homestead had recently been raided by Ferguson's militia, who had ransacked the house and stolen—among other things—the clothing of Mrs. McDowell's two sons, Colonel Charles McDowell and Major Joseph McDowell. The Tories described how they would first make her sons beg for their lives, and then murder them. Unfazed, the old lady gave them the sharp edge of her tongue, reminding them prophetically that ". . . in the whirligigs of life, they might, sooner or later, have a little begging to do themselves."[19]

The next day the combined force, now swelled to about 1,400 by more North Carolinians under the brutal but effective Colonel Benjamin Cleveland, rode out of Quaker Meadows. The day's march would cover eighteen to twenty hard miles to a campsite near the crest of South Mountain.

Astute leaders, Shelby and Sevier realized that their unwieldy command might be undone by its own success in recruiting militia. There were five colonels in camp, with no clear commander. Being what they were, the always unruly militiamen were restive. "The little disorders and irregularities which began to prevail among our undisciplined troops, created much uneasiness in the commanding officers—the Colonels commanding the regiments." Charles McDowell was the senior Colonel, but many were not confident of his physical fitness for the arduous campaign. In a shrewd bit of politicking (for which he later claimed full credit) Shelby argued for Colonel William Campbell of Virginia—an experienced officer with the largest regiment—to be nominally in overall command. Charles McDowell would ride to ask General Horatio Gates (still in regional command despite the Camden debacle) to send a general officer to come and take overall charge, leaving his brother Major Joseph McDowell in command of his regiment.

"On the morning after the appointment of Col. Campbell, we proceeded towards Gilbert Town [NC], but found that Ferguson, apprised of our approach, had left there a few days before."[20]

Even as the over-mountain men and the North Carolinians marched to help them, a rancorous power struggle was playing out within the South Carolina militia.

James Williams had carried the news of the victory at Musgrove Mill to the governor in exile, James Rutledge, in North Carolina. Purportedly Rutledge had rewarded Williams with a brigadier's commission which would effectively have given him command of all active South Carolina militia. Even Williams' staunchest defenders point out that there is no preserved paper record of this appointment.[21]

There is also no record to support his detractors' claims that Williams himself claimed full credit for the victory at Musgrove's Mill. Rutledge would hardly be the first—or last—politician to erroneously reward the bearer of good news. At any rate the claims against Williams are based upon the vitriolic memoir of William Hill, propagated by Draper.

Back in South Carolina at Sumter's camp on the Catawba River, Williams had his commission read aloud, and the huge uproar it caused and its immediate impact would seem to suggest that those present accepted that some sort of document did indeed exist. The ego of Sumter, who had been elected brigadier by some of his fellows (but had not in fact been commissioned by the governor) could not tolerate this. Hill wrote that ". . . much to his [Williams'] well deserved mortification they all to a man knowing his recent conduct in deserting his post and embezzling the public property as before mentioned refused to have any thing to do with him or his commission and if he had not immediately left the camp he would have been stoned out of it."[22]

Of course this is patently false, since at least Brandon's regiment and Williams' own Little River troops followed him.

What is established is that Sumter arranged a rump election to appoint a delegation to hurry to a meeting with Governor Rutledge in Hillsborough to assure that he, not Williams, would be granted overall command of the South Carolina militia. Not content just to stack the deck with loyal followers (Hill excepted; he was too weak for the pace of travel Sumter would set), Sumter absented himself on the eve of one of the decisive battles of the Revolution to accompany the delegation.

At about the same day—30 September—that the over-mountain men left Quaker Meadows, the South Carolina militia marched out searching both for them and Ferguson. In his memoir Hill had by now reduced Williams' command to "the few followers" who skulked along at the rear of the marching column, and elaborated that ". . . such was the spirit of animosity cherished by the Sumter men against Williams and his followers, that they shouted back affronting words—even throwing stones at them, the whole day."[23]

All other factors aside, this episode—covered in five pages of great (if dubious) detail by Draper and repeated by subsequent historians—beggars the imagination. These were hard men, and Brandon had a reputation for violence when provoked. The idea that he—and others of the Second Spartan Regiment—would passively accept being repeatedly insulted and pelted with rocks seems incredible. More germane, not a single memoir or pension record of the officers or men in either Williams' or Brandon's command mentioned the dispute, much less being stoned.

As early as 4 October the over-mountain men had encamped near Gilbert Town. They had good intelligence that Ferguson was moving south, presumably toward the big base at Ninety Six, but they were still uncertain of his location or destination. Ferguson's actual intent was to link up with Cornwallis, and he was already dispatching couriers to entreat Cornwallis to send help.

The South Carolina militia was encamped northeast of Gilbert Town at Flint Hill, and Hill's narrative—again elaborated upon by Draper—made much of the continuing heroic efforts by himself and Colonel Edward Lacey (who made no mention of any such goings-on) to stymie Williams' and Brandon's obstinate treachery as late as Thursday, 5 October.

Hill also accused Williams and Brandon of riding out toward the mountains, i.e., westward, and returning the next morning, 5 October. In Hill's version of events Williams and Brandon rode out to intercept Sevier and Shelby, and attempted to persuade them to move toward Ninety Six ". . . where his own interests [i.e., his properties, long since destroyed] were centered . . ." and accused Williams of attempting to divert those commands ". . . simply for the sake of Tory booty. . . ." Hill went on to recount that Lacey was dispatched to Shelby and Sevier's camp expressly to expose Williams' knavery.[24]

Shelby made no mention of any such meeting with Williams and Brandon. The only shred of independent evidence that might corroborate Hill's accusation is Lacey's comment that "They [Shelby and Sevier] also had later assurance, from two [unnamed] men, that Ferguson had gone to the British post at Ninety-Six. . . ."[25]

Lacey himself made no mention of any Williams-Brandon conspiracy, but he is far more informative in that he provided an insight as to how the *ad hoc* command functioned. "In a consultation between [Colonels] Lacey, Hill, Williams, Brandon, Roebuck, Hammond, Hambright, Graham, Hawthorne, and Chronicle, it was agreed upon, that an express should be sent to Colonels Campbell, Cleaveland, McDowell, Shelby, and Sevier, to let them know Col. Ferguson's whereabouts, position, force, &c; inviting them to come on, unit their forces and attack Ferguson on King's Mountain.

"Most fortunately for the American cause, Col. Edward Lacey rode that express, sixty miles in one day; late at night he entered the Whig camp, and was taken prisoner and blind-folded; he begged the sentinel to conduct him immediately to the Colonel's quarters, where he introduced himself as Colonel Lacey. They at first repulsed his advances, and took him to be a Tory spy. However, he had the address at last to convince them he was no imposter. . . ." After a quick bite to eat and riding a fresh horse, he rode back with a plan to rendezvous at The Cowpens on 6 October.[26]

Lacey further recalled that earlier that evening Campbell had informed

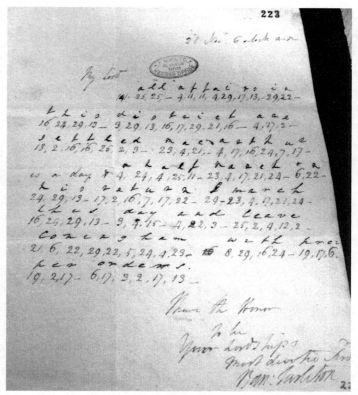

Whig partisans frequently intercepted British couriers, severely disrupting operations. For security, British commanders resorted to numerical substitution codes in critical correspondence.
—BRITISH NATIONAL ARCHIVES

the other Colonels that he was breaking off the apparently futile chase, and was returning west of the mountains. The men from the western settlements were undoubtedly apprehensive over the Cherokee threat. Upon learning that Ferguson was within reach, however, Campbell quickly changed his mind.

What is established is that detachments from Brandon's Second Spartans were monitoring chokepoints and scouring the countryside as scouts, but there is no evidence that either Brandon or Williams ever left the camp even to check on these parties. Benjamin Merrell: ". . . in September 1780 he again Volunteered under Capt. Robert McGomery [Montgomery] and went in pursuit of Ferguson & his party marching from the Same place crossing the Catawba River at the Tucadejah [Tuckaseegee] ford then up the East side of said River to Baiteys ford then up the south fork of Catawba thence crossing Broad River at the Island Ford thence to the

Cowpens thence across Broad River at the Cherokee Ford from which place our company were permitted to return home to Join in the pursuit on the next day but before the time [. . .] for starting the intelligence [w]as received that Ferguson had been defeated and we were not called out at that time. . . ." John Moor often told his wife he was guarding a crossing on the Catawba River at the time of the battle of King's Mountain and ". . . was in hearing of the Battle and was marched up to the Battle Ground Immediately after the close of the fight and was appointed with others to take charge of the Prisoners." William Pelham was scouting at the time of King's Mountain, and had likely been moved from Gavin Gordon's company to George Aubrey's company,* Pelham's widow was unclear on the timing of the change. Some in Robert Montgomery's company were not aware of the battle until 11 October.[27]

While the soldier-politicians were bickering and maneuvering, the ranks of the regiments were being swelled by some very unlikely recruits. Elisha Parker had been wounded and captured at Danbury, Connecticut during March 1777, shipped south, and spent three years in a Charleston Harbor prison hulk before escaping in June 1780. Penniless, nearly naked, and friendless, Parker was trying to work his way home. With roving Tory bands scouring the countryside, many such refugees found it expedient to work their way home by enlisting in a militia unit, travelling as far as that unit went toward home, and then joining the next unit closer to home. Parker joined Brandon's regiment and marched back south with it.[28]

On 5 October the first militia contingents arrived at the Cowpens rendezvous, straggling in over the late afternoon and early hours of the night. The owner of the Cowpens property was a prosperous Tory named Saunders. Saunders was ". . . at the time, in bed—perhaps not very well, or feigning sickness; from which he was unceremoniously pulled out, and treated pretty roughly. When commanded to tell at what time Ferguson had passed that place, he declared that the British Colonel and his army had not passed there at all; that there was plenty of torch pine in his house, which they could light, and search carefully, and if they could find any

---

*Pelham misidentified Aubrey as "Avery"; other pensioners place Aubrey himself at King's Mountain, but the company had routinely been subdivided. Pelham's usual assignment as a scout was to patrol the Indian Line from Otterson's Fort.

track or sign of an army, they might hang him, or do whatever else they pleased with him. . . ."[29]

Thomas Young recounted that some of the over-mountain men were already at the Cowpens: "I was under the command of Col. Brandon. Late in the evening, preceding the battle, we met Colonels Campbell, Shelby, Cleaveland, and Sevier, with their respective regiments, at the Cowpens, where they had been killing some beeves."[30]

Lacey instead recorded that ". . . a little before sun-down the mountain men came up."[31]

These conflicting accounts as to who arrived in what sequence suggest that in all likelihood the arrival of units at the rendezvous was not as simple as has been assumed by many historians following Draper's lead. Probably the long columns, the inevitable stragglers, Brandon's scouting parties, foragers, and others filtered in over the course of many hours.

Joseph Kerr—described only as "the cripple spy," a member of Williams' command, and recommended by Colonel Steen as "faithful and efficient"—had several days before been dispatched to ascertain Ferguson's strength and whereabouts. Kerr's account on his return could stand as a model for modern efficiency in espionage.

Kerr ". . . found the British and Tories encamped about one hundred yards apart, and their arms staked up and no sentinels." In this single detail Kerr clearly mistook Ferguson's handful of American Volunteers, in their red-coats, for British Regulars. "This declarant gained easy access to them by passing himself as a Tory—as Tories were then numerous in that part of the country. He believes, but in this he may be mistaken, that Ferguson's strength, including British and Tories, was not exceeding 1,500. He ascertained from the Tories that they intended on the evening of that day to go from Quinn's old place to the top of Kings Mountain and remain there a few days in order to give protection to all the 'rebels' who would join Ferguson's standard. After obtaining this information and making these discoveries this declarant returned the next day to Cols. Sevier, Shelby, Cleveland and Steen having stayed all night at the house of a Tory who lived 10 miles from Quin's old field. He reached our encampment about sunset."[32]

Kerr's report was corroborated by another spy, Enoch Gilmer, "a shrewd, cunning fellow" who posed as a mentally deranged stranger.[33]

The Patriots now had hard intelligence that Ferguson was encamped on Brushy Ridge. It was a location familiar to many of the locals as there was a hunting camp located there; open areas like that where Ferguson planned to camp was prime deer habitat.*

After a hasty meal a conference of the colonels pared down the unwieldy force by leaving about half, men on foot and those with exhausted or weakened horses, at The Cowpens to follow along as best they could. Estimates of the size of the total force that left The Cowpens vary wildly. Most have accepted the counts by Shelby (910) or Hill (933) because of their seeming precision, but with undisciplined militia from numerous units milling about in the dark, and units coming and going at different times, no one was taking a precise head count.[34]

Eager to catch Ferguson, it would be a fast and harrowing night march through rough terrain ". . . of about twenty seven miles, or perhaps only twenty six. . . ." by Kerr's estimate. Kerr was remarkably accurate; the distance was probably about 26.5 miles estimated from modern topographic maps.[35]

The details of the march from the Cowpens to the Brushy Ridge battle site are even more problematical. Most accounts of the battle would have the Patriot militia undertaking the harrowing night march in a single long column, probably two horsemen abreast. This assumption is contradicted by first-person accounts, and the feat is simply impossible. The problem is familiar to any military leader or traffic engineer.

Moving columns of even well-disciplined troops under adverse conditions results in a sort of slinky-toy motion. One individual slows or stops for whatever cause, and traffic piles up in a wave that propagates backward down the column. When the individual who stopped moves forward again there is a hesitation before each successive individual behind can resume moving. Men (or trucks or horses) speed up to catch the individual ahead, opening huge gaps in the column. Parts of the column are stopped, while others run to catch up, imparting a constant and exhausting stop-and-go

---

*King's Mountain is a prominent topographic feature in North Carolina. The battle was actually fought on the northeastern extension of Brushy Ridge some 4.7 miles south-southwest in York County, SC. The area is very rural, and the closest town of any size is Grover, NC (population 708) 5.9 miles away by road.

pace. The effect would have been magnified by darkness, rain, and mud-slickened trails, and exacerbated by stronger or weaker horses, poor visibility, fatigue, debilitating cold, and a host of other issues.

A simple arithmetic calculation—the length of a typical horse and the natural following distance that horses like to maintain—indicates that under *ideal* conditions a double-column of about 900 mounted men would be over 1.2 miles long. The unwieldiness of such a column of untrained militiamen in near-total darkness and rain is mind-boggling. It is also contradicted by memories of the participants.

Many individuals did not record the details of the final leg of the march to King's Mountain, but others provided cogent descriptions with approximate times at which they passed specific landmarks.

James Collins was in Chronicle's command, a force that had been trailing Ferguson for some days. Chronicle was probably hottest on Ferguson's trail, as Collins recorded crossing the Broad River at Cherokee Ford late on Friday 6 October, probably before dark. "The spies brought news that he had crossed Broad River at a place called the Cherokee Ford, and had made a stand. . . ." The information was outdated, as the spies reported, "He had taken a position at a small distance down the river, below the crossing place. . . ." when in fact Ferguson was by this time already at Brushy Ridge.[36]

If so, Chronicle's regiment was the first to face the hazards of crossing the water barrier at Cherokee Ford. The pursuing militia had to be extremely wary of potential ambushes set by outriders from Ferguson's column.

The importance of water crossings is little appreciated today, but to be caught in the middle of a river with no cover at hand was disaster. Any unit caught divided on the opposite sides of a river could be cut to pieces in detail. Incredibly, Ferguson had not picketed the various fords, chokepoints that any approaching enemy would have to negotiate.

Collins: "On Friday evening, we came to the river, with the full expectation of meeting them, and being attacked in crossing: we passed over, but no enemy appeared. The enemy had moved on, I think about nine miles, and made a stand at a place called King's Mountain. . . ." Safely across the river, "We had encamped at for the night, on the ground the enemy had left [Ferguson's old campsite on the eastern side of the Broad River]. . . ."[37]

Collins described this easily recognizable, recently occupied site as "...
a position at a short distance down the river, below the crossing place; having the river on one side, a high rocky ridge on the other, and a large old
field fronting where we must of necessity cross the river."*

In 1842 militiaman Silas McBee of Brandon's regiment remembered
tarrying until darkness, and a night march. "There was an Englishman of
the name of Saunders and his ungathered corn crop of perhaps fifty acres
was harvested in about ten minutes. Some of his beeves were killed and
roasted. Here at the cowpens, being pretty well fatigued fine range along
a hill, the army lay an hour to refresh, the horses being pretty well fatigued.
Saunders corn was a timely Godsend. We marched on twelve miles in
pitchy dark.† A drizzly rain commenced. The road was pretty good. We
progressed slowly."[38]

Thomas Young gave a more detailed account overall, and said that
"We then proceeded on towards the Cherokee Ford on Broad River where
the enemy was said to be. We traveled on till late at night; we then lay
down to sleep without any attention to order that I could perceive." Young
also recalled a much longer rest period than McBee. "When I awoke in
the morning, Joseph Williams, the little son of Col. Williams was lying at
my back. We arose and pushed on &crossed the Broad River at Cherokee
Ford. The enemy were not there.[39]

Though the accounts differ in detail, both agree that Brandon's command paused to rest at some point on the west side of the Broad River
before pressing on to Cherokee Ford.‡

The regiments from North Carolina, and particularly those from far-

---

*Draper, *King's Mountain* (p. 229) places this site "Some three miles above the Cherokee
Ford . . ." but Collins' description is quite explicit. It closely corresponds to a topographic chokepoint slightly downstream from the location where Ford Road (west
bank) and Cherokee Ford Road (east bank) drop down to the river level. This is immediately upstream of where Doolittle Creek enters the river, and is an almost ideal position from which to defend the river crossing. The valley of Doolittle Creek forms a
gently rising, though winding, ramp-like path through the rugged land along the river
and onto the gentler upland terrain.

†The distance from the Cowpens to the old Cherokee Ford, near the present-day town
of Cherokee Falls, SC, was actually about 16.75 miles/27km by the most direct feasible
route.

away Virginia and Tennessee, were not so fortunate. Eager to have done with Ferguson, the decision was made to march at night through unfamiliar terrain. Benjamin Sharp of Campbell's Virginia command was typical. The men ". . . ate a hasty meal of such provisions as we had procured, and, by dark mounted our horses and after marching all night, crossed the Broad River by the dawn of day. . . ."[40]

Andrew Creswell of Campbell's command: ". . . we struck camp at the Cowpen but did not get leave to eat our beef till we took up the line of march which lasted all night."[41]

This comment is interesting, since it suggests the lurching stop-and-go night march set an average pace of about 1.5 miles per hour. Worse, this group ". . . began their march about 9 o'clock but it proved a very dark & raining night the path being small & the woods very thick, the troop got scattered & dispersed through the woods thus wondering [wandering] the whole night, that when morning appeared the rear of them was but 5 miles from the Cowpens. . . ."[42]

A cold rain began at some point, although accounts vary slightly about the time the drizzle commenced. Despite the bone-chilling rain, the ill-equipped militiamen wrapped anything they could—their blankets and their coats—around their powder and the firing mechanisms of their weapons to protect them from the wet.

---

‡Tennessean Colonel Isaac Shelby said that "just after dark" Williams had marched off to attack 600 Tories rumored to be nearby, despite being "much opportuned to abandon that object," and arrived at Cherokee Ford *after* the Tennessee contingent; see Dunkerly, *The Battle of King's Mountain—Eyewitness Accounts* (p. 70). No other accounts corroborate this.

CHAPTER **10**

KING'S MOUNTAIN, 7 OCTOBER 1780: THE DAY OF BATTLE

*Nobody ever defended anything successfully, there
is only attack and attack and attack some more.*
—GEORGE S. PATTON

THE PURSUERS HAD UNDOUBTEDLY HOPED TO CATCH
Ferguson early in the day, but it was not to be. His last known position
was still about 9.5 miles (15km) away from the most advanced Patriot unit,
and about 900 feet (275m) higher in elevation, with much rugged country
still to cross.

As dawn neared the rain was still falling (Young said that after crossing
the river about dawn "It commenced raining on us"), and the Patriot troops
were strung out over at least twelve miles (19km) of forest trails. Chronicle
was across the river and rested, Williams and Brandon crossed sometime
around dawn. The main body was still unaware that Patriot troops were
on the far shore: Gilmer was sent ahead to scout the crossing. A short while
later Gilmer's booming voice was heard singing *Barney Linn* at the top of
his lungs, a signal that the crossing was clear.[1]

Becoming lost forced the tail of the main column ". . . to march un-
commonly hard which caused many of the horses to give out as but few of
them were shod. . . ." This observation is also interesting in that it indicates
that men with lame or weakened horses (or men still lost in the forest) further reduced the number that had departed the Cowpens.[2]

Because of the rain the Broad River was now flowing high and fast.
Men with larger and stronger horses were assigned to cross at the upstream

side of the ford, their horses forming a barrier to the flow, though Draper says, "Not much attention was paid to the order." The entire force crossed without a single man being unhorsed.[3]

The signs of Ferguson's destructive passage were clear. "We passed a meeting house, around which the Enemy had cut off the tops of the chestnut trees to get the fruit," Young recalled.[4]

Sending Gilmer ahead again, the column stopped to loot a cornfield, the famished men eating the raw ears of corn. Just before mid-day it began to rain more heavily, and the rapid pace and continuous cold rain was taking its toll on the men and horses. Several of the colonels proposed breaking off the pursuit. Shelby reportedly swore that "I will not stop until night, if I follow Ferguson into Cornwallis' lines," apparently ending the matter.[5]

At about noon the weather front passed. The incessant rain ceased, and the day turned clear with "a fine cool breeze."

The columns pressed on, gathering intelligence from the local residents as they went. They overtook the spy Gilmer at one house, where he was posing as a Tory to gain the confidence of some women. One told Gilmer that she had taken some chickens to Ferguson at the old hunting camp about three miles (5 km) away just that morning. Colonel Campbell maintained the ruse, seizing Gilmer, throwing a noose over his neck, and dragging him out to be hanged in the front yard. Major Chronicle argued that they not hang him where his ghost would haunt the house, so Gilmer was marched out of sight down the road and released to ride ahead.

With increasingly precise intelligence as to where Ferguson was camped, and his approximate strength, another conference of the colonels concocted a typical frontier battle plan, familiar to all from Indian fighting. The force would divide into two columns, surround Ferguson's camp on the ridge, and attack from all sides to assure that no one escaped. The only issue was whether the Patriot numbers were sufficient to surround a numerically superior enemy. It is relevant to point out that in all likelihood additional men had been lost through horses going lame, becoming lost in the wilderness, and so forth. A few men like Christopher Brandon admitted that ". . . after joined Col Williams to go to Ferguson's [defeat crossed out] King's Mountain but my horse tiring I was left behind and did not get up in time to be in the battle." The stronger among the men on foot, as well as those on weaker horses, were following behind the main column, but the total strength was probably well below the commonly accepted force of about 900.[6]

Colonel William Graham of the South Fork Regiment learned that his wife was perhaps fatally ill a few miles away. After another conference—this time more heated—Graham, with David Dickey as an escort, was released from duty. Major William Chronicle took command of the regiment. Chronicle was not the senior major, but he was familiar with the ground; Chronicle said, "Come on, my South Fork boys."

Some of Sevier's men were screening the main column, and managed to capture some of Ferguson's few scouts. Harder intelligence came from the capture of fourteen-year-old John Ponder. Lieutenant Colonel Frederick Hambright recognized the boy as a member of the well-known Tory family, and immediately arrested him.[7]

Ponder was carrying another dispatch from Ferguson to Cornwallis, giving his strength as about 1,000 militia and 100 uniformed Provincials. The officers concealed Ferguson's superior numbers from their men. Ponder also revealed that Ferguson was wearing a blue and white checked duster, a light overcoat, to protect his uniform. In his thick accent Hambright told his men, "Well poys, when you see dot man mit a pig shirt over his clothes, you may know who him is, and mark him mit your rifles."[8]

Further last-minute intelligence was obtained through a released prisoner from Brandon's regiment. Thomas Young recalled that "We came to a field where it was said we were to have some beeves killed." Food was always much on the mind of the hungry militiamen. "Here we met George Watkins, a Whig, who had just been paroled by the Enemy. He gave our officers information that we were within half a mile of Ferguson's party on the top of Kings Mountain, & of their position."[9]

James Collins later wrote, "Near two o'clock in the afternoon we came in sight of the enemy, who seemed to be fully prepared to give battle at all risks."[10]

At this point yet another hasty conference divided the force into two columns, to be led by Colonels Campbell and Cleveland's regiments. Campbell's column would invest the southeastern side of the elongated ridge, Cleveland's the northwest. (James Collins recalled three columns, under Cleveland and Sevier, Campbell and Williams, and Shelby and "Hamright.")

A final order was given for the men to dismount; horses were tied and men detailed out to act as horse-holders. Only a few senior officers would ride. Young recalled that "Orders were immediately given to tie our blankets behind us, pick & prime," so blankets, coats and any other loose gear were tied to the saddles.

Incredibly, apart from a few scouts, Ferguson had posted strong pickets only at the base of the ridge, and was still unaware of the danger only half a mile (about a kilometer) away. With darkness fast approaching it was imperative to attack while Ferguson could still be taken unawares.

As previously noted, Ferguson had taken up a position on a bald ridge. Beginning in the nineteenth century many critics have questioned why he chose this particular spot to tarry—and thus even inadvertently accept battle. In all probability his militia simply needed recuperation after hard marching. It may have been that he indeed thought it a strong defensive position, given the fighting abilities of his militia. Probably his remark that it was a strong position and that "all the rebels in hell could not drive him from it" was pure braggadocio, but Ferguson's decision has been the subject of considerable speculation.[11]

It is dangerous to try and read the mind of a man dead for over two centuries, but standing on the ground, seeing it as Ferguson saw it—without benefit of modern topographic maps—is informative. The extension of Brushy Ridge is located within a stone's throw of the old colonial-era road that Ferguson's baggage wagons would have to follow. To the naked eye the ridge easily dominates all the immediately surrounding terrain, with the exception of a small knob to the southwest, which would prove significant in the fighting to come. The position had a readily accessible open campsite atop the northeastern end of the ridge, and a spring and small stream on the northwest side provided a reliable water supply.

To continue the march into the gentler terrain to the east or northeast would invite attack by a possibly larger, and certainly more mobile, force while on the move, with few sites so well-suited for defensible nightly camps. With his experience in light infantry operations, and probably mindful of Braddock's disastrous defeat and retreat at Monongahela in 1755, these were risks Ferguson likely weighed. All in all, Brushy Ridge probably seemed the best spot to accept battle.

Examination of the terrain at the King's Mountain battle site also reveals a position totally unlike the perspective map shown in Draper (facing page 236). Draper's map was drawn in an era before modern topographic mapping, and did not benefit from the analysis of a skilled topographic sketch artist of the type that had proven so useful in the Civil War of 1861–1865. In fact the topography is in many ways the reverse of the depiction, and is a tadpole-shaped hill significantly higher on the southwest, tapering to a lower extension with a more rounded top to the northeast. The crest slopes gently from the high end to the broader, flatter-topped northeastern end. Draper's other illustration (facing page 209) is the actual King's Mountain, higher and far more rugged, and miles apart to the northeast.

Florid nineteenth-century accounts that mention men tumbling to their deaths from the cliffs and lying shot dead among the rocky crags are complete hooey. There are rock outcrops along the flanks, particularly at the steeper northeastern end, but the ridge top is gently rounded, with scattered stone outcrops, most no larger than a man's body. The northeastern

At the time of the King's Mountain battle the narrow, rounded crest of northeastern Brushy Ridge was barren of trees, and contrary to popular myth does not have rocky crags. This view is looking southwest toward the highest part of the ridge.—AUTHORS

extension of Brushy Ridge is simply one non-descript ridge among many.

Our description of the dispositions and battle are based on the US Geological Survey's Grover NC-SC 7.5 minute quadrangle map (2013), and examination on the ground. Google map and similar programs are not particularly useful because of the wooded and fairly subtle topography.

Ferguson had established the main part of his camp on the northeastern end where the ridgeline is lower, more rounded, and less rocky—in other words, more comfortable for the officers. This was the position for his more reliable uniformed Provincials. The militia was strung out along the higher and narrower ridge crest extending some 1,000 feet (305 m) to the southwest.

Inexplicably, Ferguson not only failed to position pickets at some distance from the camp, but he did not use his baggage wagons to laager the camp, erect any sort of breastworks, or fortify the camp in any way, though he was clearly concerned about being attacked. Perhaps he thought that possession of the high ground, and the open terrain to deploy his better-disciplined troops, provided sufficient advantages.

Like most British officers, Ferguson relied heavily upon the bayonet, though most of his newer militiamen had only rudimentary training with the weapon. Several Patriots described Ferguson's reliance upon bayonet charges, and Hill gave a description of the improvised bayonets that equipped many of Ferguson's militia: ". . . he trusted much to the bayonet, and as proof of this he had trained his men to that purpose & those with which he could not furnish with this weapon he had contrived a substitute by getting the Black-smiths to make long knives to answer this purpose, with a tang put in a piece of wood to fit the calibre of the gun & a button to rest on the muzzle of the piece."[12]

Certainly Ferguson himself must have been of two minds. One of his preserved dispatches to Cornwallis (others were intercepted) expressed both confidence but also asked for reinforcement—"Three of four hundred good soldiers, part dragoons, would finish the business."[13]

Ferguson's total troop strength is not precisely known. The most accurate period assessment was supposedly based on a captured ration strength report: 1,125, though as many as 200 may have been absent on foraging expeditions.[14]

As was typical, the Whig leaders addressed their men in "pep talks" that were actually designed to shame potential laggards. James Collins, now inexplicably in Chronicle's regiment, was quite candid: "Each leader made a short speech in his own way to his men, desiring every coward to be off immediately; here I must confess I would willingly have been excused, for my feelings were not the most pleasant—that may be attributed to my youth, not being quite seventeen years of age—but I could not well swallow the appelation of coward. I looked around; every man's countenance seemed to change; well, thought I, fate is fate, every man's fate is before him and he has to run it out. . . ."[15]

Campbell visited the various regiments, reportedly saying that ". . . if any of them, men or officers, were afraid, to quit the ranks and go home: that he wished no man to engage in the action who could not fight; that as for himself he was determined to fight the enemy a week if need be. . . ."[16]

The officers were under no illusions as to their men's ability to withstand a Loyalist bayonet charge. In a lengthy address Colonel Benjamin Cleveland admonished his men in part that "Every man must consider himself an officer, and act from his own judgment. Fire as quick as you can, and stand your ground as long as you can. When you can do no better, get behind trees, or retreat: but I beg you not to run quite off. If we are repulsed, let us make a point of returning and renewing the fight: perhaps we may have better luck in the second attempt than the first."[17] Cleveland's recollection of his own speech may have improved it in the retelling, but the concepts ring true to the principles of frontier warfare.

Brandon urged his Second Spartans to begin with an "Indian halloo" and fight their way up the hillside.

Approaching the southwestern end of the ridge—probably along the valley of Stonehouse Creek—some units became temporarily lost among the broken, heavily wooded ground. There are significant discrepancies as to Patriot unit dispositions between Draper's original map and later interpretations, particularly that of the National Park Service. For our purposes we have reinterpreted the Park Service map, and the reader is free to view Draper's map in light of the topography described.

Subtleties of the ground not apparent on topographic maps profoundly influenced how the battle played out. With the shortest distance to traverse, Shelby's and Sevier's commands easily moved into position along the southwestern end. Shelby's men would have the easiest task. Although at this point the military crest is far down the slope, almost at the creek bottom, they would attack up a long, gentle topographic ramp against some of Ferguson's lesser-trained militia.*

To their left Williams' command—including Brandon's Second Spartans—faced a steeper slope. The military crest is high up the ridge slope near the topographic crest, with good fields of fire for the defenders. On the right or southeast, Campbell, McDowell, and Winston would have to circle around the ridge. Here the military crest is even higher up the ridge, so that the attackers would be exposed to long-range fire as they moved along the lower slopes, and have to climb long, steep slopes under fire.

The hardest task faced Cleveland, Chronicle, and Winston. They would not only have the longest approach march, under fire, but then have to attack up the lowest but steepest and rockiest slopes defended by Ferguson's best troops.

Brandon's Second Spartan Regiment charged up this slope on the northwestern side of Brushy Ridge, under fire from Loyalist troops. The large battlefield monument atop the ridge is barely visible through the trees at left.—AUTHORS

---

*As opposed to the highest, or topographic, crest the military crest is the highest point on a slope from which the base of the slope can be directly observed and brought under fire.

Once the march began any sort of communication or coordination was impossible, so the plan was that when the center regiments of each column were in position the signal for a coordinated attack would be a "frontier war whoop, after the Indian Style," and the commencement of firing.

As fate would have it some of Ferguson's men at last spotted Shelby's men (who had far less distance to traverse) moving into position and opened a galling but ineffective fire at long range through the trees. Collins said, "The shot of the enemy soon began to pass over us like hail; the first shock was quickly, and for my part, I was soon in a profuse sweat."[18]

On the other side of the ridge Campbell threw off his coat and bellowed, "Here they are, my brave boys; shout like hell and fight like devils!" Recalling his experience at Musgrove Mill, DePeyster remarked to Fergu-

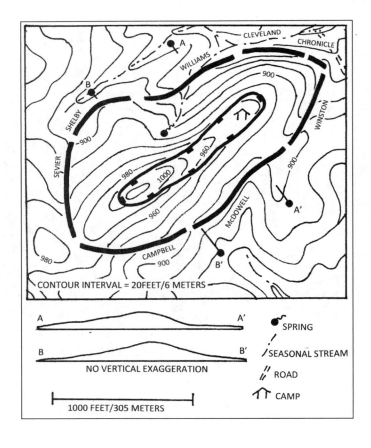

son, "These things are ominous—those are the damned yelling boys."[19]

Although Draper relentlessly excoriated James Williams and downplayed the number of men in his command, he did acknowledge that among the "good and experienced partisan officers" were Brandon, Hammond, Hayes, Roebuck, and Dillard. Pension records suggest that Brandon may have had 200 or more men at the battle, making the Second Spartans one of the larger contingents.*

Draper did not assign any particular chronology to the battle, and many of the events he relates are clearly out of any logical order in his narrative. The following is our attempt to reconstruct a generalized course of this chaotic battle as it relates to the Williams-Brandon command, based on terrain analysis and pension records.

In the usual frontier warfare fashion, the Whigs infiltrated among the trees and small rock outcrops, presenting poor and fleeting targets in the low light under the trees. In contrast, the Loyalists were positioned on open ground and probably often silhouetted against the afternoon sky—precisely the conditions modern infantry are taught to avoid. The Loyalists also had the disadvantage of firing down a steep slope, which usually causes men to fire high of the target. As a result ". . . the English shot whistled over the heads of the Americans, rattling among the trees and cutting off twigs, while the bullets of the mountaineers produced dreadful effects. . . ."[20]

Private Thomas Young ". . . ran up. I found three men lying down behind a chestnut tree. I met with Ben Hollingsworth; we got down behind a tree & fired till the Enemy cut nearly all the bark off the tree above us. Hollingsworth says 'it won't do here; we shall be killed.' Some of the bark fell in my eyes, & we got into another place where we could stoop and be safe until we loaded. I then rise up and fire with effect."[21]

In Brandon's command William Giles and William Sharp, neighbors and kinsmen, were fighting their way up the slope when Giles was struck in the neck by a shot and collapsed. ". . . a musket ball passed through the

---

*Pension records place 49 Second Spartans at the battle, so Hill's estimate of 40 or so total in Williams' command is patently absurd. By one analysis, about one in fifteen South Carolina militia veterans survived to file a pension claim (see Babits, *A Devil of a Whipping*, p. 33). We have used a very conservative one in four survivors. This supersedes a previous estimate (Gilbert and Gilbert, *Patriot Militiaman in the American Revolution*, p. 42).

back of Giles' neck, and he fell as if dead. Sharp, who was his neighbor, friend, and relation, said 'Poor fellow, he is dead but if I live a short time longer, I will avenge him.' After firing his rifle several times, he saw Giles rise up, rest upon his elbow, and commence loading his gun. He was on his feet again, fought through the battle, and lived to a good old age. The ball had passed through his neck, and *creased* him only." Together Giles and Sharp resumed fighting their way up the hill.[22]

James Collins in his old age was amazingly candid about the fighting, and his ability with his musket: "Whether I effected any thing or not, is unknown to me. My first shot I ever doubted, for I really had a shake on me at the time; but that soon passed over, and I took the precaution to conceal myself as well as I could, behind a tree or rock, of which there were plenty, and take as good aim as possible."[23]

As Collins implies, the marksmanship of the Patriots was probably not so remarkable and benefited much from nineteenth-century romanticism. Some of the more fantastic accounts describe dozens of Loyalists lying among the imaginary rock crags, each with a bullet hole through the forehead. This was clearly not the case. Patriot ammunition expenditure was immense, and at best only about one in every thirty or so rounds found its mark.

Three times the Loyalists on the higher part of the ridge counterattacked Sevier and Campbell's commands. If interviews by Draper are credible, the counterattacks were not at all coordinated. Patriot units under Sevier, Williams, Lacey, and Winston were not counterattacked at all. James Collins recalled that in Chronicle's command, immediately to the right of Winston, "We soon attempted to climb the hill, but were fiercely charged upon and forced to fall back to our first position; we tried a second time but met the same fate. . . ."[24]

The counterattacks were disciplined. The Loyalists ". . . reserved their fire until the termination of their pursuit; and having discharged their rifles, they retreated with great precision, reloading as they retraced their steps— as they had learned very skillfully to do by the example and instructions of Ferguson. . . ." In each case the Whig militia returned to the attack when the Loyalist militia withdrew back up the slope.[25]

From the configuration of Ferguson's position and the accounts of the battle it is clear that pressure from Shelby, Sevier, and Campbell eventually pushed the less-disciplined Loyalist militia off the higher ground at the southwestern end of the ridge. This would have pinched Williams' command, forcing him left along the ridge to the northeast. The effect was to create a powerful force pushing down the topographic ramp along the ridge crest, while other commands formed a blocking force that cut off any chance of escape for the beleaguered Tories.

Thomas Young of Brandon's regiment was still a boy of sixteen, and "I well remember how I behaved. Ben Hollingsworth and I took right up the side of the mountain, and fought our way from tree to tree, right up to the summit. I recollect I stood beside one tree and fired until the bark was nearly all knocked off and my eyes pretty well filled with it. One fellow shaved me pretty close, for his bullet took a piece out of my gun-stock."

Less experienced than his elders, Young made a potentially fatal error. "Before I was aware of it, I found myself apparently between my own regiment and the enemy, as I judged from seeing the paper which the Whigs wore in their hats, and the pine twigs the tories wore in theirs, these being the badges of distinction." Young elaborated on this: "I heard our regiment haloo, & looked round & saw our men; about a dozen of them shook hands with me. A little fellow by the name of Cherry gave me a sound scolding for my conduct, & told me to stick with him or I would be Killed. I did stay with him for some time."[26]

William Hill depicted James Williams as a laggard and coward who appeared only after the battle was over, but Thomas Young's account flatly contradicts this. "I had seen him but once before that day—it was early in the beginning of the action, as he charged by me at full speed around the mountain. Toward the summit a ball struck his horse under the jaw, when he commenced stamping as if he were in a nest of yellow jackets. Colonel Williams threw the reins over the animal's neck—sprang to the ground and dashed onward."

As often happened, Young then encountered a kinsman on the other side. "I had two cousins in this battle on the Tory side—Col. [William] Young and M. [Matthew] McCrary, whose father was a prisoner with the British on Edisto Island, & his mother [Young's mother's sister] made Matthew turn out with Ferguson's army for fear his father would be hung."[27] Whether this would have guaranteed the elder McCrary's safety is questionable.

The Second Spartans pushed into the edge of the Loyalist camp. "Just after we had reached the top of the hill, Matthew saw me, ran & threw his arms around me. "Matthew had apparently discarded his own musket, for "I told him to get a gun and fight; he said he could not. I told him to let me go, that I might fight."[28]

The other commands were also pushing relentlessly against the north-eastern part of Ferguson's perimeter, despite the loss of key officers. Major William Chronicle, leading Graham's South Fork Regiment, was fatally wounded. Frederick Hambright took a ball through the thigh, severing arteries, but remained in the saddle to avoid spooking his men. But it was not the kind of battle that required hands-on leadership anyway.

As Ferguson's men were pushed into an ever-tighter perimeter, many began to lose hope. Tradition has it that some began to raise white cloths, and that Ferguson personally slashed many of the flags down with his sword.[29]

Ferguson, probably accompanied by two officers, attempted to escape capture by breaking through the Patriot lines. Distinctive in his checkered duster and wielding his sword in his left hand, he was easily recognizable. Numerous men claimed the honor of having killed him. Several men in Sevier's command claimed to have shot Ferguson, and even Silas McBee said, "The troops had been cautioned to pick Ferguson off, they being told he used his sword in his left hand, his right being rendered nearly useless from a wound received in some form of fight before the American war. I did not need the caution—I knew him, having often seen him, and I aimed a shot at him."[30]

Draper's map places Ferguson's death site on the other side of the ridge from that attacked by Williams' command, and in the sector of the Loyalist position attacked by McDowell's command. What is documented is that he was shot at least six times. One account described wounds in his thigh, another that shattered his already paralyzed right arm, and a mortal head wound. Several accounts—written long afterward—suggest that Ferguson's foot hung in a stirrup, his panicked horse dragging him along the ground.[31]

In the final extremity Ferguson's survivors were pushed into a tiny perimeter. "With their men forced into a huddle near their tents and wagons, the surviving British officers could not form half a dozen of them together; and the demoralized Tories were being shot down like sheep at the slaughter."[32]

With Ferguson's death command passed to Captain Abraham DePeyster. He attempted to surrender, but in the heat of battle surrender is often difficult. Draper rightly discounts several of the more romanticized accounts, and his version—that the first two mounted British officers who raised token white flags were shot down—is plausible. By this time individual Loyalists were pleading for quarter.

The Loyalist resistance had been fiercer and more effective in the northeastern sector, and only toward the end of the fight were Chronicle and Hambright's men able to make headway. Collins: "We took to the hill a third time; the enemy gave way; when we had gotten near the top, some of our leaders roared out, 'Hurra, my brave fellows! Advance! They are crying for quarter.'"[33]

The Patriot militiamen were having none of it. Shelby recorded only that "Our men, who had been scattered in the battle, were continually coming up, and continued to fire, without comprehending, in the heat of the moment, what had happened." Sevier's son Joseph, who thought his father had been killed, shouted, "The damned rascals have killed my father, and I'll keep loading and shooting till I kill every son of a bitch of them." Most of the militiamen just kept on killing, shouting, "Give them Buford's play!" Many were taking their personal revenge for previous rape, arson, robbery, and murder.[34]

Part of the confusion may have been, as Draper describes, that many of the Loyalists were raising white flags on ramrods or gun barrels. But the naivete of Draper and other nineteenth-century writers also largely fails to allow for the fact that many of these men were from a culture with a long history of brutal warfare. They had a lengthy cultural history of no-quarter asked or granted battles of annihilation.

Finally Shelby rode into the deadly space between the two lines, shouting "Damn you, if you want quarters, throw down your arms!" Campbell knocked one Patriot militiaman's weapon upward saying, "Evins, for God's sake don't shoot! It is murder to kill them now, for they have raised the flag!" and went on along the line shouting, "Cease firing! For God's sake, cease firing!" DePeyster excoriated Campbell, calling the actions of the Patriots "damned unfair," but the firing did die down.[35]

Pressed into an area of about sixty by forty yards, the Tory prisoners were ordered to lay down their arms, remove their hats, and sit down as a token of submission. They were quickly surrounded by ranks of cheering Whigs.

One last act of tragedy and murder was to play out. Colonel James Williams had commandeered another horse, and as he rode up to the mass of prisoners, he was shot in the groin, reportedly wheeling his horse and exclaiming, "I'm a gone man!" William Hill implied that Williams had been shot down by some of Lacey's men for his supposed cowardice and perfidy, but not even Draper accepted this argument.[36]

Thomas Young: "The moment that I heard the cry that Colonel Williams was shot, I ran to his assistance, for I loved him as a father; he had ever been so kind to me, almost always carrying a cake in his pocket for me and his little son, Joseph. They carried him into a tent, and sprinkled some water in his face. As he revived, his first words were 'For God's sake boys, don't give up the hill!' I remember it as well as if it had occurred yesterday. I left him in the arms of his son Daniel, and returned to the field to avenge his fall."[37]

There are several possibilities as to who actually shot Williams, most likely either some of the still-resisting Tories, or far less likely members of a Tory foraging party who had rushed back to arrive at the end of the fighting, fired on the Whigs from behind, and then fled into the forest.

At any rate Campbell believed that the shots came from either advanced scouts of the feared Tarleton who, it was rumored, was rushing to the scene, or from some die-hard prisoner. Campbell gave orders for the men of Williams' and Brandon's commands to fire on the prisoners.* Still keyed-up from the fighting and seeing their commander gunned down, Williams' men probably needed little prompting. One of Brandon's lieutenants, Joseph Hughes, later stated that ". . . we killed near a hundred of them after the surrender of the British, and could hardly be restrained from killing the whole of them." At the prompting of one of his officers, Shelby ordered the prisoners moved to another spot, leaving their weapons behind on the ground.[38]

Several Loyalists found the mortally wounded Ferguson and carried him to a position on the south side of the ridge, where he died. Many of

---

*This may be another of Draper's attributions of all bad things to Williams' command. In such a small space men from other commands doubtless joined in the slaughter.

the victors were so curious that some of the wounded Whigs were carried to see his body. Young James Collins was already aghast at the carnage: ". . . the situation of the poor Tories appeared to be really pitiable; the dead lay in heaps on all sides, while the groans of the wounded were heard in every direction. I could not help turning away from the scene before me, with horror, and though exulting in victory, could not refrain from shedding tears. . . ." When Collins examined Ferguson's corpse he observed that ". . . seven rifle balls had passed through his body, both of his arms were broken, and his hat and clothing were literally shot to pieces."[39]

Ferguson's body was plundered for souvenirs, a common enough practice in war. A tradition has arisen that some of the "mountaineers" defiled the corpse, urinating on it. There is no mention of this by any actual participant in the battle, only Tarleton's oblique reference: "The mountaineers, it is reported, used every insult and indignity, after the action, and exercised horrid cruelties on the prisoners that fell into their possession."[40]

The aftermath of the battle was as usual, horrific. Benjamin Sharp: "The battle closed not far from sundown, so that we had to encamp on the ground, with the dead and wounded, and pass the night amid groans and lamentations."[41]

CHAPTER 11

KING'S MOUNTAIN AFTERMATH

It was the joyful annunciation of that turn of the tide of success which terminated the Revolutionary War, with the seal of our independence.
—THOMAS JEFFERSON

THE NEXT MORNING THE VICTORS WERE IN LITTLE better condition than the vanquished, after days of relentless marching, short rations, and a violent battle. Thomas Young's plight was typical: "I had no shoes, and of course fought this battle barefoot, when it was over, my feet were much torn & bleeding all over.

"The next morning we were ordered to fire a round. I fired my large old musket, charged in the time of battle with two musket bullets, as I had done every time. The recoil in this case was dreadful, but I had not noticed it in the battle."[1]

James Collins: "Next morning, which was Sunday, the scene became really distressing; the wives and children of the poor Tories came in, in great numbers" to recover their dead and wounded. "We proceeded to bury the dead, but it was badly done; they were thrown into convenient piles and covered with old logs, the bark of trees, and rocks; yet not so as to secure them from becoming a prey to the beasts of the forest, or the vultures of the air; and the wolves became so plenty, that it was dangerous for any one to be out at night . . . also, the hogs in the neighborhood, gathered in to the place, to devour the flesh of men. . . ." Passers-by saw ". . . all parts of the human frame, scattered in every direction" a few weeks later.[2]

The spy Joseph Kerr found James Williams and "This declarant well remembers conversing with him after the battle. He knew he must die and did so cheerfully resigned to his fate."[3]

The Patriots were now wary of Tarleton. Benjamin Sharp: "The next day, as soon as we could bury our dead, and provide litters to carry our wounded, we marched off to regain the upper country for fear of being intercepted by a detachment of the army of lord Cornwallis, for we were partly behind his quarters, being between him and the British garrison of Ninety-Six. A British surgeon, with some assistants, were left to attend their wounded; but the wounded Tories were unprovided for, and their dead left for their bones to bleach on the mountain." (Here Sharp is probably making a distinction between Ferguson's red-coated Provincials and his militia).[4]

The victors moved quickly to avoid possible pursuit. Seventeen captured baggage wagons, tents and other unwanted or heavy plunder were burned.[5]

Highly-prized weapons and supplies were divided up among the militiamen. Many officers acquired swords for the first time. James Collins: "In the evening , there was a distribution made of the plunder, and we were dismissed. My father and myself drew two fine horses, two guns, and some articles of clothing, with a share of powder and lead. . . ."[6]

In addition to his soldiers' weapons, Ferguson had additional muskets and other weapons intended to equip new recruits—a total of 1,200 to 1,500 firearms by various accounts. Such a windfall could not be abandoned, so the flints were removed and the weapons piled. The prisoners were paraded past the pile and each was made to select two to carry along on his march into captivity.[7]

Some of Campbell's men remained to inter the Whig dead, carried to the flats near the base of the ridge and buried in adequate graves. Two men from the regiment told Draper that the site was ". . . a small elevation, some eighty or a hundred yards south-east of Ferguson's head-quarters; large pits were dug, and a number of the slain were placed together, with blankets thrown over them, and thus hurriedly buried."* Ferguson's body

---

*It is almost impossible to determine who or how many Patriots were killed. The King's Mountain monument lists Lieutenant Colonel James Steen as killed there; he was most likely killed in Rowan County NC, probably in the late summer of 1781.

was wrapped in a raw cattle hide, and buried near where he fell. Rumor had it that one of his two laundress/mistresses, "Virginia Sal, a red haired lady," was buried with him.[8]

The Patriot wounded were carried to whatever safety could be arranged, and some men like Robert Henderson of the Ninety Six district militia ". . . remained here ten or fifteen days, attending on the wounded."[9]

Like most of the badly wounded, Williams was placed in a litter suspended between two horses. The continual swaying and jouncing on the rough trails must have been agonizing.

Silas McBee: "The mountaineers marched October 8, twelve miles, where Colonel James Williams died at Fondrin's [Fondren] plantation and was buried with the honors of war."

Though not entirely accurate (Williams was buried the next day near Buffalo Creek), McBee's account gives an insight into the mindset of the militia. "Next morning early the army commenced its march for their homes west of the mountains. . . . fearing that Cornwallis who was only thirty miles off would march with his whole army to intercept them and take the prisoners. They did not know that Cornwallis—panic struck at the moment he heard of Ferguson's total defeat, marched in great confusion to Winnsboro. . . . I have to smile when I tell of how Cornwallis was running in fright one way, and the Americans eagerly fleeing the other way."[10]

The column marched through the jagged terrain east of the Broad River, about twelve miles from the battle site. Sharp: "That afternoon we met Capt. Neil coming on with his detachment, and encamped for the night on a large deserted Tory plantation, where there was a sweet potato patch sufficiently large to supply the whole army. This was most fortunate, for not one in fifty of us had tasted food for the last two days and nights, that is, since we left the Cowpens. Here the next morning we buried colonel Williams, who had died of his wounds on the march the day before. We still proceeded towards the mountains as fast as our prisoners could bear."[11]

Encumbered by wounded and recalcitrant prisoners, whose best interests lay in retarding the march, progress was slow. The diary of Lieutenant Anthony Allaire, one of the prisoners, recorded that although one day's march was 32 miles, most days covered from one to nine miles (1.5 to 14.5km). On some days no progress was recorded. The number of militia was inadequate to guard the host of prisoners, and escapes were common.[12]

The Whig commanders agonized over the slow pace, possible pursuit by Tarleton, and the chronic shortage of food. Thomas Young: "After the battle we marched upon the head waters of Cane Creek, in North Carolina, with our prisoners, where we all came very near starving to death. The country was very thinly settled, and provisions could not be had for love or money." The countryside had also been heavily plundered by the armies of both sides. "I thought green pumpkins, sliced and fried, about the sweetest eating I ever had in my life!"[13]

Benjamin Sharp seemed particularly concerned about food. "During the whole of this expedition, except a few days at the outset, I neither tasted bread nor salt, and this was the case with nearly every man; when we could get meat, which was but seldom, we had to roast and eat it without either: sometimes we got a few potatoes, but our principal rations were ears of corn, scorched in the fire or eaten raw. Such was the price paid by the men of the Revolution of our Independence."[14]

The prisoners were fed raw corn and green pumpkins, another source of complaint by Allaire, although clearly the guards were not dining that much better.[15]

Colonel Cleveland was the source of many complaints of vindictive cruelty. Brandon was solicitous of his own men's welfare, but had a reputation for violence. In one incident of attempted escape, William Hill (again, not the most reliable of sources) said that the exasperated Brandon ". . . a rough, impulsive Irishman, discovering that one of the Tories, who had been carrying a couple of the captured guns, had dodged into a hollow sycamore by the road-side, dragged him from his hiding place, and completely hacked him to pieces with his sword."[16]

Although such measures might offend modern sensibilities, the militiamen probably thought little of it. On 12 October Allaire bitterly recorded in his diary that, "Those villains divided our baggage, although they had promised on their word we should have it all." The column had that day stopped in Gilbert Town, where the prisoners were confined in an open-air pen used to house Patriot prisoners when Ferguson had occupied the village a month earlier. When one Tory woman was asked what was to be done with the Patriot prisoners, she had replied, "We are going to hang all the damned old Rebels, and take their wives, scrape their tongues, and let them go." Tongue-scraping was a period punishment for blasphemy;

the offender was gagged, the tongue pulled out of the mouth and scraped raw and bloody with the sharp edge of a piece of iron or wood. The locals thought turn about fair play, and had little sympathy for their oppressors-turned-captives.[17]

The column marched on to Bickerstaff's Plantation, and on Saturday, 14 October, Campbell—under considerable pressure from the likes of Colonel Cleveland—convened a drumhead court-martial to try some of the Tory militiamen. Allaire vehemently condemned the trial, and many later writers have described it as barbaric. What has to be borne in mind is that during their term of ascendancy the Loyalists had instigated Chero-kee raids and committed robbery, arson, rape, and murder in the King's name. Some had deserted Patriot units while on active service (the two men who deserted to warn Ferguson were among the accused). All these can be capital crimes under modern military law.

Shelby recorded, ". . . a week after the battle, they were informed by a paroled officer, that he had seen eleven patriots hung at Ninety Six a few days before, for being Rebels. Similar cruel and unjustifiable acts had been committed before. In the opinion of the patriots, it required retaliatory measures to put a stop to these atrocities."[18]

Vengeance aside, some particularly unsavory prisoners presented a quandary. If held as prisoners they might be paroled or exchanged, released to resume preying upon Patriot families. There was of course no function-ing judicial system in South Carolina, but under North Carolina law two magistrates could convene a felony trial. Thomas Young recalled that, "After the battle was over we hung nine, against whom sufficient proof was made out that they had murdered Whigs previously."[19]

Various accounts disagree on the number eventually condemned to hang—from thirty to forty. Various men were reprieved through the inter-vention of influential Patriots, usually neighbors or relatives. One of Sevier's neighbors was twice reprieved. James Crawford had deserted and carried the news of the over-mountain force to Ferguson; when they did not at first appear Ferguson ordered him hanged for bringing false information, the sentence to be carried out late on 7 October. Condemned again, Sevier intervened to save him. His fellow deserter, teenager Samuel Chambers, was reprieved because of his youth and the belief that Crawford had misled him.[20]

Most accounts agree that the condemned were divided into three groups, and by torchlight swung up on ropes three at a time from a large oak tree. In his diary Lieutenant Allaire wrote bitterly that nine ". . . fell victim to their infamous mock jury. Mills, Wilson, and Chitwood died like Romans. . . ." This seems unlikely since these were not drop-hangings; the victims were hoisted up to slowly strangle. One particularly venomous Tory-hater, Captain Patrick "Paddy" Carr of the embittered Georgia refugees, famously remarked that, "Would to God that every tree in the wilderness bore such fruit as that!"[21]

The grisly proceedings were thrown into confusion when the fourth trio was about to be strung up. Although the tale is somewhat garbled, one of the condemned was Billy Pearson. By one account, "Brandon stepped up when they were hanging a parcel of Tories. One man, a vile Tory named Pearson, had a bridle rein round his neck, just to be swung off. Brandon said to him, 'Billy, if you promise to fight on our side, I will save you.' Brandon swore Pearson to be true. Billy Pearson was a good Whig to the end of the war."[22]

The last-minute reprieve is problematical, but there were many such interventions by senior officers. Genealogical research suggests Brandon likely had Pearsons as neighbors, and probably several in his regiment. Since he had almost certainly sent his nephew, young Matthew McCrary, home to his mother after he was captured at King's Mountain, he may have found it politically expedient to pardon Pearson.[23]

In this group Isaac Baldwin had been convicted of not only robbing families of their food, clothing, and bedding, but flogging them bloody, then leaving them tied to trees as prey to wild animals. Thomas Young: "Nine were hung, and the tenth was pinioned, awaiting his fate. It was now nearly dark. His brother, a mere lad, threw his arms around him, and set up a most piteous crying and screaming, as if he would go into convulsions. While the soldiers were attracted by his behaviour, he managed to cut the cords, and his brother escaped." At this point Shelby intervened to propose ending the proceedings, and Campbell—as senior officer present—pardoned the remainder.[24]

Undoubtedly many felt the point had been made, and in fact the indiscriminate execution of prisoners held by the British later ceased.

Unaware that both Cornwallis and Tarleton had turned away, the

Patriot leaders rushed to put the swiftly-rising Catawba River behind them to block pursuit. The prisoners were driven hard. Allaire's diary recorded: "Sunday, 15th—Moved on at five o'clock in the morning. Marched all day through the rain—a very disagreeable road. We got to Catawba and forded it at Island Ford about ten o'clock at night. Our march was thirty-two miles. All the men were worn out with fatigue and fasting—the prisoners having no bread or meat for two days before. We officers were allowed to go to Col. McDowell's, where we lodged comfortably. About one hundred prisoners made their escape on this march."[25]

Allaire conveniently omitted that McDowell's aged mother, the matron of Quaker Meadows, extended a charity quite unlike that shown her when Ferguson's men plundered her home in September.[26]

With the flooded river protecting their rear, the Patriots could at last relax a bit. As was the usual practice, many of the militia simply went home after the battle. James Collins: "It seemed like a calm, after a heavy storm had passed over, and for a short time, every man could visit his home, or his neighbor, without being afraid. After the result of the battle was known, we seemed to gather strength, for many that had before lay neutral, through fear or some other cause, shouldered their guns, and fell in the ranks; some of them making good soldiers." Thomas Young: "From this point we marched over into the Dutch [German] settlements in the fork of Catawba and recruited, until we joined Gen. Morgan at Grindall Shoals." And finally "We were all nearly starved in this trip. When I got home to my Mother's, I buried the few rags I had left in consequence of the abundance of the lice with which they were infested."[27]

Some of the militia volunteered to escort the prisoners on into Virginia. Campbell discharged many of his Virginians. Campbell, Shelby and Cleveland drafted a report on the battle. The remaining Tennesseans left on a forced march back over the mountains, as always fearful of an uprising by the Cherokee.

Thomas Brandon thanked Elisha Parker, the Connecticut refugee who had briefly joined up with the Second Spartans, and sent him on his way.[28]

CHAPTER 12

BLOODY BAN TASTES DEFEAT: BLACKSTOCK'S FARM, 20 NOVEMBER 1780

Wars may be fought with weapons, but they are won by men. It is the spirit of men who follow and of the man who leads that gains the victory.
—GEORGE S. PATTON

CORNWALLIS WAS DETERMINED TO ELIMINATE THE PESKY Gamecock by fair means or foul. His favorite tool—Tarleton—was fruitlessly chasing the Swamp Fox, so he assigned Major James Wemyss the task, with about 100 mounted infantry from the 63rd Regiment of Foot and 40 or so of Tarleton's Green Dragoons, but with orders not to risk his force. Receiving intelligence that placed Sumter near Fishdam Ford, Wemyss devised a plan to have a few men infiltrate Sumter's camp in the hours after midnight on 9 November to kill or capture him before launching a surprise attack.

The plan miscarried. Several of Sumter's subordinates, not so convinced as Sumter that the British would not launch a surprise attack, posted strong guards and had their men sleep on their arms. Around midnight Wemyss charged into a Patriot camp alerted by the noise of his approaching horses. The initial Patriot fire shot down twenty of the British, and Wemyss was seriously wounded. William Hill was unusually frank about the revered General Thomas Sumter: ". . . two of the dragoons entered the Genls. markey while he made his escape out of the back of the markey & got under the bank of the River. . . ."[1]

Wemyss' second in command ordered a bayonet charge into the rebel camp, but his outnumbered men—caught in the light of campfires—were gunned down by Colonel Edward Lacey's Patriots concealed in the darkness among the trees.

British Lieutenant Henry Stark ordered a retreat, leaving Wemyss and other wounded to be captured. Sumter returned well after dawn. Wemyss was found in possession of a list of the Patriots he had hanged and the houses he had burned, but "notwithstanding this he was well treated by his Conquerors."[2]

It was a minor victory, but the news would help further Sumter's recruiting efforts.

Cornwallis had lost the major part of his militia at King's Mountain, and now Wemyss' red-coated Regulars had been defeated. Cornwallis laid the blame on the captive Wemyss for his impetuosity, calling him "mad." Cornwallis' situation was growing more serious by the day. On the strength of the victory at Fishdam Ford, Sumter was gathering in droves of militia recruits, and now commanded a force of a thousand or more mounted infantry that posed a serious threat to Ninety Six.

Cornwallis decided to unleash his most trusted commander, but also the most genuinely "mad." Couriers were dispatched to order Banastre Tarleton to break off his pursuit of Francis Marion, the Swamp Fox, to deal with what now loomed as the greater threat. Whether Cornwallis considered Tarleton even more impetuous than Wemyss is of course problematical. Tarleton had clearly demonstrated a propensity for frontal attacks against superior numbers, but Tarleton had one major advantage—he had never lost a fight. His successes undoubtedly blinded Cornwallis to his tactical indiscretions, his heavy handed tactics, and the cost in British and Loyalist casualties. According to the attitudes of the day the last was of little consequence anyway.

Tarleton hastened toward Brierly Ford on the Broad River with about 190 dragoons and mounted infantry of his British Legion. To reinforce him, Cornwallis dispatched his available British Regular infantry. Officer casualties had been severe, and the survivors of the ravaged 63rd Regiment of Foot were placed under Lieutenant John Money. Money, Cornwallis' aide-de-camp, was another personal favorite of the general.[3] The veteran 1st Battalion, 71st Regiment of Foot (Fraser's Highlanders) was commanded by a hardened veteran, Major Archibald McArthur. The Highlanders had been fighting in South Carolina since coming south with Clinton. The regiment had served continuously in the back country, and had acted as a bodyguard to Tarleton during his sickness.[4]

The British force would be augmented by a three-pounder (about 40mm) "grasshopper gun." These light cannons had bronze gun tubes, lighter and stronger than cast iron, mounted on light carriages. They could be moved fairly swiftly and be easily towed over rough terrain. They were well-suited to Tarleton's preferred tactics of rapid pursuit.

Among Banastre Tarleton's most important weapons were "grasshopper guns," small cannons with lightweight bronze gun tubes that could be easily towed over rough terrain, and manhandled into action by a small crew. The handspikes that stuck up above the box trail, and the way the gun hopped backward when it recoiled, inspired the name.—AUTHORS

The vast majority of Sumter's force was militia, with small detachments of State Troops and State Dragoons, and about a hundred of Colonel John Twiggs' Georgia refugees. Sumter's problem now was that the enlarged force had inevitably grown unwieldy and slower on the march.

Sumter's scouts under Georgian Captain Patrick Carr were shadowing

McArthur's Highlanders encamped at Brierly Ford, unaware that Tarleton was coming on at top speed. In his usual way, Sumter detached smaller forces. Colonel Samuel Hammond recorded:

"Intelligence to be depended upon was obtained, that a large quantity of provisions was deposited for the British army at Summers' Mills, under a small guard, and also that a party of British militia or tories were stationed at Captain Faust's, upon the waters of the ____ [blank in original]. To obtain information of the movements of our enemy, and, if possible, to get possession of and bring away or destroy the provisions stored at Summers', Colonel Thomas Taylor, of South Carolina, and Colonel Candler, of Georgia, were dispatched down the country with this object in view, and with discretional orders to suit the circumstances of the times and things. At the same time, Lieutenant-Colonel Williamson, of Clarke's regiment of Georgia, and Major S. Hammond, were detached toward Captain Faust's to attack, and if possible, to break up that station."[5]

Militiamen with knowledge of the local terrain were hastily called up to help track the British movements. William Grant, Jr., "Being still in the minute service in November he was called on again and entered the service under Capt Grant, Major Joseph McJunkin, Col Thomas Brandon by order of General Sumter to go to Fooses Ford."[6]

Militiaman John Calhoun provides a good example of the difficulty of tracking the service of militiamen who might serve in several regiments, or who might be either "loaned" to another regiment for special duty, or simply switched units to join a friend or relative in the field. Calhoun recorded early service under Colonel John Thomas Senior, then Colonel John Thomas Junior (First Spartans), and Lieutenant Colonel James White (Little River Regiment), and now was assigned to serve under Colonel William Candler of the Georgia refugee militia as a scout.[7]

Probably a good rider with a strong mount, Calhoun was one of the horsemen assigned to shadow the advancing British columns. "In this company he was sent out as a reconnoitering party to watch the motion of Cornwallis' army—came up with them at the Broad River, Shirer's Ferry— and fired & wounded a man washing in a canoe across the river—then went lower down to Buzzard's Mills there divided into smaller companies for reconnoitering and was then attached to Col. Candler's command and was ordered back to the river to watch Cornwallis' Army; just as we got there his army was just crossing to our side of the river—we had to retreat & were pursued. . . ."[8]

Sometime on the morning of 18 November Tarleton and his weary Legion troops joined McArthur's camp on the Broad River, but in typical fashion the hard-charging Tarleton spared neither his troops nor their brutalized horses. He immediately set off in pursuit of Sumter and glory. The Highlanders were ferried across by boat. The artillery and the mounted troops—with the Legion's distinctive green uniform jackets covered by dusters to conceal their presence from Sumter's scouts—crossed at a ford several miles downstream and the two forces joined up on the far bank.

The problem for Tarleton was limited mobility caused by the shortage of horses. Tarleton's legionnaires were experienced in the pursuit, and he had mounted the 63rd Regiment's 80 survivors on confiscated horses as mounted infantry. The Highlanders would have to struggle along on foot with the artillery piece.[9]

Tarleton drove his troops harder than ever in the cool weather. To maximize time in the pursuit the force would camp hours after nightfall, grabbing hastily cooked rations and a few hours' rest before setting off again in the pre-dawn hours.

The next day Tarleton dispatched sections of dragoons to scour the countryside, looking for signs of Sumter's passage and questioning the local citizenry. The Legion was not known for its benevolence, and many of these interrogations were not at all friendly. But they did bear fruit. Tarleton learned that Sumter was still unaware of the pursuing British. Sumter's military merits did not include good security, and without adequate scouts he was blissfully unaware of the danger so close on his heels.

With luck, Tarleton could fall upon Sumter's slow-moving column strung out on the march, where superior discipline, infantry trained in the use of the bayonet, and the speed and sabers of the Legion dragoons would more than compensate for superior rebel numbers.

Sumter was absolutely fixated on attacking the big base at Ninety Six. As a preliminary he planned an attack on a force of 100 Loyalists at Williams' plantation. In addition he had dispatched raiding parties hither and yon. Samuel Hammond: "On the next morning [16 October] Col. Chandler [Candler of Georgia] was detached with fifty men, declarant among the number to return & destroy said [Summer's] Mills which was effected by cutting the running gear, left there & marched all day & night to catch up with Sumpter which we did the next day at Blackstock's. . . ."[10]

Tarleton's fabled luck had deserted him. In the pre-dawn hours of 18 November a soldier from the 63rd Foot stole a horse and rode hell-bent for Sumter's camp. Whether the deserter was able to ride into camp unmolested—Sumter had repeatedly proven lax in camp security—is not recorded. At any rate Tarleton had lost the critical advantage of surprise.[11]

Joseph McJunkin: "Sumter's march toward Ninety Six was arrested by the intelligence that Col. Tarleton was following him by forced marches with the manifest intention of falling upon him. He turned to the north, which placed the Enoree River in his front."[12]

Sumter would flee from Tarleton if feasible, but in fact he had few options for an escape route. The roads were few and poor, and suitable river crossing sites fewer still. Leaving a detachment of dragoons at a crossing of the Enoree River to warn of Tarleton's approach, the Patriots broke camp and headed for the crossings of the fast-flowing Tyger River and the relative safety of the north bank. "He had barely passed this stream [the Enoree] with his main body when Tarleton's advance obstructed the passage of his rear guard. Sumter, however, pushed on and was gaining ground on his pursuer."

Militiamen were already gathering for a crack at Tarleton but the situation was chaotic, as Patriot units moved about on the trails that crisscrossed the region. Robert Long had been made prisoner after the fall of Charleston. He contrived to escape captivity at Ninety Six and joined the remnants of the Little River Regiment. Sumter had previously ". . . ordered [Captain Samuel] Ewing's company of 14 men to cross Dunkin's creek, and reconnoiter the country towards the forts the Tories had on Col. Williams' plantation; and upon our returning to Sumter's camp , he had decamped. . . ." Ewing's tiny command was adrift, but followed on the trail of Sumter and Tarleton, and ". . . upon crossing the Enoree, found Tarleton was between us and Sumter; took two of his men and escaped. This is the reason we were not in the battle of Blackstock's."[13]

If they remained on the south side of the Tyger, Sumter's army would be hemmed in by the terrain and driven northwest. Moving across broken terrain would further slow their march without bringing them any closer to safety.

Rank and file Patriots were heartened by the news of the rebel victories at King's Mountain and Fishdam Ford, and local militiamen further swelled Sumter's numbers. Some joined the column at the last minute. One local man, William Beard ". . . was at Blackstocks where Sumpter fought Tarleton, I was not under any officer there, but fell in and fought it out."[14]

In Brandon's Second Spartans, "At this time Capt. Joseph McJunkin, feeling sufficiently recruited [recovered] to take the field once again, assembled as many of his command as possible and joined Sumter at Padget's Creek, between the Tyger and Enoree Rivers. At the same time a number of the militia from Georgia effected a junction with Sumter. McJunkin was then appointed Major and received a commission as such."[15]

Captain Samuel Otterson, barely recovered from the wound that had splintered part of his arm after Hanging Rock, mustered his company.[16]

The Patriot leaders faced another harsh conundrum; the pace of the march. A long, cumbersome column of poorly-disciplined militia was bound to be slow, while Tarleton was renowned for the speed of his movements. The Patriot column would be slowed by the steep, ravine-ridden slopes and bad roads leading down to the narrow fords, while Tarleton would be able to gain ground while still moving along the relatively flat, hard ground along the ridge crests to the south. Far worse than being caught on the march would be for Tarleton to overtake the column on the flat river bottomland that surrounded the narrow fords. Any Patriot forces caught on the south bank would be trapped, their backs to the river, and cut to pieces in detail.

The chances of getting the column across with Tarleton only hours behind were minimal. If by some miracle they could cross unmolested, it would be only a temporary reprieve. In the best possible case they could elude Tarleton, but being chased is never good for morale: in all likelihood Sumter's army would simply disintegrate when the militiamen concluded it was no longer worth the candle.

Samuel Hammond had a different take on the decision to stand and fight. The detached raiding parties, a significant part of Sumter's force, were trying to overtake the main column. "Sumter reluctantly halted, refreshed his men and horses, in about a half a mile of Blackstock's field. I say reluctantly, for although the men and horses stood in the greatest need of such refreshment, yet the certain intelligence that the enemy's superior forces were briskly following his trail, urged his going forward. The safety of Colonel Taylor and his party decided him to suspend his retreat."

Most accounts say that a hasty conference of the Patriot colonels concluded that the only option was to face Bloody Ban south of the river. Colonel Thomas Brandon was on his home ground, and suggested William Blackstock's tobacco plantation as a strong defensive position. The plantation sat on a southeast-facing slope where the road—such as it was—dropped down to cross a tributary stream before climbing a small ridge and then dropping down again to Blackstock's Ford.

The plantation itself was simply a large cleared area, but it offered critical advantages. The surrounding forest would impede flanking movements by the Loyalist dragoons. Tarleton's flagging troops would emerge from the forest along the narrow road, only to face a small stream, and then climb eighty feet (24 meters) up a fairly steep slope to reach the Patriot positions. The slope itself was open tobacco fields, bare ground after the harvest, and provided ideal fields of fire for defenders.

For two centuries the configuration of this tiny battlefield has been misunderstood. Joseph McJunkin was adamant that "Botta's history of the Revolution is incorrect, in saying that Sumter's position was protected by the river in front. Sumter's position was on the south bank of the Tiger and Tarleton's advance was along the road to Blackstock's ford, which turns off to the right from the ridge road between the Enoree and Tiger. Sumter's line was alone protected by the houses and fences, and of these he made good use. . . ."[17]

Samuel Hammond better described the fire sack that Tarleton would tumble into. "In front of the buildings, a small branch of the Tiger river passed through the field, margined by small bushes, but not obstructing the view of the British movements from the hill. This water-course formed a half moon, with its concavity towards the enemy, and the ridge corresponded with this shape of the branch. Sumter had the houses filled with his troops, and there being a strong new fence on either side of the road, these afforded a tolerable cover to the most of his men."

In about 1858 Joseph Hart summed up the position very well: "The place Sumter selected was admirably chosen, and in a military point of view could scarcely be equaled in the vicinity. Covered by the woods, and supported right and left by the hill and trees, he was able to place his untried men in a position that would give them confidence. The gentle ascent immediately in his front would prevent an advantageous charge from the enemy—a move Sumter, with his undisciplined forces, no doubt much dreaded."[18]

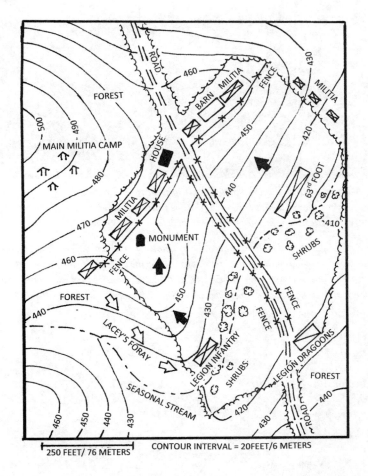

Blackstock had built well. The road ran straight up the slope, bounded on either side by fences, and the fences described by Hammond also ran along the military crest of the ridge. A veteran general could not have intentionally designed a better defensive site.

The fences were not the usual split rail construction; Blackstock had

Above: *Most of the Blackstock's battlefield is now heavily forested, but Tarleton sent his weary troops into an uphill assault against Patriot militia in defensive positions at the top of the slope at left.*—AUTHORS

Below: *At William Blackstock's tobacco plantation, the Patriot defense was anchored on a tobacco-drying barn, and a large farmhouse probably much like the 1771 Dickey-Sherer House preserved at King's Mountain State Park, South Carolina. These sturdy houses were originally designed for defense against Cherokee raids.*—AUTHORS

built sturdy waist-high log fences. Edward Lacey later said that ". . . there was a strong log fence, one notched upon another, which formed a lane where a strong picket was placed at its mouth. The fence served as a breast work. . . ."[19]

Behind the fences sat the farm buildings. Archeological evidence indicates that a sturdy log house overlooked the uphill end of the lane. A large tobacco-drying barn that anchored part of the defenses was described by Lieutenant McKenzie of Fraser's Highlanders: ". . . their left was covered by a large log barn, into which a considerable division of their force had been thrown, and from which, as the apertures between the logs served them for loop holes, they fired with security." The buildings and fences made a crude fortress, providing some shelter from enemy fire, and the slope and fences would impede the usual British bayonet charge.[20]

In his typical fashion Tarleton, in his post-battle sketch map sent to Cornwallis, would depict the farm buildings as five mutually supporting "blockhouses."[21]

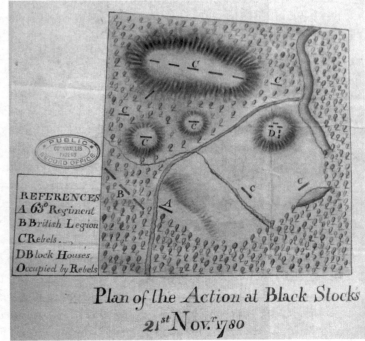

In his self-serving report to Cornwallis, Tarleton lied shamelessly. He reported his lopsided defeat as a resounding victory, and depicted the Patriot defenses at Blackstock's as several mutually-supporting "blockhouses." The fifty "rebel prisoners" he returned with were actually random men (including Loyalists) scooped up along the local roadsides.
—BRITISH NATIONAL ARCHIVES

REFERENCES
A 63° Regiment
B British Legion
C Rebels
D Block Houses
Occupied by Rebels

Plan of the Action at Black Stocks
21st Nov.r 1780

For once the pugnacious Sumter would take another man's—Thomas Brandon's—advice, fighting a defensive battle rather than charging head-long at the enemy. Arriving late in the afternoon, the militia made a typical hasty camp while Sumter and his colonels made their dispositions. Archeological finds and period descriptions suggest the main camp was below a small knob to the west of the main house, though they most likely built cooking fires at scattered positions.

Colonel S.T. Sims recorded that "Old Major Otterson told me that at Blackstock's, Sumter had his horses under a hill in his rear, & formed a line of battle in the protection of a dwelling house and several out houses, and a fence in their front. . . ."[22]

Blackstock himself was absent, fighting with another militia regiment, but his wife Mary informed Sumter, "General, I won't have any fighting around my house," to no avail.

Mary was probably yet another woman of divided loyalties. When their son married into a Loyalist family, husband William was away but returned just as the ceremony was finishing: the official ". . . cutting short the ceremony, said 'I pronounce you man and wife.' Blackstock heard it and bawled out 'I pronounce it a damned lie.' Came up very angry and said the Tories had left him nothing but his old red jacket, they might have that— & pulled it off, stamped on it, & swore that they might have it too."[23]

Several miles to the south Tarleton brushed aside the Patriot detachment under Captain Patrick Carr that was watching the Enoree fords. The Patriot dragoons were holding five Tory prisoners. The Patriot horsemen fled, leaving their prisoners by the roadside. The prisoner's hopes of rescue were brutally dashed. In his memoir Tarleton wrote that: "On his arrival near that place, he found that the advanced guard and main body of the enemy had passed the river near two hours, and, that a detachment to cover the rear was waiting the return of a patrole: The advanced guard of the British dragoons charged upon this body, and defeated them with considerable slaughter."[24]

Following their usual philosophy of "Kill now, ask no questions later," the Green Dragoons had hacked the Tory prisoners to death.

Anxious lest Sumter slip across the Tyger River, and with the short day slipping away, Tarleton pared down his force. The mounted Legion troops and Money's mounted infantry hastened their pursuit. The flagging infantry of the 71st Foot and the grasshopper gun were left to follow as best they could.

Luck was still on the Patriot side. A local woman, Mary Dillard, saw Tarleton's small advance force passing by. She rode ahead with intelligence that Tarleton had only mounted men and an estimate of his numbers. Tarleton himself corroborated this, saying that, "A woman on horseback had viewed the line of march from a wood, and, by a nearer road, had given intelligence that the British were approaching without infantry or cannon."[25]

The Patriot officers placed their main line along the fence at the military crest, dragoons and a small reserve to the rear. Sumter would observe the fight from the slightly higher ground southwest of the main house, but could move along the ridge as he chose. Patriot cavalry vedettes were thrown out to warn of Tarleton's approach. Colonel John Twiggs' Georgia refugees were placed as skirmishers, most probably sheltering in the underbrush along the creek bottom.

This was going to be a vicious fight. The Whig militia was spoiling for a chance at Tarleton and the Legion on their terms, and archeological studies at Blackstock's provide an insight into the Patriot mindset. It was common for soldiers to carry several musket- or rifle-balls in the mouth to avoid fumbling with a shot bag in the heat of battle, and it also produced saliva that reduced thirst. But many of the balls found at Blackstock's have distinctive tooth marks.[26]

Chewing the ball roughened the surface and made the flight slightly more erratic and less accurate. But when it did strike flesh, it tumbled and rolled, and the rough surface ripped a jagged wound that bled profusely and healed slowly if the victim survived. It was the eighteenth-century equivalent of a dum-dum bullet.

The cavalry vedettes were the first to spy Tarleton. Major Joseph McJunkin: "The rear guard was left some distance behind on the road. The men composing it set about getting their dinner—fires were built and dough rolled around sticks and set before the fire to bake. Just at this stage of the preparations Tarleton's force came in sight.

"Major McJunkin, who was Officer of the Day, immediately sent a messenger to Sumter to let him know that the enemy were in sight. Orders were returned to come up to the house."[27]

He later clarified this order in another memoir, saying "[Sumter] directed that the troops should abandon their cooking, and take post in and at the house."[28]

The foraging parties had somewhat closer calls. Colonels Thomas Taylor of Georgia and William Candler had successfully plundered the British depot at Summers' Mill. William White was driving one of the wagons loaded with captured flour when they arrived at the pre-arranged rendezvous, and later he told his wife that Taylor was "not a little displeased" to find Sumter missing.

"His men were very hungry, and he allowed two or three hogs to be cleaned and cooked, and some of the flour made into bread. White was engaged in baking the bread, in the fashion of Johnny cake, on a piece of pine bark, at the moment when Sergeant Ben Rowan and Major Hannah, who had been sent out by Sumter to reconnoitre, dashed up in fiery haste to bring the news that Tarleton was just at hand. The hogs and the dough were thrown into the wagon uncooked, and Rowan used to say that William drove the wagon into camp [the Blackstock's position] at a full gallop. White said that as he turned the corner of a little stable the firing commenced, and a ball passed through the sleeve of his hunting-shirt. He saw 'Irish Johnny Walker,' and asked where two individuals were, whom he called by name. He replied that he did not know, but had last seen them running over the hill. 'What shall we do?' then inquired White, and Walker answered —'Stand to them: we'll beat them anyhow.' White put three balls into his mouth to have them ready, and went into the fight."[29]

Hammond's account had the Patriots arriving at the farm barely ahead of Tarleton, but in accord with most accounts, ". . . our rear videts fired at the advancing cavalry of the enemy. Colonels Taylor and Candler at that moment drove in with their wagons loaded with flour, &c., passed our rear guard, and entered the open field at Blackstock's. At the next moment, Tarleton's legion charged on our rear guard, but Taylor and his men were safe."

Small scouting parties were also barely a step ahead of Tarleton. John Calhoun: ". . . we reached the army commanded by Brannon [Thomas Brandon] & Sumter and just joined the army at Blackstock's as the picket guard was fired on—were formed and fought in that Battle."[30]

About an hour before sunset the head of Tarleton's main column emerged into the cleared ground across the small valley from the rebel position. Tarleton was anxious to pin Sumter in place before darkness fell for fear he would slip across the river and escape in the night. McJunkin recorded that, "Tarleton having viewed Sumter's position, concluded to guard his opponent and hold him there until the balance of his force should come up. Sumter was not of the metal to submit to such bondage."[31]

For once Tarleton did not immediately fling himself headlong at the enemy. Perhaps it was because he knew he was badly outnumbered, and on unfavorable ground. But being Tarleton, attack he would. Tarleton's sketch map reveals how he deployed his force, with the 63rd Foot to the right of the road, the Legion infantry to the left, and as usual his dragoons in reserve to exploit the expected victory.

Tarleton dissembled in his memoir, saying of the Patriot defensive position ". . . this formidable appearance made Tarleton halt upon the opposite height, where he intended to remain quiet till his infantry and three-pounder arrived: To encourage the enemy to do the same as he, he dismounted the 63d to take post, and part of the cavalry to ease their horses."[32]

Money's infantry dismounted and showed themselves on the cleared slopes on the right side of the road above the south side of the creek. Meanwhile the Legion infantry dismounted and began to work their way through dense vegetation to the left of the road, probably an attempt to flank the right of the Patriot line. For Tarleton, it was an extraordinarily prudent plan, but it was an attack.

Money's men fixed bayonets and advanced down the slope toward the creek bottom. Samuel Otterson via Colonel Sims: "Tarleton let down the fence opposite them, and marched up to them in the open field. Sumter's orders were not to fire till the enemy were in sixty yards of them."[33]

Accounts vary, but it seems that Sumter took the bait. Joseph Mc-Junkin: "He [Sumter] then called for volunteers to act as the advance, and bring on the action. Col. Farr, of Union, and Major McJunkin, were the first to volunteer: they were followed by others, until the General said, 'there were enough.' They were ordered to go forward until they met Tarleton's advance, which they were to engage, and if not strong enough to resist, and hold it in check, they were directed to fall back gradually, facing about and firing as occasion might serve. These orders were obeyed; and

Tarleton's advance was continually annoyed and checked. . . ."[34]

The force, perhaps as many as 400 men, moved down to confront Money. They fired one ragged volley, apparently inflicting few or no casualties. McJunkin recalled, "The action was commenced with great spirit, the assailing party gradually yielding to superior numbers until Tarleton made a general charge with a view of pushing his adversary from his advantageous position."

In all likelihood the militia actually scampered back to the protection of the fences and buildings in the face of Money's bayonets. The sight of a fleeing enemy incited the usual bayonet charge, and Money led his men up the slope. Eighty men would try to drive several hundred with the bayonet.

When Money's line reached a position about halfway up the slope the Patriot militia opened a deadly and concentrated fire at a range of about fifty yards. The American militia as usual aimed first at "epaulets and crossbelts" to decapitate the British command structure. They succeeded in spades. Money was among the first to go down.

Golding Tinsley, a celebrated marksman in the Little River Regiment,* was with skirmishers and snipers in the trees to the British right, and claimed to have shot Money. "Several of the boys had shot at him. At length I told them to give me a crack. He was on an excellently trained horse which kept moving backwards across an *opening in the woods* [underlined in original] in front of us. As he passed this time, I fired, and he fell from his horse."[35]

Money was mortally wounded by several balls, and his two subordinate lieutenants were killed outright. Most of the NCOs and about a third of the privates were killed or wounded. Given the number of rifles and muskets trained on them, it was miraculous that any survived. Perhaps now the Patriots were shooting high when firing down slope.

The red-coated Regulars, many of whom were now recruited from the colonies to replace casualties, were trained to stand their ground, flailing away with short-range musket fire, inflicting (and accepting) hideous casualties. For a while the 63rd stood its ground in the face of the murderous

---

*Tinsley was probably another militiaman who moved to and fro between regiments; the reader should recall that he was clearly taking orders from Thomas Brandon at Musgrove Mill.

fire. "The battle continued in this position, until Tarleton withdrew his force. . . ." Their valor would avail them nothing, not even praise from their own commander. The 63rd began to fall back.[36]

On the Patriot right, near what is now called Monument Hill, Colonel Edward Lacey's militiamen slipped through the forest, coming undetected ". . . within seventy-five paces of the enemy, undiscovered, when they gave them a fire so well directed, that twenty men fell and nearly as many horses. Many of his [Lacey's] men dismounted, and would creep up so near the foe that a shot was never wasted."[37] A Legion lieutenant, identified by Tarleton only as Skinner, and his men charged into the trees, pushing Lacey back.

Meantime, the stubborn, courageous survivors of the 63rd Foot were in deep trouble. Tarleton: "Though the undertaking appeared hazardous, Lieutenant-colonel Tarleton determined to charge the enemy's center with a column of dragoons, in order to cover the 63d, whose situation was now become dangerous. The attack was conducted with great celerity, and was attended with immediate success. The cavalry soon reached the houses, and broke the Americans, who from that instant began to disperse: The 63d immediately rallied, and darkness put an end to the engagement."[38]

This whopper was probably the greatest in a long career of self-serving lies. Confined between log fences in the narrow lane, the Green Dragoons were raked by the same deadly fire that had decimated the 63rd Foot. The charge likely did not reach much more than halfway up the slope, much less break the Patriot position.

Patriot Colonel William Hill's *Memoir* is in many ways as self-serving as Tarleton's *History*, but his assessment of Tarleton's charge is probably quite accurate: ". . . their horse then advanced in the Lane to attack our body of reserve that stood between the Lane & the River where the charge was made by their horse—The Americans having the advantage of the before mentioned fence together with the thick wood just by the fence that before they got through the Lane their front both men & horse fell so fast that the way was nearly stopt up—a retreat was then ordered which was a pleasing sight for the Americans to behold—so many falling either by wounds or stumbling over the dead horses or men. They were pursued by the Americans with loud shouts of victory. . . ."[39]

Edward Lacey said, ". . . the British soldiers and horses fell so thick that their numbers, dying and dead, nearly blocked up the road."[40]

As the British retreated, Patriots under Colonels Clarke and Candler infiltrated through the woods to attack the flank and rear of Money's beaten command. Hammond said, "When this [British] retreat was ordered, Clarke and Hammond had attacked the infantry in the rear, and taken a part of their horses; but the whole retreating British force coming up, they were compelled to retire, and carried off a few infantry horses, and cut loose a number of others."

For the British the only bright spot, of which Tarleton made much in his dispatches to Cornwallis, was the near-fatal wounding of Sumter. As the remnants of the 63rd Foot retreated down the slope, a group turned to fire one last volley at their tormentors. Sumter and a small group of officers had ridden forward to observe the retreat. As the redcoats fired, Sumter turned sideways to present a smaller target. Five buckshot ripped into the right side of his chest, and a sixth entered under his right shoulder, chipped his spine, and lodged under his left shoulder. Captain David Hopkins: "Captain Gabriel Brown [of the Second Spartans] was killed on my left hand and General Sumter was on my right. It happened from one platoon of the enemy on their retreat."[41]

Sumter remained bolt-upright in his saddle, sword clutched in his paralyzed right arm. Concealing his condition, Sumter rode with the command group back up the hill, where another officer heard a rustling in the fallen leaves and realized it was blood dripping from Sumter's back and right arm. Asking Colonel Henry Hampton to sheath his sword for him, Sumter had Hampton instruct the senior colonel, Georgia refugee John Twiggs, to assume command.

Sumter was carried into the Blackstock house where a surgeon probed for and extracted the ball from under his left shoulder.

Tarleton withdrew to lick his wounds on a hilltop position about two miles to the south, probably near the present-day Spring Hill Cemetery. The 71st Foot's Lieutenant Roderick McKenzie later wrote sarcastically in response to Tarleton's published account of the battle that "the victorious Lieutenant Colonel Tarleton retreated some distance, Parthian like, conquering as he flew." In the morning Tarleton would resume the fight with the aid of the artillery and McArthur's Highlanders.[42]

With the exception of the incident in which Sumter was wounded,

Patriot casualties had been ludicrously few. Simon Davis: "We had a smart fight with the British and Tories at Blackstocks on which I providentially escaped unhurt."[43]

Twiggs sent parties of mounted men to observe and harass Tarleton in his retreat, and as lagniappe they gathered in the scattered horses that Tarleton needed so badly. The night was cold and wet, and the wounded of both sides were carried into the Blackstock house. Lieutenant McKenzie later wrote, "The wounded of the British detachment were left to the mercy of the enemy, and it is but doing bare justice to General Sumpter, to declare, that the strictest humanity took place upon the present occasion; they were supplied with every comfort in his power."[44]

Private Abraham Bolt Senior recorded, ". . . the Regiment was pursued and attacked by Lt Col Tarletons dragoons at Blackstocks on Tyger River in Spartanburg District. Col Sumpter commanded in the Battle—After a severe skirmish in which we drove the enemy back we retreated."[45]

Twiggs had his men build large campfires, and the glow could certainly be seen from Tarleton's position on the ridge-top to the south. Then the Patriots slipped across Blackstock's Ford. Not trusting to Tarleton's mercies, they carried their own wounded with them.

Joseph McJunkin: "A litter was constructed, and suspended between horses, and on this the gallant General was placed, and, followed by his whole command, crossed to the north bank of the river. He was placed in safety by his faithful and devoted followers, before they again presented themselves to the enemy."[46]

The retreat was accomplished at a quick pace. "It was thought expedient to retreat that night, though it was near sun down when the enemy quit the field. . . . Not a few of the militia lodged that night among the Storys and McIllwaines, twelve miles distant from the scene of action. The retreat was continued the next day toward King's Mountain in York District. On the way thither a part of the Whigs encamped on Gilkie's Creek. A pet Tory lived near where they lay, and some of them told him they would press him into service and take him along with them in the morning. To escape that disaster he took a chisel that night and cut off one of his toes."[47]

Having won a resounding and incredibly lopsided victory, why did Twiggs choose to slip away? Tarleton would be reinforced, and the Patriot scouts almost certainly had reported the arrival of Fraser's Highlanders and the grasshopper cannon, but the Patriots still occupied a very strong position with superior numbers. True, the militia almost always scattered after a battle. Most historians have attributed the breakup to Sumter's wound, and the collapse of morale at the loss of this charismatic leader. Lewis Turner stated, ". . . the British retreated but our officers believing the enemy would be reinforced that night ordered a retreat."[48]

The statement of Reuben Long, Sr. pointed to another issue probably much on the mind of the officers: logistics. The militia was chronically short of supplies, particularly ammunition. "Sumter finding his ammunition was exhausted retreated in the night and continued his retreat for several days when we halted and he [Long] was sent with a detachment to remove some property into Lincoln County NC. . . ." The shortage of ammunition was corroborated by William Beard: "Sumpter whipt and run Tarleton three quarters of a mile but our powder ran out."[49]

Ammunition was not the only shortage that afflicted the Patriot force. One local fifteen-year-old had ". . . run away from his mother, for the purpose of joining in such exciting scenes, literally without clothing, without arms or other equipments." After the battle he received permission to strip one of the dead redcoats, "the weather being extremely cold. The dead man was promptly undressed, and all but the red coat, promptly fitted to the person of young Robert Stark."[50]

The next morning Tarleton returned to a battlefield populated only by his own dead and wounded. Tarleton could by the standards of the time claim a tactical victory, since he was left in possession of the field. McJunkin: "In the morning after the battle Tarleton returned to the battle ground and, finding his opponent gone, hung John Johnson; a Whig who had been captured the day before. Mr. Johnson had taken protection some time in the summer, as many others had done, and when forced to fight had chosen to fight for liberty. His residence was on Tyger River in the vicinity of Hamilton's Ford, where some of his descendants may still be found."

Charles Sims, paroled after the fall of Charleston, ". . . was just recovering his health . . . and a Tory Scout surrounded the house and took him prisoner. This was probably Bill Lee,* who operated largely in this neigh-

---

*Sims repeatedly referred to "Bill Lee" but this was probably William "Bloody Bill" Cunningham.

borhood. Cornwallis was then at Spring Hill, Lexington District, on Congaree Creek. A drum-head court martial having been called, he and a young [John] Johnson . . . were condemned to die. Johnson was brother-in-law to old Maj. Sam. Otterson. He was hung on a tree near his own house. On Congaree Creek, near Cornwallis, in a Tory camp, Sims was already tied up to the limb of a tree . . . the cap had been drawn over his eyes, when an officer riding up from Cornwallis' camp, asked who that was, and on being told it was Charles Sims, he ordered him instantly to be taken down. He recognized him as an old school mate. This officer's name was Maj. George. They had been schoolmates in Virginia. George took him to Cornwallis, and procured for him not only a pardon, but a parole."[51]

After the necessary arrangements were made, Tarleton renewed the pursuit and followed as far as Grindal Shoals on Pacolet River.[52] The simple truth was that the dreaded "Bloody Ban" had been mauled—and badly.

In his reports to Cornwallis, and in his post-war memoir marked by character assassination of his former commander, Tarleton lied shamelessly about the whole episode. The Loyalists killed at the Enoree ford became a force of Patriots. The Patriot force at Blackstock's had been decisively defeated, but "A pursuit across a river, with a few troops of cavalry, and a small body of infantry, was not advisable in the night; a position was therefore taken adjoining to the field of battle, to wait the arrival of the light and legion infantry.

"An express was sent to acquaint Earl Cornwallis with the success of his troops. . . ."

Tarleton grossly inflated Patriot losses: "Upwards of one hundred Americans were killed and wounded, and fifty were made prisoners." He glossed over his own casualties, listing only three officers killed and three wounded, with forty-five enlisted killed and wounded. If there was any blame to be laid, it was to be at the feet of the dead John Money and his 63rd Foot, since "The ardour of the 63rd carried them too far, and exposed them to a considerable fire from the buildings and mountain."[53]

The embittered Roderick McKenzie was particularly incensed by Tarleton's assertion that the rebel losses included three dead colonels. "The real truth is, that the Americans being well sheltered, sustained very inconsiderable loss in the attack; and as for the three Colonels, they must certainly have been imaginary beings, 'men in buckram,' created merely to grace the triumph of a victory, which the British army in Carolina were led to celebrate, amidst the contempt and derision of the inhabitants, who had much better information." (Buckram was a stiff cloth used in bookbinding; the closest modern colloquialism would be "straw-men.")[54]

The Patriots suffered negligible casualties, although as with most of these battles it is impossible to make an accurate assessment. The maximum estimates of Patriot casualties include only about seven killed and wounded; the only officer losses were Sumter wounded, and Captains Gabriel Brown and possibly John Nixon killed. British and Loyalist losses are absolutely impossible to estimate because of Tarleton's lies and obfuscation.

Some estimates of British and Loyalist losses run as high as 90 killed and 170 wounded. Minimum estimates are 52 killed and wounded, though the same source cited two separate and consistent individual Patriots who reported British losses as "killed 92 and upwards of 100 wounded" and the other ". . . 92 dead and 100 wounded upon the field. . . ." He also cited Nehemiah Blackstock (the son of William) as saying there were burial plots "containing 81 dead British" on the property.[55]

Most sources say that fifty Patriots were taken prisoner, but the fifty prisoners Tarleton boasted of were mostly men randomly scooped up from the countryside on his return march, including Loyalists unfortunate enough to cross the Legion's path. In his frustration, Tarleton engaged in some of his typical practices. Joseph McJunkin said that Tarleton paused briefly at Grindal Shoals on the Pacolet River. "William Hodge, a peaceable citizen, resided two miles above the shoals. The next morning a little after sunrise, Tarleton with his whole army came to the house of Mr. Hodge, took him prisoner, seized provisions and provender, killed up his stock, burned his fence and house, and carried him off, telling his wife as they started that he should be hung on the first crooked tree on the road. He was carried to Camden and put in jail. Some time in ensuing April he made his escape by cutting the grating out of the window, with some others."[56]

In the aftermath of the battle Tarleton's fabrication took on a life of its own. In his memoir Tarleton preened, citing a letter from Cornwallis in which he lauded his dashing cavalryman to Sir Henry Clinton: "It is not easy for Lieutenant-colonel Tarleton to add to the reputation he has acquired in this province; but the defeating one thousand men, posted on very strong ground, and occupying log houses, with one hundred and ninety cavalry and eighty infantry, is a proof of that spirit and those talents which must render the most essential services to this country."[57]

There were celebrations in British-occupied New York, and bonfires were lighted in his honor in Tarleton's home town of Liverpool.

In contrast, most of the rank and file militiamen of the Second Spartans did not think much of the battle. Abel Kendrick in Captain Grant's company would later say only that they ". . . had a slight engagement or skirmish with the British . . ." Lewis Turner recalled only that he ". . . was in another battle at Black Stocks on Tyger River South Carolina. Genl Sumter commanded in that engagement the British forces was commanded by Tarlton. the Americans successfully [illegible], had the misfortune to get our general wounded."[58]

As it turned out, Tarleton had won neither a tactical nor a strategic victory. But that anonymous redcoat from the 63rd Foot had in fact made an enormous contribution to the Patriot cause. By sheer force of personality Thomas Sumter kept alive the fires of resistance in the revolution's darkest hours. Perhaps an indication of his charisma was that men like William Hill continued to worship him for decades. Relentlessly ambitious and jealous of prerogatives, he was not particularly gifted either tactically or strategically. He staunchly refused to cooperate with leaders of the Continental forces sent to fight in the South, and generally did little that did not personally benefit Sumter himself.

Sumter's tenacity unfortunately extended to a complete inability to learn from his own errors. He stubbornly refused to recognize that the militia could not fight the British regulars on their own terms. The defensive battle at Blackstock's had been an anomaly, but even then Sumter had succumbed to his own worst habits when he sent the militia volunteers out into the open tobacco fields to counterattack Money.

But that unknown redcoat private had removed the irascible and obstructionist Sumter from the scene at a critical juncture, and it changed the entire dynamic of the war in the South. What the cause needed now was militia leaders who would work with the Continental Army. Congress had at last steeled itself to dispatch yet another army of Continentals south, and this time there would be little political interference in the affairs of the army. George Washington would finally be allowed to choose his own Southern Department commanders.

He chose well.

CHAPTER **13**

THE CALM AT THE STORM'S EYE

The fishermen know that the sea is dangerous and the storm terrible, but they have never found these dangers sufficient reason for remaining ashore.
—VINCENT VAN GOGH

THE MILITIA'S MOST FEARED OPPONENT HAD BEEN BADLY beaten—at least on one afternoon—but the partisan war raged on.

Samuel Hammond: "General Sumter, although badly wounded, continued with his troops, carried on an uncomfortable litter, until they passed Berwick's iron works; after which, his command was divided. A part continued with the general as an escort, until they reached North-Carolina, while the Georgians, commanded by Twiggs, Clarke, Candler and B. Few, turned westward, and in a few days marched towards Ninety-Six, taking their course along the foot of the mountains."[1]

Most authors have concluded that Sumter's army disintegrated after Blackstock's, and many men did indeed just go home. Most who did so were likely from the Minute Service; William Grant recorded ". . . that night and the [militia] scattered and went home having been out not less than one month."[2]

The dispersal of part of Sumter's main force after Blackstock's was actually fairly typical. It left no large organized force to resist large enemy forces, but the militia remained active, contending with the local Tories in the bitter partisan war. The better organized militia units hung together and withdrew in good order. Lewis Turner recorded that the Second Spartans retreated ". . . eight or nine miles and encamped." John Calhoun remembered that "he was marched on to the iron works under Col. Thomas—the balance of the army crossed Smith's Ford. There he was dismissed & never after joined the regular army but was liable to be & was called on frequently after."[3]

Lewis Turner remembered, "After the battle at Black Stocks until the applicant quit the Service he was employed in skirmishing through the country sometimes in pursuit of the Tories and at others guarding the country against the British. . . ."[4] Lacey "kept the field with his mounted Infantry. . . ."[5]

Elements of the Second Spartans remained in the field. Captain Samuel Otterson: "From thence the army under Sumter crossed the Broad River and as well as I recollect divided out in scouting parties in one of which I got my arm rebroke in chase after a party of tories under [page torn] Brandon whom we killed with the exception of [those] we took prisoner. My arm being broken the last time by a fall from my horse soon got better."[6]

Robert Long left a lengthy description of his ramblings about the countryside as militia forces joined and divided, and an ever-changing force of partisans harassed the British across hundreds of square miles. Long described how three Little River companies joined with Brandon's Second Spartans the day after the battle, took charge of prisoners and delivered them across the Pacolet River to Sumter's force withdrawing into North Carolina. They then turned east and then south down the Broad River valley, skirmishing with the British.[7]

McJunkin: "After seeing Gen. Sumter out of striking distance from the enemy, the command of Col. Brandon returned to the vicinity of their own homes and took post at Love's Ford on Broad River. This position was well adapted to check the operations of the Tories on the west side of that river, and restrict their intercourse with the British Army at Winnsboro."[8]

Robert Long, with the Little River Regiment that so often cooperated with Brandon, ". . . marched to Love's Ford on Broad River. Capts. Casey, Ewing, and Harris, commanded by Col. Hayes; joined Col. Brandon there; from that to 3rd or 4th December lay by not a single day,—no, nor night either, but marching and counter-marching, occasionally crossing and recrossing Broad river, Pacolet, Tyger, and Enoree,—sometimes Cols. Brandon and Hayes together, at others detached in companies as the service seemed to require, or as the enemy receded or advanced."

From their relatively secure base in the dense river-bottom canebrakes Brandon and Hayes launched harassing raids. Long recorded that in one such raid three companies of his regiment ". . . and Capt. Blasangam [Blassingame] of Col. Brandon's, about 40 men" rode back across the Tyger and Enoree. Riding through the next night ". . . near 40 or 50 miles to Col. Dugan's place: at dark attacked Major Lantrip with about 60 Tories; wounded 8 and took 10 prisoners" and then rode back, arriving about 20 December.[9]

The efforts of the Patriot militia were largely consumed in countering the Loyalist militia. The defeat at King's Mountain might have struck a mortal blow to Cornwallis' recruiting, but diehard Tories remained numerous in the back country, and ". . . besides, Georgia was infested with them," recalled James Collins. Apparently the sizeable Ponder clan remained particularly noxious, and militia was assigned to scour the region west of the Broad River in search of them.

Collins' party captured the "very old, grayheaded" patriarch of the clan, and he was threatened with death unless he disclosed the location of his sons. As the old man begged for his life, one Whig surreptitiously called Collins aside: "'I want you to take this spear and run it through that d— d old Tory. He ought to die.' 'No,' said I, 'he is too old; besides, the colonel would never forgive me; he is a prisoner and he don't intend to kill him.' 'Oh,' said he, I can easily plead you off with the colonel'; then putting his hand in his pocket he drew out a purse of money, saying, 'Here is twenty dollars—[showing the silver]—I will give you this to kill him.' I felt insulted. I thought he underrated my real character, and thought that through my youth and inexperience, he would bribe me to do a deed that he himself would be ashamed of. . . . the poor old Tory was set at liberty, after getting a friendly admonition from the colonel."[10]

Brandon had established a home guard company to counter Loyalist depredations, and a prominent figure was the indefatigable William Kennedy, Sr. "Although Kennedy had no commission, the men of his neighborhood acknowledged him as their leader, and their feet were ever in the stirrups at his bidding. His efforts were mainly directed against the British and Tory scouts that made plundering excursions into the Districts of

Union and York, which was very frequent when the British army under Cornwallis was encamped near Winterboro [Winnsboro]. Against the Tories, he was ever in the field, and they never could surprise him."[11]

Joseph McJunkin: "To illustrate the course pursued by the tories to the deserted wives and children of the whigs, and the spirit of their daughters, the following incident may be mentioned. A tory Colonel, of the name of Moore, from North-Carolina, being informed that Sumter was wounded, and that therefore his strong arm was not stretched out for the protection of the country, accompanied by his band, made a descent upon Union District, and visited the house of Samuel McJunkin, the Major's father. All the males were absent; they passed there the night; in the morning, they were joined by some South-Carolina tories, among whom was Bill Haynesworth. When about to leave, they stripped the house of provisions, bed clothes and wearing apparel. The last article taken was a bed-quilt, which Bill Haynesworth placed upon his horse. Jane McJunkin [the Major's sister] seized it, and so did Bill. They pulled and exerted themselves; the other tories amused themselves, by crying out, well done, woman—well done, Bill. The Colonel, struck with the strength and courage of the young woman, swore, if she could take it from him, she should keep it. In the course of the struggle, Bill lost his feet, and fell prostrate on his back. Jane put one foot upon his breast, and wrested the quilt from him. Bill, crestfallen and defeated, had to retire without his share of the spoils."[12]

Although the episode sounds comic, in the severe back country winter the absence of food and protection from the cold—average low temperatures in January are 30F (-1C) and can plunge to -5F (-21C)—could well be a death sentence for a family.

After Blackstock's the long-suffering Ann Kennedy took in her badly wounded cousin William Kennedy (there were a *lot* of William Kennedys, including her father and brother). "He was conveyed to the house of Wm. Kennedy, Sr., to be taken care of. It was not long after this event, that the tories again visited their house; but not finding Wm. Kennedy, Sr., or his sons at home they commenced searching through the house for plunder, when they found Wm. Kennedy, the cousin of Ann, in bed. The tories held a consultation to decide whether or not they would kill the wounded soldier. One of them remarked: 'Let him alone, he will die in a few days any how.' The tories were so exasperated at not finding the father and brothers of Ann at home, that they soon began plundering the house. They cut a web of cloth out of the loom, ripped open the feather beds and scattered the feathers to the four winds and made saddle blankets of the cloths and bed ticks. They robbed the ladies of their finger rings and other jewelry. They had taken nearly all the bedclothes except a blanket which Ann's mother had folded up, placed in a chair and was sitting on it. A tory seized hold of it and attempted to draw it from under the old lady. She begged him not to take the last blanket she had for herself and children. Ann could brook the insult no longer. She seized the tory by the arm pushed him out of the door and gave him a kick as he went. This so provoked him that he snatched a gun from the hand of one of his comrades and swore he would shoot her, but the captain interposed and prevented him from committing the rash act and advised him never to kill as brave a woman as she was.

"The tory then ran into the house picked up a fire brand from the hearth, swore he would burn the house and attempted to set fire to a pile of flax in the corner of the house; again Ann interfered and threw him out of the house. The captain then requested him not to burn the house as they had got everything that was worth taking; so the tory threw the fire brand at her with all vengeance, which struck her on the hand breaking the bones therof, which made her a cripple for life. Fearing that other tories might not prove so lenient to her wounded cousin, should they make another visit to their house, she made a litter and with some of the family, placed him on it and carried him to the forest where she made him a bed in a fallen tree top where she dressed his wounds and waited upon him until he recovered, which was some three or four weeks. Not long after this, the neighborhood was so annoyed by the tories, that a few resolute whig women assembled together and wrote a note to General [Daniel] Morgan, who was then stationed near the Pacolet Springs in Spartanburg to send a company to Union to subdue the tories, but no one manifested a willingness to be the bearer of the note, until Miss Ann Kennedy stepped up and volunteered her services to carry it. She concealed the note in her stocking—pinned a sunbonnet around her head—mounted a pony—rode about sixty miles—delivered the note to General Morgan and returned home in safety."[13]

Charles Sims had been in hiding for months, but an unusually bitter winter was coming on. "Sims had been for a time fed in the woods by his

[Eli Cook's] wife. Cook knew also of his hiding place, and a deep snow having fallen, he was fearful that Sims would freeze—went and brought him in, and concealed him in his hay loft, which stood near his house. He had his arms with him. One bright moon-light night a Tory scout [party] rode into the old Quaker's yard, and demanded to know where Sims was concealed? Sims heard every word that was spoken; he believed his time had come, thinking that the old Quaker had betrayed him. But he was quickly reassured. Cook managed the difficulty with admirable skill. 'Am I not a King's man; having in any right to think I would conceal a rebel? Am I Sims' keeper?' These inquiries were made so rapidly and earnestly that the Tories were completely deceived, and searched no farther for their victim. Sims all the time lay in a few feet of them, his gun and pistol cocked, prepared to sell his life dearly, if the Quaker had proven traitor. He had with him in the hayloft an old English shotgun of the Queen Anne Model, very long, and of large bore, which he carried through the war—it is still in the possession of his family." Sims finally gave up and fled to Virginia as a refugee. He later sent a messenger to collect his family, and the family remained in Virginia until the end of the war.[14]

In October newly arrived Patriot General Nathanael Greene was faced with seemingly insurmountable problems. One was the conundrum that had thwarted commanders on both sides: in a countryside picked clean of supplies, he could not feed his army. The rump of Gates' army at Charlotte supplied itself by plundering the locals, and many of the troops were practically naked. Despite Cornwallis' plan to move north, the militia in South Carolina would have to continue to entangle him long enough for Greene to rebuild his army.

Of necessity Greene violated a fundamental military principle, and in the face of a foe superior in ability if not in numbers, he would divide his force. The main army would remain to the east while Morgan, with the light troops and Lieutenant Colonel William Washington's cavalry—about 82 men, detachments from the 1st and 3rd Continental Light Dragoons—would move to the west to threaten Ninety Six.

Joseph McJunkin: "In the early part of December, Col. Brandon, Major McJunkin, and such forces as they could collect, took post at Love's ford, on Broad River, to prevent intercourse between Cornwallis, who was still at Winnsboro' [SC], and the loyalists west of Broad River. While there, a scout under the command of Capt. [John] McCool, was ordered to cross Broad River, and attack the tories on Sandy River." The exact site of the skirmish is unknown, but McCool and William Grant's companies probably ventured about ten miles into enemy territory.

Joseph McJunkin, referring to himself in the third person: "While lying there, says Major McJunkin, a scout was sent over to Sandy River [east of the Broad River] under Capt. Joseph McCool. The party was worsted in conflict with the Tories in that section and Daniel McJunkin, the Major's brother, was taken prisoner and carried off to Winnsboro. 'At my insistence,' says the major, 'Col. Brandon sent a flag to Lord Cornwallis proposing to exchange Col. Fanning, who was a prisoner with us, for Daniel McJunkin. This proposition was rejected by His Lordship, and Daniel was sent forthwith to the jail in Camden.' Here he remained until April, when he escaped in company with William Hodge . . ."

McJunkin went on to describe the conditions in the British prison at Camden in terms eerily similar to those in a Nazi death camp of another era. ". . . the jail at Camden was literally crammed with men from the time of the defeat of Gen. Gates until the following spring; that for a considerable time in the autumn of 1780 not a morsel was given them to eat save pieces of pumpkins gathered from the troughs where horses had been fed. These remnants of horse feed were brought in baskets once a day and thrown into the jail among the prisoners, and it often occurred that some of them failed in getting a single morsel even of this fare. . . . All of them prisoners of war, and of course many of them murdered by this process of—shall I call it slow torture?"[15]

Daniel would remain a prisoner ". . . until about the last of April, 1781, when he and some others made their escape, but nearly perished for the want of food, before they reached their friends."[16]

The task of foraging for Daniel Morgan's Flying Army was delegated to those most familiar with the region, the militia. Christopher Brandon: "After Morgan encamped at Grindall shoals, we were kept pretty busy in procuring provisions for his army."[17]

The Blackstock's triumph emboldened the Whigs, and no Tory outpost was safe. On 11 December, Loyalist David George penned a rambling, despairing dispatch to Cornwallis complaining about the ranging Patriot militia. George had been gathering provisions for Cornwallis' hard-pressed army. ". . . I had gone to the Trouble of fixing up three Waggons and teams to set off to Charles Town; had got some of my load in; and was about to finish Loading the last Waggons; on thursday Last when There came up a Number of arm'd Rebels; seizd all The Horses they cou'd find that was fit for service Drive of two of the Waggons and plunderd me of many things; Took me a Prisoner. . . ." The raiders took wagons and prisoner across the Broad River ". . . to where the rebel colonel Brandon lay with as they told me [with] about two hundred or three hundred and fifty men who lay at one John Cunninghams in the fork Between Broad and Packolate Rivers."

George went on at length to describe rebel plans to construct storehouses and a fort on at the headwaters of Turkey Creek, referred to "Brandon's defeat of Ferguson," and ". . . while they had me a Prisoner among them they were inform'd that their Wives was to be sent of out of this Province; I heard many of them swearing that if their wives was sent off; they wou'd come in and carry of the Subjects Wives and Children . . ." His grammar and handwriting deteriorated as he went on." I fear they will ruin me totally if soon there is not a stop put To their coming in a-mong us and I am afraid to offer to move a way; for if I was to offer to move of & the Rebels was to hear of it they woud follow me and take of every thing I possess Brandon and Lacey might be Very Easily Driven of Brandons men is always scouting about the Bearer [courier] is Very uneasy a waiting for me. . . ."[18]

The setback that had befallen Tarleton did not distract Cornwallis from his primary mission: to destroy Greene's army or drive it out of the Carolinas. He still had the intact 23rd and 3rd Regiments of Foot and the 2nd Battalion of the 71st Foot. Major General Leslie's 1,500 men (two battalions of the Foot Guards, and the von Bose Regiment with a detachment of *jagers*) were now available. More questionable were the hundred or so demoralized infantry and 40 or so Green Dragoons who had escaped the Blackstock's Farm debacle. Tarleton's Green Dragoons had proven themselves of little value in a stand-up battle. Still, Cornwallis had cause for optimism. Such a small but professional force could be more than a match for either Greene or Morgan if they could be brought to bay.

Every morsel that the Patriot partisans gathered in was one less to feed Cornwallis' destitute army, and Cornwallis had men scouring the countryside for rebel bands. On 20 December Major Archibald McArthur of

the 71st Foot wrote describing difficulties posed by the Patriots comman-
deering transport. "A Person arrived here [yester?]day who left Turkey
Creek two Days ago & says the Rebels had pressed all the Waggons in that
neighborhood & gave out they were [illegible] sent to Salisbury for Salt."
The emboldened Patriot bands were also now confident enough to establish fixed bases, as McArthur went on that "I have the Honor to send your
Lordship a sketch of the Ground where the Rebels have made the Redoubt
on Turkey Creek, Lieut. McDonald has made it from the information of
Mr. Lane who was at the Place when Prisoner."[19]

Unfazed by his drubbing at Blackstock's, on 24 December the inde-
fatigable and always upbeat Tarleton wrote Cornwallis that "I have sent
H__[blank in original] out to enquire about the other side. I have just got
Intelligence from 2 of my People about the state of the Roads &c. on this
side thro Murphy's Settlement up the Broad River to Sandy River & the
Cross Roads—the Roads are good, Forage likewise is to be obtained—"[20]

Cornwallis was continually bombarded with urgent dispatches that
showed mounting British concern for the safety of Ninety Six. On 30
December Brigadier of militia Robert Cunningham (Bloody Bill's cousin
and the garrison commander at the fortified Williams Plantation) wrote
"Sir From undoubted Authority Genl. Morgan is now at Pacolett with
5,000 of the Virginia Riflemen all on foot; am convinced he is joined By
[illegible], Brandon, and Pickens, who lead forth all the frontiersmen from
long Cane—the destination of this force I cannot yet learn by the best
Intelligence. Believe Ninety Six to be their object."[21]

On the same day David George, from his position on the north bank
of the Tyger, reported that his sister-in-law had infiltrated the Whig camp.
"She understood from Captain Francis Princes and Henry Princes wives;
That they were a Waiting for Colonel Morgan & Colonel Washing Who
was on their march. . . ." with intent to attack Ninety Six or Augusta with
3000 men. Later that day George reported additional intelligence ". . . I
have heard a few moments ago Morgan & Washington had joind the party
that lay at Grimes Mill yesterday. . . . I am well informed they intend to
march as fast as they can to Ninety Six. I don't believe they have as many
men as reported to my Wife's sister: they have call'd in Brandons; Lyles;
Hayes' [and] Clarks Regiments & they were all together in camp yesterday.
. . ."[22]

The only preserved letter from Colonel Thomas Brandon dates from this period. (The asterisk is an annotation by Lyman Draper.)

Camp near the Mouth of the Packlet,
4th Decr. 1780.

Honor^d Sir:

I received yours of the 2nd instant this morning by Colonel Hays, and am greatly obliged to you for the men you sent, and shall strictly adhere to the contents of your letter.

I have sent a party after wagons, and at this moment agoing to detach off two parties after provisions. I have not collected any at this time, for the British march^d down Packlet to Col. Henderson's Plantation, and was on Fairforest within eight miles of my house. Col^o. Moore and a strong party of Tories march^d through my settlement, and rob^d and plundered many people, and myself amongst the rest.

I still keep post on Broad river. When Maj^r Farr returned from your camp, and informed me it was your desire for me to collect provisions, I [illegible] immediately proceeded to that business, but heard of a party of Tories on Sandy River I proceeded after them, and fell in with a small party—we Killed three and wounded three, most notorious villains. The British who were at Blackstocks have returned to Cornwallis.

I had certain intelligence from Col. Williams* last Friday, and there were no British there, and only about forty Tories, and they busy employed [at?] Killing and barreling beef. I dont believe there are any British of this side of 96. The person who informed me is a man of truth.

As to the wagons you sent for, it will be out of my power to furnish with as many you sent for; however I will send as many as I can get, and as soon as possible. I hope it will be in my power to furnish you with a quantity of beef and pork.

I am, Dear Sir,
Y^r. Hbl^e. Sevt—
Thos. Brandon

*Meaning Col. Jas. Williams' Fort or place on Little River.[23]

On Christmas Day of 1780 the man who Ann Kennedy sought rode into the militia camp at Grindal Shoals. He, more than any other man, would decide the outcome of the war in the South. He led only a motley force of 500 or so men: a battalion of 300 hardened Continentals from Delaware, Virginia, and Maryland; Virginia, North Carolina, and South Carolina State Troops; and Virginia militia, many of them disciplined former Continentals.

Brigadier General Daniel Morgan was a veteran of the French and Indian War, when he had served as a civilian "waggoner," or teamster. In 1755 Morgan assaulted an overbearing British officer during the retreat from Fort Duquesne, and was sentenced to 500 lashes—a death sentence for a weaker man. By some miscount, Morgan received only 499. The incident instilled a lingering hatred for the British officer class, and in later years Morgan would sometimes show his scars and tell others that the British still "owed him one." Morgan survived to serve as a rifleman in the Virginia militia, and prospered after that war, rising to the rank of captain in the militia.[24]

Upon the outbreak of the revolution he raised a company, Morgan's Riflemen, and distinguished himself in the Arnold Expedition before being taken prisoner in the disastrous defeat at Quebec City. Exchanged in 1777, he was surprised to be given command of a Virginia regiment of Continentals, then the Provisional Rifle Corps. Morgan excelled in further actions, including the Saratoga battles (19 September and 7 October, 1777). Morgan grew increasingly disillusioned by Congressional interference that elevated less competent—but politically connected—officers to high rank, and perhaps by Horatio Gates' usurpation of Benedict Arnold's role in the Saratoga victory. He resigned from the army in June 1779, and wisely declined a subordinate command in Gates' new southern army. Agreeing to re-enter service after the Camden debacle, Morgan was at last promoted to Brigadier General in October 1780, and joined the army then at Hillsborough, North Carolina.

Congress had at last come to its senses and also allowed George Washington to promote his own choice for commander of the Southern Department. He chose another anachronism, businessman and "Quaker general" Nathanael Greene. Despite a limp that caused competitors to question his fitness for command, in 1774 Greene organized a local militia company

Brigadier General Daniel Morgan knew the limitations and strengths of militia, analyzed Tarleton's usual tactics, and designed an unusual defense in depth that resulted in decisive victory at The Cowpens. Morgan, a former militiaman, habitually wore the hunting uniform of the militia even when commanding Continentals. From a portrait by Alonzo Chappel.
—NARA

(which got him voted out of his meeting-house) and learned military skills through extensive reading. Proving himself tactically competent and a superlative administrator under difficult conditions, Greene quickly earned Washington's trust and very rapid promotion. On 3 December 1780 Greene succeeded Gates in command at Charlotte, North Carolina, with the unprecedented provision that he was answerable only to Washington. Greene was in direct command of all forces from Georgia to Delaware, and in effect second in command of the Continental Army.[25]

It was an unusual team. Morgan would soon prove to be one of American history's tactical geniuses. Greene would prove himself to be that most unusual of generals—one who lost every battle but won the war.

In a series of dispatches Greene listed forces to expect and instructed Morgan ". . . you will employ against the enemy on the West side of the River, either offensively or defensively as your own prudence and discretion may direct, acting with caution, and avoiding surprises by every possible precaution. I give you the entire command in that quarter, and do hereby require all Officers and Soldiers engaged in the American cause to be subject to your orders and command. The object of this detachment is to give protection to that part of the country and spirit up the people—to annoy the enemy in that quarter—collect the provisions and forage out of the way of the enemy, which you will have formed into a number of small magazines, in or near the position you may think proper to take." (16 December 1780)

Despite Greene's clear instructions, Sumter persisted in issuing orders to the militia that contradicted Greene.

In other dispatches a clearly apprehensive Greene advised Morgan that Cornwallis was being reinforced by 2,000 redcoats marching laboriously from Charleston to Camden. He repeatedly admonished Morgan to be alert to avoid surprise, join with him if threatened by Cornwallis' force, and advised him that a supply of tents, hatchets, and "particularly shoes are coming on." (29 December 1780)

"If you employ detachments to intercept supplies going to Ninety-Six and Augusta, it will perplex the enemy very much. If you think Ninety-Six, Augusta or even Savannah can be surprised . . . you may attempt it. But don't think of attempting either unless by surprise. . . ." Clearly, though, Morgan's main mission was distraction. " If you could detach a small party to kill the enemy's draught horses and recruiting cavalry upon the Congaree, it would give them almost as deadly a blow as a defeat." (8 January, 1781)[26]

As the Patriot militia continued to gnaw at the British and Loyalist strength, some of the small skirmishes were almost comic. One very dark night Samuel Clowney and a slave "of remarkable fidelity to his master, and withal a strong Whig" were approaching a crossing of Kelsey's Creek near present-day Spartanburg when they heard a party of mounted men approaching on the other bank. Hatching a quick plan, Clowney sent his man into the underbrush. When the men were in mid-stream, Clowney challenged them to identify themselves, and they replied "Friends to the King!"

Clowney ordered them to give up their arms or be shot down, shouting as if in command of a large force, and the slave made an enormous racket. They gathered up the enemy weapons and marched the prisoners to camp where they "were much chagrined when they found their captors were only two in number, while they were five."

The two Patriots marched their prisoners into Morgan's camp about eight miles away. When Morgan inquired as to exactly how two men had captured five, Clowney replied dryly, "Please your honor, I surrounded them."[27]

Despite Sumter's intransigence, the militia in South Carolina played their part. On 26 December the militia crossed the Pacolet, heading south toward the trading post at Hammond's Store, deep within the Ninety Six District. The purpose was to break up a force of Tories plundering and harassing the local Whig families. Robert Long: "Col. Washington's 84 cavalry, and Cols. Brandon and Hayes about 200 militia, rode that night about 16 miles and next day [27 December] about after crossing Tyger and Enoree, attacked Col. Moore and about 500 Tories on Bush River. . . ." The exact site of the store is now unknown, and other sources estimate the Tory force at about 250, under a Colonel Thomas Waters.[28]

Thomas Young: "We came up with them at Hammond's store; in fact, we picked up several scattering ones, within about three miles of the place, from whom we learned all about their position. . . . When we [were] in sight, we perceived that the tories had formed in line on the brow of the hill opposite to us. We had a long hill to descend and another to rise. Col. Washington and his dragoons gave a shout, drew swords, and charged down the hill like madmen. The tories fled in every direction without firing a gun. We took a great many prisoners and killed a few. Here I must relate an incident which occurred on this occasion. In Washington's corps there was a boy of fourteen or fifteen, a mere lad, who in crossing Tiger River was ducked by a blunder of his horse. The men laughed and jeered at him very much, at which he got very mad, and swore that, boy or no boy, he would kill a man that day or die. He accomplished the former. I remember very well being highly amused at the little fellow charging round a crib after a tory, cutting and slashing away with his puny arm, till he brought him down."[29]

Long summarized that they ". . . killed and wounded a great many, took 40 or 50 prisoners, and dispersed the rest and also Will Cunningham's with 100 more a mile or two from Moore's camp; and on the next day the fort at Williams' plantation."[30]

On 4 January Morgan reported the Williams Plantation action to Greene by post: "Gen. Cunningham, on hearing of Waters' defeat, prepared to evacuate Fort Williams, and had just marched out with the last of his garrison as a party consisting of about forty Militia Horsemen, under Col. Hayes, and ten dragoons under Mr. Simmons, arrived with an Intention of demanding a Surrender. The Enemy's force was so superior to theirs they could effect nothing more than the demolition of the Fort."[31]

Washington's raiders rode back north to find militia rallying to join Morgan. Long recorded meeting "Cols. Thomas and Roebuck with 200 men," and "Col. A. Pickens just escaped from the Tories at Ninety-Six, and 95 men with him." (Pickens had not escaped, but repudiated parole.) Pickens assumed command of a brigade that also included Brandon's and Hayes' regiments, crossed to the south of the Pacolet, and ". . . moved down Fairforest as a body of observation, and to encourage our friends to turn out, which they did then considerably after Moore's defeat."[32]

As usual, the prickly—and invalid—Sumter continued to refuse to co-operate with Greene or Morgan. As late as 19 January Greene was still trying to soothe him, and in a letter wrote that ". . . among other things he [Morgan] mentions some embarrassment which has arisen from an order of yours to Colonel Hill, not to obey any order from him unless it came through you." Greene went on to explain the necessity to avoid a potentially "fatal delay" in relaying orders, and that it would be "very extraordinary, if a captain should dispute an order from his general, because it was not communicated through his colonel." In military protocol Sumter as a militia general, and Hill as a colonel, would have been subordinate to equivalent ranks of Continentals, yet another point of offense to Sumter and Hill.[33]

Greene's pleadings were to no avail.

CHAPTER 14

THE COWPENS, 17 JANUARY 1781

Just hold up your heads, boys, three fires and you are free. . . .
—DANIEL MORGAN

WHATEVER THE FACTS OF THE OBSCURE FIGHT, THE Hammond's Store pinprick had far-reaching consequences. Now thoroughly alarmed, and not knowing Greene's plans, Cornwallis did not know Morgan intended to avoid battle. Morgan posed a potential threat to Ninety Six, while Greene maneuvered to pose a threat to the bases at Camden and Charleston. So Cornwallis instructed Tarleton to break off his futile pursuit of the Swamp Fox, Francis Marion, in the lowlands, move inland, and destroy Morgan. He thus divided his own army, pursuing Greene while Tarleton chased Morgan.

On 12 January Andrew Pickens, at Fairforest Meeting House, was informed by scouts that Tarleton was on the move, and immediately set off to join with Morgan. The next day Greene posted a dispatch to Morgan, informing him that "Col. Tarleton is said to be on his way to pay you a visit." Morgan ". . . beat a retreat. Marched up the road towards Cowpens, and Pickens up Pacolet through the hills; camped that night, the 13th, on a very high hill. 14th joined Morgan, camped together that night, Cols. Thomas and Roebuck also with 200 men . . ."[1]

By the 16th Tarleton was hot on Pickens' trail, his men pausing only to forage and commit their usual depredations. Angelica Mitchell Nott: "At the time Tarleton was going to the Cowpens, some Tories came to my aunt's with whom I lived & burnt the top of our tent. It was a rail pen covered with straw. Tarleton camped at aunt Beckham's on this march." She later added that "At the time Col. Tarleton came to aunt Beckham's, they (that is the enemy) took all the bedding save one quilt. Soon afterwards a party of Tories came & took that away." The Patriot militia ". . . marched close order all day till in the night; set the woods on fire, which no doubt retarded Tarleton's pursuit each time at least a fourth of an hour. . . ."[2]

Among Morgan's many difficulties was communicating with and re-assembling his scattered forces. Joseph McJunkin: "At this time Genl Pickens was encamped between Fairforest and Tyger to watch the movements of Tarleton and give information to Genl Morgan. I was sent as an express to Genl Morgan, Morgan then sent an express to Col Washington who was then at Wofford Iron Works to inform him of Tarleton's approach and to meet him at Gentleman Thompsons. The next morning (the 17th of January 1781) Tarleton attacked Morgan at the Cowpens. . . ."[3]

Militiamen were arriving from all quarters, and Joseph McJunkin's officer messmates included a major from Georgia and a Colonel Glenn of the Newberry Militia. On the morning of the 15th Glenn recounted a nightmare to his messmates. He had confronted a giant snake, and cut it in half with his sword; "the head had escaped, but the tail lay powerless at his feet." Professing to be no "construer of dreams," McJunkin told him that "the snake Tarleton" would be defeated, lose most of his force, but "the head effect his escape in safety."[4]

Thomas Young recalled that after Hammond's Store, "We then returned to Morgan's encampment at Grindall Shoals, on the Packolette, and there we remained, eating beef and scouting through the neighborhood until we heard of Tarlton's approach. Having received intelligence that Col. Tarlton designed to cross the Packolette at Easternood Shoals above us, Gen. Morgan broke up his encampment early on the morning of the 16th, and retreated up the mountain road by Hancock's Ville, taking the left hand road not far above, in a direction toward the head of Thickety Creek. We arrived at the field of the Cowpens about sun-down, and were then told that there we should meet the enemy. The news was received with great joy by the army. We were very anxious for battle, and many a hearty curse had been vented against Gen. Morgan during that day's march, for retreating, as we thought, to avoid a fight. Night came upon us, yet much remained to be done."[5]

Morgan arrived at the Cowpens late on 16 January, and established a hasty camp. Samuel Hammond: "Orders had been issued to the militia, to have twenty-four rounds of balls prepared and ready for use, before they retired to rest. A general order, forming the disposition of the troops, in case of coming to action, had also been prepared. . . . This order was transmitted verbally.[6]

Sumter was still stirring the pot, bypassing his superior Morgan and essentially instructing the faithful William Hill not to cooperate with Morgan. Greene was still exhibiting Quaker sensitivities, advising Morgan that, "I will write General Sumter on the subject, but as it is better to conciliate than aggravate matters where everything depends so much on voluntary principles, I wish you to take no notice of the matter, but endeavor to influence his conduct to give you all the aid in his power. Write him frequently and consult with him freely. He is a man of great pride and considerable merit and should not be neglected. If he has given such an order, I persuade myself he will see the impropriety of the matter and correct it in future, unless personal glory is more the object than public good, which I cannot suppose is the case. . . ." He again instructed Morgan to give battle only if certain of victory, to "Put nothing to the hazard, a retreat may be disagreeable but not disgraceful." (19 January)[7]

Sumter's intransigence aside, one of Morgan's difficulties was now organizational; the forces available to him swelled during the night as more local militia arrived. Following the news of King's Mountain and Blackstock's, the locals were eager to put an end to Tarleton, or just to seek the relative safety of joining a larger force. James Collins had been in a contingent hunting out local Tories. "It was not long until became necessary for us to seek safety by joining Morgan, who was encamped at the Cowpens, but we were not permitted to remain long idle, for Tarleton came on like a thunder storm. . . ."[8]

Christopher Brandon had been about six miles away, and "On the 16th, we joined Morgan at the Cowpens—it was dark when we arrived, and they were making up fires to *show large*. It was a still night, and it was all quiet, yet beneath this quiet, deep anxiety."[9]

Morgan's other critical need was to augment his cavalry. Washington's small force of Continental dragoons would be no match for Tarleton's British Legion and 17th Light Dragoons, so Morgan formed an *ad hoc* formation of militia dragoons. Thomas Young: "It was all important to strengthen the cavalry. Gen. Morgan knew well the power of Tarleton legion, and he was too wily an officer not to prepare himself as well as circumstances would admit. Two companies of volunteers were called for. One was raised by Major Jolly of Union District, and the other, I think, by Major McCall. I attached myself to Major Jolly's company. We drew swords that night, and were informed we had authority to press any horse not belonging to a dragoon or an officer, into our service for the day."[10]

Preparations took the better part of the night. "It was upon this occasion I was more perfectly convinced of Gen. Morgan's qualifications to command militia, than I had ever before been. He went among the volunteers, helped them fix their swords, joked with them about their sweethearts, told them to keep in good spirits, and the day would be ours. And long after I laid down, he was going about among the soldiers encouraging them, and telling them that the old wagoner would crack his whip over Ben. [Tarlton] in the morning, as sure as they lived.

"'Just hold up your heads, boys, three fires' he would say, 'and you are free, and then when you return to your homes, how the old folks will bless you, and the girls kiss you, for your gallant conduct!' I don't believe he slept a wink that night!"[11]

Christopher Brandon: "About daylight, I recollect Morgan's coming up to our fire, where Col. Brandon lay stretched on the ground (for we had no tents) and I well remember his morning salutation 'Get up, my fellows,—why here asleep, and the British almost in sight.' We were up in quick time and formed in order, and I'm sure there never was a set of men more anxious for battle. I was in Col. Brandon's Regiment, and marched into the line in quick time."[12]

As usual Tarleton had roused his men well before dawn. Morgan had placed outposts along all the approach roads, and the first clash took place in the pre-dawn darkness. Thomas Young: "Our pickets were stationed three miles in advance. Samuel Clowney was one of the picket guard, and I often heard him afterwards laugh at his narrow escape. Three of Washington's dragoons were out on a scout, when they came almost in contact with the advanced guard of the British army; they wheeled, and were pursued almost into camp. Two got in safely; one poor fellow, whose horse fell down, was taken prisoner. It was about day that the pickets were driven in."[13]

Knowing Tarleton's penchant for early rising, Morgan had also roused his men, and by dawn the Patriot forces were standing in their revised positions. Thomas Young: "The morning of the 17th of January, 1781, was bitterly cold. We were formed in order of battle, and the men were slapping their hands together to keep warm—an exertion not long necessary."[14]

Private James Collins was standing in the main militia line. "About sunrise on the 17th January, 1781, the enemy came in full view. The sight, to me at least, seemed somewhat imposing; they halted for a short time, and then advanced rapidly, as if certain of victory."[15]

Modern analysts consider Morgan's battle plan brilliant, but it was not always so. Fifty years later Morgan was "severely censured for his choice of ground and for risking a battle under what appeared to be the most adverse of circumstances," confronting a numerically superior enemy on flat, open ground with the Broad River behind "to cut off all retreat in the case of misfortune. . . ."[16]

But Morgan knew militia all too well, and had other factors to consider. "I would not have had a swamp in view of my militia for any consideration. They would have made for it, and nothing could have detained them from it. As to covering my wings, I knew my adversary and was perfectly sure I should have nothing but downright fighting. As to retreat, it was the very thing I wished to cut off all hope of. I would have thanked Tarleton had he surrounded me with his cavalry. It would have been better than placing my own men in the rear to shoot down all those who broke from the ranks. When men are forced to fight, they will sell their lives dearly, and I knew that the dread of Tarleton's cavalry would give due weight to the protection of my bayonets and keep my troops from breaking as Buford's regiment did. Had I crossed the river, one-half of my militia would immediately have abandoned me."[17]

The battle at the Cowpens has often been depicted as maneuver on a flat tableland, with orthodox and simplistic maneuvers. Private Thomas Young described the Cowpens as ". . . almost a plain with a ravine on both hands, and very little under growth in front or near us." Colonel Samuel Hammond's description was more elaborate. "The ground on which the troops were placed, was a small ridge, crossing the road nearly at right angles. A similar ridge, nearly parallel with this, lay between three hundred and five hundred yards in his rear." This very low ridge is not clearly expressed on a topographic map, but crosses the Green River Road near the junction with the old Coulter's Ford Road. "The valley between this was made by a gentle slope; it was, of course, brought within range of the eye; passing from one to the other ridge, the land was thickly covered with red oak and hickory, with little if any underbrush."[18]

Although the terrain appears flat to the untrained eye, Morgan masterfully deployed his militia on the small ridge at left of the Green River Road, with his main force of Continentals concealed behind the ridge. When the militia withdrew as Tarleton expected, they lured him into a deadly trap.—AUTHORS

Period accounts of the topography must be viewed critically. Several accounts refer to "ravines" bounding the battle site, but examination of the ground reveals that these are actually gentle slopes down to adjacent creek bottoms. The ground was apparently much wetter (springs mentioned in contemporary accounts have since disappeared) but even in 1781 these boundaries were marked more by changes in vegetation—the transition from open ground to adjacent canebrakes—than by topography. Today the transition from the edges of the old battlefield to the "ravines" formed by the head of Island Creek and the Long Branch of Island Creek on the southwest and a headwater of Suck Creek on the northeast (the names are those used on the US Geological Survey topographic maps) is imperceptible, and defined only by the change from the mown park area to adjacent fields and forest. Still, the combination of the very slight changes in elevation, dense canebrakes, and heavy rains that immediately preceded the battle would have rendered the adjacent terrain effectively impassable to Tarleton's dragoons.*

The Cowpens battlefield proper as it is preserved today is also deceptive. It is important to remember that in 1781 the open area as described by Hammond was an unimproved pastureland, and not the manicured, closely-mown park with widely-spaced mature trees of today. Today a man

Today the Cowpens battlefield is a closely-mown park, but in 1781 it was unimproved pastureland like this undeveloped part of the park, overgrown with waist-high native grasses and dotted with trees and shrubs that further concealed Morgan's troop dispositions.—AUTHORS

---

*The proximity of these canebrakes is interesting in light of Morgan's statement that he would not want to position militia where they could flee into a swamp. His comment is probably more indicative of his pessimistic view of the militia's reliability.

on horseback can, from the position of the old forest margin where Tarleton debouched into the pastureland, see most of the Patriot militia positions. The terrain is gently rolling, but in 1781 it was covered with native grasses that grew almost waist high, interspersed with trees that limited sight range. Removal of vegetation and constant grazing by cattle may have resulted in erosion and compaction that have actually slightly subdued the topography, but that of course is impossible to evaluate. The primary point is that Tarleton did not have the clear view of Morgan's entire layered defense that the modern visitor sees.

A clue to the question of sight range was provided by Landrum, who saw the battle site from horseback in a more pristine state and ". . . has taken some pains to inspect it." Historian Landrum noted that "The only rising ground of any note on the whole field is a little eminence a short distance in the rear of the ridge, where the main line formed. *This is of sufficient height to cover a man on horseback placed in the rear of it.*" [italics added][19]

In contrast to Thomas Young's description of only limited underbrush in the area of the militia line, the Continentals recalled being positioned among pines, whose evergreen foliage blocked out the sun—and limited sight range.[20]

Much has been made of the fact that the relatively open Cowpens battle site was narrow and bounded on both sides by the "ravines," swamps, and canebrakes. The fact was that even given the limited size of the battlespace, Morgan did not have sufficient numbers to form an orthodox linear defense, one formation deep, with the flanks anchored on the swamps. His flanks would of necessity be left hanging, and in fact Tarleton would flank both sides of Morgan's defense.

Morgan's genius was to (1) use the subtleties of the topography and the fighting styles of his troops to organize what would today be called a collapsing defense in depth, and (2) to use a rear-slope defense for his main line of Continentals that maximized surprise and shock potential when Tarleton's troops stumbled into it. He also played upon Tarleton's penchant to go head-on at the enemy, relying upon the discipline and bayonets of his redcoats.

The details of Morgan's deployments, and the course of the battle, have been the subject of considerable speculation. As a framework we use the description presented by Lawrence Babits, except where our interpretation of the Second Spartans' role differs in detail.* Christopher Brandon provided the general description of the deployment. "The Continentals under Howard, were formed across the road, and Brandon's regiment on the left of the Continentals, and Col. McCall on the [extreme] left flank. Col. Roebuck was on the right wing, while McDowall with a party of Mountaineers, amounting to some 60 or 70 in number, were stationed sixty or eighty yards in advance of the line as "Sharp Shooters," to begin the fire. The cavalry formed in the rear of the left wing of the Regulars. The Pickets were three miles in front of the main line, and were run in, very closely pressed."[21]

Morgan's first line was actually rifle-armed skirmishers, a relatively orthodox tactical arrangement. Their position on a gentle forward slope ahead of the militia line took advantage of the longer effective range of the rifle to inflict a few casualties, try to disrupt the British command structure by targeting officers and NCOs, and thereby disrupt the enemy's unit cohesion. Given the militia's usual practices, this was probably not the neat open-order spacing of trained light infantry, but loose gaggles of men.

Young: "The regulars, under the command of Col. Howard, a very brave man, were formed in two ranks, their right flank resting upon the head of the ravine on the right. The militia was formed on the left of the regulars, under the command of Col. Pickens, their left flank resting near the head of the ravine on the left. The cavalry formed in rear of the centre, or rather in rear of the left wing of the regulars."[22]

The first ridge is actually a low rise to the Patriot right, or west side of the Green River Road. It was occupied by the standing ranks of Pickens' militia, armed with rifles and muskets, arrayed along the rise and extending onto the lower ground to the east side of the road. As previously noted the Second Spartan Regiment was on the left of the militia line, but the command arrangement has caused some historical confusion. Thomas Brandon himself—with a strong horse and better-equipped to serve as a dragoon—was detailed out to augment Washington's small force of dragoons. This

---

*As with a number of more recent historians, Babits consistently refers to Brandon's command as the Fair Forest Regiment, perhaps in reference to Brandon's early 1781 relocation and construction of the Fair Forest Creek blockhouse. Members of the command consistently referred to it as the Second Spartans or Lower Spartans, spun off from the First Spartans and recruited from the "Brown's Creek Irish" settlements. This also avoided confusion with Daniel Plummer's Tory Fair Forest Regiment.

left Lieutenant Colonel William Farr in direct command of the men on foot in the militia line, though Brandon seems to have been incapable of resisting the urge to move back and forth between the two contingents. To Brandon's right was Hayes's Little River Regiment, with their right flank on or near the road.

Babits attributes the internal arrangement of the Second Spartans' six companies to a perceived right-to-left order according to the traditional "standing to right of line" precedence where the more "senior" formation deploys on the right, with seniority descending to the left. Babits' deployment diagram places Benjamin Jolly's company, under temporary command of the highly regarded nineteen year-old Lieutenant Joseph Hughes, on the extreme right. This was in fact Brandon's old company from the First Spartans, and chock full of his relatives. However Brandon's most experienced company commander (Robert Faris) was on the extreme left, the third most senior captain (William Grant) second from right. In all probability Brandon paid little attention to military etiquette, but may have placed his most reliable companies to anchor the ends of his line. This would have serious consequences for Hughes.[23]

All this would have effectively screened Howard's third, and main, line from direct British observation. This third line positioned on the rear slope of the small rise included Morgan's best troops—veteran Continentals, disciplined Virginia militia (many of whom had earlier served as Continentals), along with a few Georgia refugee militia.

Christopher Brandon's account is of interest in that he addressed the sight range that day. "The battle field was almost a plain, with little or no undergrowth. On our left flank was a miry branch, in front of which the 'Long cane' men under McCall were stationed. A slight rise on the ground prevented our seeing the enemy, until they came within eighty yards of us."[24]

Scots historian David Stewart, writing in 1825, may have drawn in part from American sources, but still provides an interesting insight into the British perception of the battlefield: "On the morning of the 17th January 1781, intelligence was received that General Morgan was in front, with his force drawn up on a rising ground, thinly covered with pine trees; the front line being on the crown of the rising ground, and the second 400 paces in rear of the first line."[25]

When Tarleton emerged from the forest into the more open pastureland, even from horseback he would have seen only the Patriot skirmishers and Pickens' single line of militia, generally easy meat for his resolute redcoat infantry and dragoons. The Patriot main line of resistance, and certainly Washington's cavalry reserve, would have been invisible. All Tarleton's experience dictated that a couple of musket volleys followed by a bayonet charge would cause the militia to flee in disorder, to be ridden down and butchered by his dragoons.

Morgan's plan in fact depended heavily upon allowing the militia to be driven back by Tarleton's attack, but to withdraw in an orderly fashion. Their specific orders were to fire only two volleys at the oncoming British, and then withdraw around the flanks and through deliberate gaps in the line of Continentals. The militia had a designated rally point in a low swale behind the left flank of the Continentals, and their horses were tied nearby.

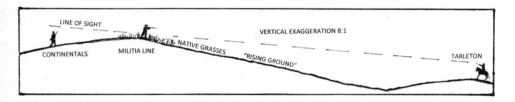

The most exposed Patriot militia position was the open eastern flank, where Anderson and Brandon's commands would have to withdraw around the left flank of the Continentals. This flatter ground would expose them to easy attack by Tarleton's dragoons if their retreat was not orderly, and it was one of the riskier parts of Morgan's plan. If the militia panicked and kept going toward the river several miles away it would leave the Continentals isolated, as at Camden.

True to expectation, Tarleton decided to go head-on at the Patriot position before one of his best units, McArthur's 1st Battalion, 71st Regiment of Foot (Fraser's Highlanders), was deployed. Positioning his two grasshopper guns to guide on the road, he formed a single line of infantry extending from side to side of the field. Tarleton seems to have recognized the vulnerability of the Patriot left, and positioned his 17th Light Dragoons on both flanks to take advantage of this slightly more open ground and exposed flank. His favored British Legion dragoons would be held in reserve to exploit the expected victory.

Inexplicably, Colonel Joseph Hayes' Little River Regiment advanced toward the British, opening a gap in the militia line, then moved backward to close the gap. As ordered, the skirmishers—militiamen from North Carolina and Georgia—opened a desultory fire on the advancing British, and then retreated toward the militia line firing as they fell back. Hammond's Georgians withdrew to the Patriot left, filling in the gap to the left of Brandon's regiment. So far it was developing as the fairly orthodox battle that Tarleton expected.*

Joseph McJunkin recalled Morgan continuing his efforts to steady the militia line, walking behind and advising them, "Boys, squinney [squint] well and don't fire until you see the whites of their eyes."[26]

From his position Private Thomas Young could hear Morgan's booming voice. "About sun-rise, the British line advanced at a sort of trot, with a loud halloo. It was the most beautiful line I ever saw. When they shouted, I heard Morgan say, 'They give us the British halloo, boys, give *them* the Indian halloo, by G—'; and he galloped along the lines, cheering the men, and telling them not to fire until we could see the whites of their eyes. Every officer was crying don't fire! for it was a hard matter for us to keep from it.

"I should have said the British line advanced under cover of their artillery; for it opened so fiercely upon the center, that Col. Washington moved his cavalry from the center towards the right wing." Musket balls and shot from Tarleton's grasshopper guns were apparently overshooting the Patriot infantry and falling among the dragoons.

Despite Morgan's admonitions, some of the nervous militiamen opened fire. Young: "The militia fired first. It was for a time, pop—pop—pop— and then a whole volley. . . . I have heard old Col. Fair [Farr] say often, that he believed John Savage fired the first gun in this battle. He was riding to and fro, along the lines, when he saw Savage fix his eye upon a British officer; he stepped out of the ranks, raised his gun—fired, and he saw the officer fall."[27]

---

*Major Samuel Hammond made it quite clear in his pension application that this regiment was being reorganized as cavalry under newly-commissioned Colonel James McCall. McCall and 25 to 30 men already equipped as cavalry were detached to augment Washington's dragoons, and Hammond commanded the remaining men on foot. Samuel Hammond FPA S21807.

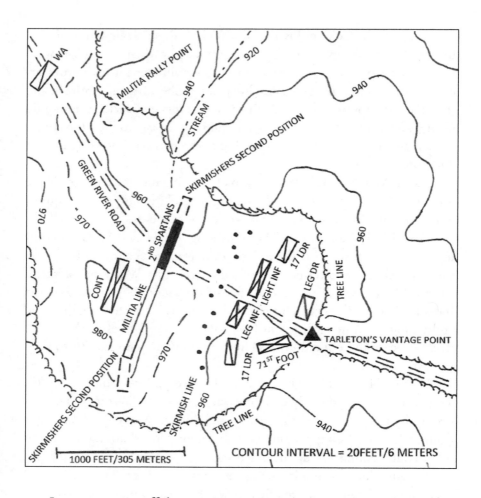

In a supporting affidavit to a pension application, Thomas Young was more precise. "A British officer rode up toward the advance guard of Morgan's Army, & calling them in a loud voice 'Dam'd Rebels' and ordered them to disperse—John Savage instantly raised his rifle and the British officer fell [from] his horse mortally wounded. This fact has fixed the services of John Savage indelibly upon my memory."[28]

The British Light Infantry assailed Brandon's regiment on the Patriot left, and the two sides exchanged fire at close range—normally a severe disadvantage for the Patriots. Standard British tactical doctrine was to "charge the fire"—fire one or two volleys and then charge with the bayonet when confronted by riflemen with their slow to reload weapons or by Patriot militia untrained with the bayonet. Somehow the Second Spartans got off a second ragged volley, stopping the Light Infantry in their tracks.

From there the action became a general engagement all along the line. In historian David Stewart's account from the British side, the Patriot militia acquitted themselves well. "The British were hastily formed: the Fusiliers, the infantry of the Legion, and the Light infantry, were in front; the Highlanders and Cavalry formed the Reserve. The line was ordered to advance rapidly, as soon as it was formed. Exhausted by running, it received the fire of the enemy at the distance of thirty or forty paces. The effect of the fire was considerable: it produced something like a recoil, but not to any extent. The fire was returned, but not with vivacity or impression; and it continued ten or twelve minutes in a state of balance, both parties keeping their ground. The Light infantry made two attempts to charge, but were repulsed with loss. The action making no progress, the Highlanders were ordered up. . . ."[29]

The din of the growing battle could be heard for miles. Angelica Mitchell Nott: "I heard the noise of the battle at the Cowpens. My aunt & I had gone to milk—a noise like the burning of a cane brake commenced. My aunt says, 'There, the action has commenced.' We got on the fence and remained until 12 o'clock without milking or breakfast, or thinking of it once."[30]

On the American side, James Collins observed that "We gave the enemy one fire, when they charged us with their bayonets; we gave way and retreated for our horses. . . ." Morgan was taking a great many risks. At Camden the panicked militia had stampeded through the Continentals, causing that disaster. Babits states that the main line of Continentals and Virginia militia and the two flanking battalions were stepped back, leaving gaps for most of the retreating militia to pass; after the militia had rushed through, the center battalion would move back to close the gaps and present a continuous line.

This was apparently such an unexpected and skilled maneuver that Stewart remarked upon it, although the execution was described differently: ". . . the Highlanders were ordered up; and, rapidly advancing in charge, the enemy's front line moved off precipitately; and the second, which had as yet taken no share in the action, observing confusion and retrograding in their front, suddenly faced to the right, and inclined backwards; a manoeuvre by which a space was left for the front line to retreat, without interfering with the ranks of those who were now to oppose the advance of the Highlanders. . . ."[31]

The British 7th Regiment and Legion Infantry in the center were less battered than the Light Infantry, but the militiamen of Roebuck, Hayes, and Thomas's commands were still able to execute a fairly orderly withdrawal. Stewart's sources clearly misinterpreted the planned withdrawal as "confusion." However the maneuver was accomplished, it allowed the militia to fall back without disrupting the Continentals.

Hammond's and Brandon's commands on the far left had staggered the Light Infantry but were still in a far more perilous position. They were to withdraw across the open ground to their rear, around the open flank of the Continentals. In his book "Strictures on Lt. Col. Tarleton's History," Roderick MacKenzie quoted the British Annual Register of 1781: "their second line having opened on the right and left, as well to lead the victors [i.e., advancing British] on, as to afford a clear passage to the fugitives," indicating withdrawal around the open flanks of the Continentals.[32]

Perceptions of the militia withdrawal varied. Christopher Brandon was one of those who recalled an initial, fairly orderly withdrawal to a position on the left flank of the Continentals. "With a shout they came on in a beautiful line, and a solid flame of fire burst from one end to the other. Our orders were for only one third to fire at a time, but the anxiety of the men was so great, that many of them broke ranks, and rushing forward, jumped behind trees, and commenced the fight on their own responsibility. The violent shock from the British, drove us back a hundred yards, but, loading as we went, we wheeled, and opened up a fire so destructive, that the British recoiled, and we pressed forward until we were on the high ground with the Regulars again—who, brave fellows, had maintained their position."[33]

The bloodied British Light Infantry was slow to react. British captain MacKenzie, while acknowledging the horrific casualties inflicted by the Patriot militia, laid the blame squarely on Tarleton. "The infantry were not in condition to undertake the fugitives; the latter had not marched thirty miles in the course of the last fortnight; the former, during that time, had been in motion day and night. A number, not less than two-thirds of

the British infantry officers, had already fallen, and nearly the same pro-
portion of privates; fatigue, however, enfeebled the pursuit, much more
than loss of blood." MacKenzie believed this afforded Morgan the opportunity to reorganize his militia.[34]

The British dragoons were not so slow. Despite MacKenzie's misplaced
criticism, fifty horsemen of the 17th Light Dragoons that Tarleton had stationed to exploit just such an opportunity thundered down upon the militiamen. An orderly withdrawal in the face of cavalry pursuit would have
taxed the capabilities of far more disciplined troops. The Light Infantry
rallied and some joined the chase.

Most were like James Collins: ". . . Tarleton's cavalry pursued us; ('now,'

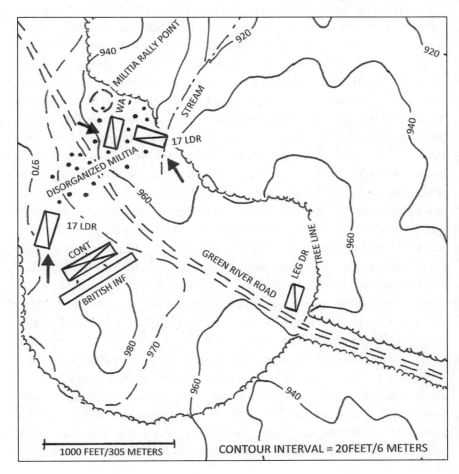

thought I, 'my hide is in the loft;') just as we got to our horses, they over-took us and began to make a few hacks at some, however, without doing much injury."[35]

With the greatest distance to cover, Joseph Hughes' company did not escape so easily. As the British 17th Dragoons got in among the fleeing militiamen, the flint fell out of Hughes' weapon. ". . . he was attacked by a couple of British dragoons; he seized a small sapling, and with this de-fended his head from the strokes of one, and with his rifle warded off the blows of the other. One of the Savages, a comrade from his neighborhood, ran to his assistance, and having shot one of the Dragoons, Hughes clubbed his rifle and soon dispatched the other."[36]

Somewhere in the melee Hughes' hand was slashed by a dragoon's sword. Christopher Brandon: "When the militia fled, and Tarleton pursued them with his cavalry, Brandon, who had been separated from their respec-tive corps in a furious charge around Morgan's left flank, was near Hughes while the militia were retreating in confusion. 'Hughes,' said [Thomas] Brandon, 'saved the battle of the Cowpens.' I saw how it occurred. Hughes could run faster than any man I ever knew. He was also a man of great per-sonal strength. As the company to which Hughes belonged fled, pursued by Tarleton's cavalry, Hughes with drawn sword would pass them, face about and order them to stand and often struck at them with is sword to make them halt. He called to them in a loud voice, and said: 'You damned cowards, stand and fight; there is more danger in running than fighting, and if you don't stop and fight we will all be killed.' But they continued to run by him in the utmost confusion. He would again pursue them, pass them, his speed of foot being so much greater than theirs—face about—meet them and again order them to halt. He at last succeeded. The com-pany halted on the brow of the slope, some distance from the battle line, behind a clump of young pines that partially hid them from the cavalry of Tarleton. Others joined them instantly for self protection against the charge of the cavalry. Their guns were instantly loaded. Morgan galloped up and spoke words of encouragement—in a moment the British cavalry were at them—they delivered a deadly fire at only ten paces distance; many saddles were emptied, and the cavalry recoiled at the unexpected assault. At this moment Col. Washington charged—the battle was restored, and the charge of Col. Howard of the Maryland Line completed the victory."[37]

Another account stated that Hughes was a man demented. "I have heard John Savage say that Hughes looked like a mad bull in the time of the battle of Cowpens. He was large, strong and active, and would be ahead; he sweated and foamed at the mouth."

The charge into Hammond's command and the Second Spartans had thrown the British dragoons into disarray, and James Collins wrote that, "They, in their haste, had pretty much scattered, perhaps thinking they would have another Fishing creek frolic, but in a few moments Col. Washington's cavalry was amongst them, like a whirlwind, and the poor fellows began to keel from their horses, without being able to remount. The shock was so sudden and violent, they could not stand it, and immediately betook themselves to flight; there was no time to rally, and they appeared to be as hard to stop as a drove of wild Choctaw steers, going to a Pennsylvania market. In a few moments the clashing of swords was out of hearing and quickly out of sight. . . ."[38]

Christopher Brandon recounted a generally similar tale. "At that moment, a charge was made by the British cavalry, and we were forced to retreat. We retreated almost three hundred yards, I know I was very tired, when Col. Brandon pushed toward Col. Washington, to inform him of our condition, and immediately Washington charged the British Cavalry, which being in disorder, was unable to withstand the shock, and was soon thrown into wild confusion."[39]

Thomas Young: "Just as the charge was made upon Tarleton's cavalry, I fell in with Col. Brandon who accompanied Washington in the charge. I was just about engaging a British dragoon, when Col. Brandon darted between us & killed him, & told me to follow him. We charged through the British cavalry till they left the ground. The bugle then sounded, & we partly formed. . . ."[40]

The apparent confusion and withdrawal of the Patriot militia had as usual also precipitated a pursuit by the British infantry. Morgan was everywhere, steadying the Continentals who were taking casualties from stray rounds that overshot the militia line and trying to control the militia withdrawal. The formation of the 71st Foot broke up as they charged headlong after the swiftly retiring Patriot militia. The Highlanders crested the small rise only to unexpectedly confront the closed ranks of Howard's Continentals, ready and waiting among the scattered pine trees. The Continentals

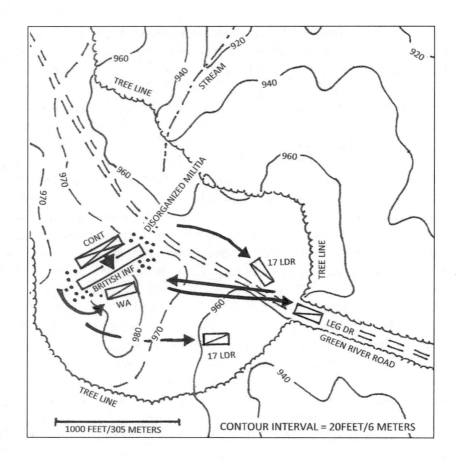

and Virginia militia blasted the gaggle of Highlanders at point blank range.

David Stewart: "But the confusion was only in the front line; for Colonel Howard, commanding the enemy's Reserve, threw in a fire upon the 71st when within forty yards of the hostile force. The fire was destructive; nearly one-half of their number fell; and those who remained were so scattered, having run over a space of five hundred yards at full speed, that they could not be united to form a charge with the bayonet, "the mode of attack in which their superiority lay."[41]

The 71st was not as disorganized as Stewart recorded. They quickly reformed as best they could, and the disciplined Highlanders and Continentals flailed away at each other with volleys of musket fire at close range. Stewart: "They were checked; but they did not fall back immediately, probably expecting that the first line and [Legion] cavalry would push forward to their support. This did not happen; and, after some irregular firing between them and Colonel Howard's Reserve, the front line [i.e., the militia] of the latter rallied, returned to the field, and pushed forward to the right flank of the Highlanders, who now saw no prospect of support, while their own numbers were diminishing, and the enemy increasing."

The Patriot numbers engaged along the main line were increasing because Washington's charge had provided a respite for the militia foot soldiers to rally.

In this swirling dogfight events were unfolding at a pace that no commander could completely control. The Highlanders were at least holding their own. Their extended left flank overlapped Howard's right, posing the danger of envelopment and attack from the flank and rear. The standard procedure in such an event was for the defenders to refuse the flank, i.e. have the rightmost unit wheel back about a pivot point on its own left, thus bending the defensive line back at a right angle to present the unit's front to the enveloping enemy.

Howard ordered it done, but it was a difficult maneuver, and in the confusion it very nearly fell apart. Captain Andrew Wallace ordered his Virginia Light Infantry Company to wheel and turn to refuse the flank, but somehow the order was misunderstood and the Virginians commenced an orderly withdrawal across the rear of the main line.* Seeing that company retiring, the rest of the Patriot troops on the right began to about face and retreat.

Several accounts disagree in the details of what transpired next, but the fact is that Colonel Washington, in his rides to the Patriot front, had observed the British disarray and exposure. "They are coming on like a mob, give them a fire and I will charge them," was his advice to Morgan.

The Patriot main line had been falling back in good order, probably in the belief that the movement was a shift to a new position on the next low rise to the rear rather than a general retreat. At that moment the reformed militia appeared above the rise, coming to the aid of the Continentals. "Face about, give them one fire and the victory is ours," shouted Morgan as he rode along the retreating line.[42]

---

*Wallace was later killed in the battle, and the reason for the confusion remains a mystery.

The 71st—indeed all the British infantry line—was indeed "coming on like a mob," disorganized and running in pursuit when the Patriot line suddenly faced about and delivered a withering point-blank volley. The shock to the oncoming British was devastating, and to take advantage Howard ordered the Continentals and Virginians to fix bayonets and charge.

The oncoming militia infantry joined in the attack. James Collins: ". . . by this time both lines of the infantry were warmly engaged and we being relieved from the pursuit of the enemy began to rally and prepare to redeem our credit, when Morgan rode up in front, and waving his sword, cried out "Form, form, my brave fellows! Give them one more fire and the day is ours. Old Morgan was never beaten." We then advanced briskly, and gained the right flank of the enemy, and they being hard-pressed in front, by Howard, and falling fast, could not stand it long. They began to throw down their arms, and surrender themselves as prisoners of war."[43]

Christopher Brandon claimed little credit for the militia in the final spasm. "By this time, the militia had rallied and returned to the fight—but very little had we to do with the fighting after that—the charge of the Continentals and the Cavalry being made, the day was won."[44]

Most accounts credit the re-formed militia, and particularly the mounted militia, with a greater role. Thomas Young was now with Washington's dragoons: "After the second forming, the fight became general and unintermitting. In the hottest of it, I saw Col. Brandon coming at full speed to the rear, and waving his sword to Col. Washington. In a moment the command to charge was given, and I soon found that the British cavalry had charged the American right. We made a most furious charge, and cutting through the British cavalry, wheeled and charged them in the rear. In this charge, I exchanged my tackey for the finest horse I ever rode; it was the quickest swap I ever made in my life!"[45]

Young, in another recounting: "At this moment the bugle sounded. We, about half formed and making a sort of circuit at full speed, came up in rear of the British line, shouting and charging like madmen. At this moment Col. Howard gave the word 'charge bayonets!' and the day was ours. The British broke, and throwing down their guns and cartouch boxes, made for the wagon road, and did the prettiest sort of running!"[46]

The tactical situation had been suddenly reversed. Now Morgan's line had overlapped the British flanks, and like the Romans at Cannae they stood in danger of encirclement and utter destruction by a *smaller* force.

Only MacArthur's hard-pressed Highlanders and the handful of artillerymen maintained at least some semblance of discipline, but they were abandoned by the rest of Tarleton's force. David Stewart's account included the interesting observation that, "They [the Highlanders} began to retire, and at length to run, the first instance of a Highland regiment running *from* an enemy!!! This retreat struck a panic into those whom they left in the rear, who fled in the greatest confusion: order and command were lost; the rout became general; few of the infantry escaped; and of the cavalry, who put their horses to full speed, not a man was taken. . . . The fate of the action was decided by the destructive fire of the Americans' second line. The Highlanders, when they were checked and repulsed, being five hundred paces in advance of the others, stood at some distance in the rear, after they retreated, and had formed into some compact order. If they had been supported, they might have made a soldier-like retreat, or taken a position till relieved by Lord Cornwallis's army."[47]

Most accounts agree that the gunners ". . . abandoned by the cavalry, supported only by a few fugitives of the infantry, seemed resolved to surrender their guns only with their lives." But "There was no time to parley. . . . ," and most accounts indicate the gunners died to a man.

The most scathing criticism was leveled at Tarleton's favored Green Dragoons of the British Legion. "These dragoons never fought well; they had repeatedly hacked to pieces a flying, unarmed, or supplicating enemy, but neither at Blackstock's, in this affair, or any other did they ever do any thing to distinguish themselves in fair conflict."[48]

Tarleton's personal bravery could not be faulted; he did rally about fifty straggling dragoons and tried to help the gunners, only to clash with Washington's dragoons. Although beloved of artists and highly romanticized, this was a minor action that occurred after the battle was decided. After the brief fight with Washington's dragoons, Tarleton and his followers fled and could not be overtaken.

Tarleton's rashness had resulted in another stunningly lopsided defeat. As usual casualties are difficult to accurately determine. Tarleton grossly exaggerated Patriot losses. Tarleton's retreating party came upon Loyalist militiamen plundering baggage wagons and ". . . the wrath of the mortified dragoons was let loose upon all those who were not fortunate enough to make good their retreat." These unfortunates were included as casualties inflicted on the Patriots.

Patriot estimates are undoubtedly more accurate. One period account listed Patriot losses as 11 killed, and 61 wounded. British losses were counted as 150 dead, 200 wounded prisoners, and 500 other prisoners, and more accurate British records ultimately compiled indicated a total loss of 784.[49]

Christopher Brandon, like many, observed that the Patriot fire had been unusually effective, and remarked: "A braver set of fellows never lived than the Long Cane men. After the battle I saw and counted eighteen Britons lying side by side, not a length apart, who fell under their destructive fire."[50]

James Collins' observations were more personal. "After the fight was over, the sight was truly melancholy. The dead on the side of the British, exceeded the number killed at King's Mountain, being if I recollect, three hundred, or upwards. . . . This day, I fired my little rifle five times, whether with any effect or not I do not know. Next day after receiving some small share of the plunder, and taking care to get as much powder as we could, we (the militia) were disbanded and retreated to our old haunts, where we obtained a few days rest.[51]

CHAPTER **15**

COWPENS AFTERMATH

*I run as fast backwards as forwards to convince
our enemy that we are like a crab. We can run
in any direction, as long as it is away.*
—NATHANAEL GREENE

THE ACCIDENTAL RETROGRADE MANEUVER HAD SAVED
the day at Cowpens, and created consternation among contemporary military experts. Much later in his "Strictures," Roderick MacKenzie quoted the Marquis de Chastellux, who praised Morgan's "modesty and simplicity" and expressed "astonishment" at the tactic. "But after the first discharge he made so dangerous a movement, that had he commanded the best disciplined troops in the world, I should be at a loss to account for it. . . . It depended on General Morgan alone to have claimed the merit, and to have boasted of one of the boldest stratagems ever employed in the art of war. This is a merit however he never claimed. . . . Whatever was the motive of this singular manoeuvre, the result of it was the defeat of Tarleton, whose troops gave way without a possibility of rallying."[1]

Morgan was rightly praised for this victory by Governor Rutledge (who took the opportunity to implore Morgan to recover his seized slaves from Ninety Six). Even Sumter appended a terse note to a communiqué: ". . . could ascertain their number to a man if I knowed what had escaped the defeat of Col. Tarleton. Upon which happy event I most heartily congratulate you." (28 January)[2]

More significant were the accolades from the Virginia House of Delegates, and the Continental Congress. But Morgan was suffering from sciatica that made riding agony. From the camp near Guilford Courthouse, Nathanael Greene wrote a brief note: "General Morgan, of the Virginia line, has leave of absence until he recovers his health so as to take the field again." (10 February)[3]

As usual, in the immediate aftermath of the battle the militia scoured the countryside for the lucrative British baggage trains. Private Thomas Young: "After this Major Jolly and seven or eight of us, resolved upon an excursion to capture some of the baggage. We went about twelve miles, and captured two British soldiers, two Negroes, and two horses laden with portmanteaus. One of the portmanteaus belonged to a paymaster in the British service, and contained gold. Jolly insisted upon my returning with the prize to camp, while he pursued a little farther. I did so. Jolly's party dashed onward, and soon captured an armorer's wagon, with which they became so much engaged that they forgot all about me. I rode along for some miles at my leisure, on my fine gray charger, talking to my prisoners, when all at once I saw, coming in advance, a party, which I soon discovered to be British. I knew it was no time to consider now; so I wheeled, put spurs to my horse, and made down the road in hopes of meeting Jolly and his party. My horse was stiff, however, from the severe exercise I had given him that morning, and I soon found that they were gaining upon me. I wheeled abruptly to the right into a cross road, but a party of three or four dashed through the woods and intercepted me. It was now a plain case, and I could no longer hope to engage one at a time. My pistol was empty, so I drew my sword and made battle. I never fought so hard in my life. I knew it was death any how, and I resolved to sell my life as dearly as possible.

"In a few minutes one finger on my left hand was split open; then I received a cut on my sword arm by a parry which disabled it. In the next instant a cut from a sabre across my forehead (the scar of which I shall carry to my grave), the skin slipped down over my eyes, and the blood blinded me so that I could see nothing. Then came a thrust in the right shoulder blade, then a cut upon the left shoulder, and a last cut (which you can feel for yourself) on the back of my head—and I fell upon my horse's neck. They took me down, bound up my wounds, and placed me again on my horse a prisoner of war.

"When they joined the party in the main road, there were two tories who knew me very well—Littlefield and Kelly. Littlefield cocked his gun, and swore he would kill me. In a moment nearly twenty British soldiers drew their swords, and cursing him for a d——d coward, for wanting to kill a boy without arms and a prisoner — ran him off. Littlefield did not like me, and for a very good reason. While we were at Grindall Shoals with Morgan, he once caught me out, and tried to take my gun away from me. I knocked him down with it, and as he rose I clicked it, and told him if he didn't run I'd blow him through. He did not long hesitate which of the two to choose.

"I asked Kelly not to tell the British who I was, and I do not think the fellow did. Col. Tarlton sent for me, and I rode by his side for several miles. He was a very fine looking man, with rather a proud bearing, but very gentlemanly in his manners. He asked me a great many questions, and I told him one lie, which I have often thought of since. In reply to his query whether Morgan was reinforced before the battle? I told him 'he was not, but that he expected a reinforcement every minute.' 'He asked me how many dragoons Washington had.' I replied that 'he had seventy, and two volunteer companies of mounted militia—but you know they won't fight.' 'By G-d!' he quickly replied, 'they did to-day, though!' I begged him to parole me, but he said, 'if he did, I should go right off and turn to fighting again.' I then told him he could get three men in exchange for me, and he replied 'Very well, when we get to Cornwallis's army, you shall be paroled or exchanged; and mean while, I'll see that your wounds are taken care of.'"[4]

In another narrative, "Tarleton's party went on & overtook Jolly & his party; they made their escape, but Deshaser & McIlton* had been taken by Tarleton before I was. McIlton was slightly wounded in the head, fainted & was left near a house, taken care of by a woman. This lady gave Washington information of McI's being there, & McI. told them that I was a prisoner with Col. Tarleton & cut all to pieces."[5]

Riding with Tarleton, Young recalled that, "Tarleton turned towards Hamilton's Ford, on the Broad river. Just before night a man rode up very

---

*Draper's handwritten notes are exceptionally illegible on this name, but it was likely Sgt. James McIlton, documented by audited files and stub indents as a member of Jolly's company.

fast & hallooed as he past us, 'Washington is coming like hell.' This produced a good deal of consternation."[6]

Young was probably all too familiar with what life in a British military prison was like, and equally wary of the limited possibilities of parole or exchange for a teenaged private. "It was now very dark, and the river was said to be swimming. The British were not willing to take water. Col. Tarlton flew into a terrible passion, and drawing his sword, swore he would cut down the first man who hesitated. They knew him too well to hesitate longer. During the confusion, a young Virginian by the name of Deshaser (also a prisoner) and myself, managed to get into the woods. In truth a British soldier had agreed to let us escape, and to desert if we would assist him in securing the plunder he had taken.

"We slipped away one at a time up the river, Deshaser first, then myself. I waited what *I* thought a very long time for the British soldier, and he came not. At last I began to think the British were across, and I gave a low whistle—Deshaser answered me, and we met."[7]

Young was feeling the effects of his wounds. "I was almost dead with thirst, having drank nothing but some vinegar given me by a British soldier.* Deshaser lifted a little water in his hands & held it to my mouth. We left the river & proceeded toward a ford on Pacolet, with which I was acquainted.[8]

"It was now very dark and raining when we came to the Packolette. I could not find the ford, and it was well, for the river was swimming. We therefore made our way up the river, and had not gone far before we approached a barn. It had a light in it, and I heard a cough. We halted and reconnoitred, and finding it occupied by some British soldiers, we pressed on and soon arrived at old Captain Grant's, where I was glad to stop. The old man and his lovely daughter washed and dressed my wounds, and in looking over the bag of plunder which the soldier had given us, they found a fine ruffled shirt, which I put on and went to bed. I shall never forget that girl or the old man for their kindness!" Young had survived the adventure of a lifetime on the day of battle, his seventeenth birthday.[9]

Young complained that he was ". . . very feeble through fatigue, the loss of blood, and the soreness of my head and arm.[10]

---

*Vinegar has been used to reduce thirst since Biblical times.

"On the next day I left with Deshaser, and arrived at home that evening, where I was confined by a violent fever for eight or ten days; but thanks to the kind nursing and attention of old Mrs. Brandon, I recovered. I now slept in the woods for about three weeks, waiting for some of the whigs to come in and commence operations. I was concerned about a horse. The British soldiers, when they took me, dismounted me from the fine charger I captured at the Cowpens, and put me on a pacing pony.* One day I met old Molly Willard riding a very fine sorrel horse, and told her we must swap. She wouldn't listen to it—but I replied that there was no use in talking, the horse I would have, and the exchange was made not much to the old woman's satisfaction, for she didn't love the whigs; I don't believe the Willards have forgiven me for that horse swap to this day.

"Soon after this I joined a detachment of whigs under Col. Brandon, and scouted through the country till we reached the siege at Fort Motte."[11]

The day after 18 January, Samuel Otterson's company stumbled across a large party of British stragglers at Love's, killing one and capturing twenty-two. Otterson's courier duties had caused him to miss the battle, ". . . but in his attempt with the party under his command to regain Morgan he learned the defeat and retreat of Tarleton and pursued about a hundred of them until night at which [illegible] all of his men had fallen off by their horses giving out except ten men where we overtook the enemy killed one took twenty two white prisoners and twenty seven negroes, sixty head of horses, 14 swords, and 14 braces of pistols." In his 19 January report to Greene, Morgan listed altogether ". . . one travelling forge, thirty-five baggage wagons, seventy negroes, and upwards of 100 dragoon horses, with all their musick. They destroyed most of the baggage which was immense."[12]

Some of Tarleton's behavior in the aftermath of the Cowpens debacle seemed out of character. Although like most British officers he considered common soldiers mere assets to be used and if necessary expended, he wrote to Morgan, "The action of the 17th instant having thrown into your hands a number of British Officers and Soldiers I primarily request of you that Attention and Humanity may be exhibited towards the Wounded

---

*A pacing horse or pony moves both left legs and then both right legs together, in a rocking motion like that of a camel. It is a gentle, soothing ride at a walk, but at any faster pace the rider is thrown violently from side to side.

Officers and Men, for whose assistance I now send a Flag, Doctor , and the Surgeon's Mate of the Seventh Regt. I secondly desire you to inform me of the Number And Inability of the Prisoners . . ." adding "P.S.—I have sent some money for the use of the prisoners." (19 January)

The Highland officers who escaped death or captivity were scathing in their criticism of Tarleton. Scottish historian David Stewart: "The dispositions made by the enemy on this occasion appear to have been judicious; and the conduct of the American Colonels, Howard and Washington, in wheeling and manoeuvring their corps, and in throwing in such destructive volleys on the Highlanders, would have been creditable to the most experienced veterans. The former success, which had uniformly attended the numerous enterprises of the officer who commanded the British on this occasion, had given him a degree of confidence that in a great measure led to the disaster which followed. The troops were hurried into action, without any previous examination of the ground, or of the disposition of the enemy; and so strong was the impression on the minds of the officers of the Highland regiment that the fault did not lie with their men, that they made a representation to Lord Cornwallis, not to be employed again under the same officer. His Lordship complied with their request."[13]

This second and even more severe debacle still did not shake Cornwallis' faith in Tarleton, however. He would remain a prominent figure until the surrender at Yorktown.

Unlike Young and Collins, some militiamen were detailed out to various necessary duties in the aftermath of the battle. Samuel Otterson ". . . then marched to the Island Ford on the Broad River, Lord Corn Waslas pursuing to retake the prisoners. Morgan marched in haste to the Catawba. We then directed our course to the South Yadkin and crossing both Yadkins, Morgan directed the So. Carolina troops to return and defend their own state which we done and formed a camp near Union Court House. At this time Genl Sumpter was making way down in the his country and ordered Col Brandon to meet him on the east side of the Congaree River, which Brandon attempted, I being one of his Majors."

Christopher Brandon ". . . then marched with the prisoners to Rowan County North Carolina. I then returned home again to Union District under Col Brandon and then joined Col Pickens and [from?] that to the [cease?] of the war at different times was under Sumpter, & Colo Lacey, &

Brandon." John Albritton ". . . was sent to guard prisoners after the battle to a place called Gilbert or Guilford in NC, & after delivering the prisoners, he was taken a prisoner by the Tories under Captain Lee, and was detained until August 1781, and made his escape from them at Dorchester South Carolina & returned home after being out eight months."[14]

William Kenedy: "After the battle of Cowpens a detachment of forty men were ordered out by General Morgan to view the British lines among whom was this petitioner as one of said party, and in that expedition the party were attacked and this petitioner was wounded in the arm and under the left nipple, the bullet ranging out through the back, that he was unable for Service for some time and the Tories Being So Troublesome he was compelled in this Situation a great part of his Time To Lay out in woods concealed that so soon as he was able he joined the army again . . ."[15]

Richard Addis ". . . continued in an irregular scouting service until the entire cessation of the Hostilities" and John Biddie ". . . was employed afterwards in various services and scouting tours until a very short time before the end of the war." Abraham Bolt, Sr. ". . . was detained to attend the wounded when the army moved on to NC and did not overtake the army till after the battle of Guilford Courthouse."[16]

These activities were part of what would become known as the Race to the Dan.

THE RACE TO THE DAN, 18 JANUARY–14 FEBRUARY 1781

From his camp on Turkey Creek, on 18 January Cornwallis penned a lengthy account of the Cowpens affair to Sir Henry Clinton in which he praised Tarleton for valorous attempts to rally his failing troops at Blackstock's, and for "recapturing" the baggage train where Tarleton's dragoons butchered the Loyalist militia.[17] Meantime, he believed that if Morgan continued to stand in place British forces could still destroy his force.

In fact Morgan had no intention of pushing his luck. And fortune— in the form of British confusion and paranoia—smiled upon the Patriot leader. The "Race to the Dan" was on and he had a head start. Morgan headed east, herding his mass of prisoners toward Ramsour's Mill to put many river crossings between himself and his pursuers, before turning north toward Virginia. The loss or demoralization of so many of his dragoons hampered Cornwallis in efforts to fix Morgan, and he mistakenly set out to the west, exhausting his men in marching over the muddy roads. Discovering his error, Cornwallis briefly rested his men, turned east and resumed the pursuit.

Morgan crossed the Catawba at Beattie's Ford on 23 January, sending the prisoners north under the escort of militia whose enlistments had expired, and leaving detachments at all the river crossings to delay Cornwallis and report his progress. In the attempt to catch Morgan, Cornwallis destroyed most of his baggage and kept only four wagons as ambulances, plus salt and ammunition. Cornwallis burned his own baggage as an example to his officers, and the enlisted men's precious rum supply was sacrificed.

Greene realized that his primary mission, to lure Cornwallis back into the South Carolina interior and prevent him moving into Virginia, had failed. Concerned about Cornwallis' rapid pursuit, he undertook a dangerous ride north to rendezvous with Morgan and assume command of that force, with instructions for the main army to follow. With his usual eye for logistical detail, he sent word ahead to assemble all possible boats for a crossing of the Dan River, the major water obstacle just across the southern boundary of Virginia.

On 1 February Cornwallis decided to force a crossing of the Catawba at Cowan's Ford. Although the pre-dawn crossing took the Patriots by surprise, a guide led many of Cornwallis' troops into deep water. The Patriots were driven off, and Cornwallis reported only four dead. But locals reported fourteen drowned men in a single fish trap, and estimated British losses of at least over a hundred.[18]

The roads—alternating between muddy in the day and icy at night— were clogged with refugees. Tarleton ranged through the countryside, fomenting terror in incidents like the attack on refugees and militia milling about at Torrence's Tavern (1 February). Characteristically, Tarleton reported an attack upon 500 hundred or more Patriot militia ready for battle. He admonished his troops to "remember the Cowpens" and they "broke through with irresistible velocity, killed nearly fifty on the spot, wounded many in the pursuit. . . ." Another British officer reported seeing fewer than ten Patriot casualties. If so, the vaunted Green Dragoons, with seven killed and wounded, did not fare that well in an attack upon civilians and an unorganized foe.[19]

Torrential rains now turned the roads into quagmires and swelled rivers like the Yadkin into raging torrents. Risky as it was, Morgan pushed his army across in boats at Trading Ford. The pursuing redcoats arrived to find only abandoned wagons and a militia rearguard that exchanged a few shots, and then fled to cross the river elsewhere in canoes. To salt the wound, the British could see boats on the far shore, but could only fire a few cannon shot across the wide, rain-swollen stream. Cornwallis sent Tarleton to search for other crossings, and headed west to cut Greene off from the upstream fords of the Dan. But Greene was headed for the boats waiting at the downstream ferry crossings.

The Patriot dragoons of "Light Horse Harry" Lee's Legion and the light troops of Colonel Otho Holland Williams continued to skirmish with and delay Cornwallis. In one final sprint the Patriots ran for the Dan River crossing and the waiting boats, crossing on 14 February. Arriving at the crossings the next morning the troops at the head of the British column could only stare at the roiling waters of the Dan River.

Greene had fled, but Cornwallis was stranded in North Carolina, 240 miles from his logistical base at Camden, with a wrecked army. He had driven the Patriot regular armies out of the Carolinas, but now faced the conundrum of the dog that finally caught a car; what was he to do with his prize?

For his part Greene also faced problems. His continuing mission was to firmly pin Cornwallis in the Carolinas. While Greene's troops briefly feasted and enjoyed the hospitality of Virginia, Cornwallis established his base at Hillsborough, North Carolina. The citizens there came to gawk at the British, but both food and new recruits were minimal.

On 22 February Greene crossed back over the Dan and began to harry the British, further disrupting their recruiting efforts. Finally on 15 March Greene faced Cornwallis at Guilford Courthouse. In the day-long battle described as "long, obstinate, and bloody" Cornwallis prevailed, but the cost was enormous. The British Southern Army was gutted, and the leader of the opposition in the British Parliament quipped that "One more such victory would prove the ruin of the British army."[20]

Greene had lost the battle but scored a strategic victory.

CHAPTER **16**

GRINDING DOWN THE BRITISH

We fight, get beat, rise, and fight again.
—NATHANAEL GREENE

BRANDON'S BLOCKHOUSE

As Tory power began to wane in the aftermath of King's Mountain and Cowpens, wealthy Tory Thomas Fletchall abandoned his properties along Fair Forest Creek, probably before January 1781. Thomas Brandon quickly moved south into the area and established a blockhouse garrisoned by a permanent guard company composed of men from the various companies on rotating duty. Brandon's confiscation of Fletchall's mills and property has in more recent times led some to revile him as a plunderer, but seizure of abandoned properties was common. It was also a prudent move to preserve local infrastructure. Mills were necessary to convert grain into useable flour or meal, and were particularly important when the state's government in exile could provide neither supplies nor funds. The facility was variously known as Brandon's Blockhouse or Brandon's Bullpen; bullpen suggests that it was also a facility for holding Tory prisoners.[1]

Captain William Young ". . . was ordered to take command of a Block house called Brandon's Blockhouse on Fair Forest Creek which he did as captain and continued there until peace was made and during this time served eighteen months."[2] Private Samuel Smith was one of the men who garrisoned the blockhouse and ". . . under Captain Jas. Woodson, about two months, was out repeatedly at other times on Scouting Services. . . ."

Apparently some men on parole served in this capacity. Joseph McJunkin stated that ". . . a call for duty was so urgent that all the true friends of liberty repaired to remain on parole duty and stand as minute men ready to the call of any and every officer and place to do duty in favor of their Country, and that Charles Tankersly was one of that class. . . ."[3]

William Kennedy Sr. remained a prominent figure in the guard company stationed at the new blockhouse: "The celebrated partisan officer Gen'l. Thomas Brandon, then Col. Brandon, lived in Union District [three words illegible] at Fairforest Shoal, five miles South of Unionville. Brandon, Kennedy, and their comrades made Union District literally a battleground. Brandon, however, was frequently removed to a distance at the head of his regiment, and Kennedy and his partisans kept the field in his absence."[4]

After the crossing of the Yadkin River on 3 February ". . . he [Morgan] advised a portion of the South Carolina Militia to return and defend their homes in the best manner they could. The regiments of Brandon and Thomas accordingly did return."

The Second Spartans' mission was to protect the Whig families in the area, but Sumter sent orders to recruit as many men as possible and join him east of the Congaree. "In obedience to this requisition Brandon proceeded into the vicinity of Granby, where he understood that a superior force of the enemy were manoeuvering with a view to prevent his junction with Sumter, hence he deemed it expedient to effect a retreat toward home." Ever since Brandon's Defeat (June 1780), Thomas Brandon had proven astute in avoiding fights he could not win, and he again chose to operate independently of Sumter. "When out of the reach of pursuit he received intelligence from Col. Roebuck that he designed to attack a body of Tories in the direction of Ninety Six. . . .

"Brandon immediately detached part of his force under the command of Major McJunkin to co-operate with Roebuck. . . ."[5]

MUDLICK CREEK EXPEDITION, 2 MARCH 1781
The Battle of Mudlick Creek was another effort to capture Williams Fort, the stockade garrisoned by redcoats and Tory militia that had resisted capture before Cowpens. On 2 March Colonel Benjamin Roebuck took two companies of his battalion of the First Spartans with a complicated plan

to lure the more numerous enemy out of the position. Lieutenant Colonel Henry White led mounted men who fired on the position, then rode away. The enemy took the bait and gave chase with cavalry and infantry, and Patriot foot soldiers hidden nearby easily captured the stockade.

White's detachment lured the pursuing Tories into an ambush, and after a confused hour-long fight the Tories tried to flee back to the stockade only to find it in Patriot hands. White was wounded and a Captain Robert Thomas was killed.

Although they did not arrive in time to participate in the attack, the Mudlick Creek expedition would have dire consequences for the Second Spartans. On 2 March Joseph McJunkin's detachment was returning from Mudlick. "On his return he and Lawson, one of his men, scouting at a distance from the rest of the party, rode up toward a house at night. At the gate they were confronted by three Tories. Fight or die was the only alternative. He and Lawson presented their rifles at two. Lawson's gun fired clear and killed his man. The Major's gun fired also, but was a mere squib [a spluttering misfire] and produced no other effect than to set fire to adversary's shirt. As Lawson's antagonist fell he jumped down, picked up his gun and shot down the other Tory and passed his sword through his body. The Major's fire so disconcerted his adversary that he [the Tory] missed him. The Major charged sword in hand; his adversary fled." The muzzle flash of McJunkin's rifle had set fire to the Tory' shirt, and "His flight on horseback soon caused his shirt to burn like a candle. This light so alarmed McJunkin's horse that he could not make him charge the fugitive. After running him a mile to get a blow at him he ran his horse alongside. At that instant the flying Tory drew a pistol, fired, and the ball struck and broke McJunkin's sword arm. His sword was, luckily, fastened to his wrist by a leather string. As his arm fell powerless by his side he caught the sword in his left hand and drew it off his sword arm, and with a back-handed blow as their horses ran side by side he killed his man. Lawson's second man recovered, notwithstanding he was shot and run through with a sword."[6]

McJunkin ". . . continued his march to Brandon's camp that night. Here his pain became so excruciating that some of his soldiers cut the ball out of his arm with a dull razor." With Tories still roaming the countryside it was too dangerous to stay in a house, so McJunkin was carried to a dense thicket on a remote part of Brown's Creek. When his arm became infected

". . . one of his fellow soldiers by great exertions and personal danger succeeded in bringing Dr. Ross to his place of concealment. The name of this soldier was David Brown."[7]

Roebuck's party was ambushed and captured. Matthew Patton: "That on 16th (or 18th) March 1781 he was taken prisoner and supposed he may then have lost his commission as it was usual for officers to wear their commissions around their necks. In his being taken it may have been lost and that then there were taken 13 prisoners: Ralph Smith, Samuel Smith, John Elder and his sons, James, Thomas, & John, Charles Bruce, Landon Farrow, Samuel Farrow, James Eames, John Blaylock, Benjamin Roebuck, & himself. They were then taken back to Mud Lick and Four of them (viz.) Landon Farrow James Elder Charles Bruce and himself were tried and condemned [and] as Rebels were ordered to have been executed on the next day at 10 o'clock. Charles Bruce was the first spared for some reasons and then the other three were finally pardoned after having endeavoured in vain to extort some information from them against others, and then sent on to 96 Jail where they remained until July as well as he remembers."[8]

Roebuck was sent to the infamous jail at Ninety Six, and later to the even worse prison hulks in Charleston harbor.

In another in the chain of disasters, "A party consisting of eight persons was on a scout. They were John Jolly, Wm. Sharp, Wm. Giles, Old Richd. Hughes, his son John, James Johnson, an Irishman, Charles Crane, and a man named Allbritton. They stopped at old Leighton's, near Fairforest, not far above the mouth. Leighton was of doubtful politics, inclined however to the strongest side. The house was in the middle of the plantation & passed by a lane. At the time this Scout stopped at the house, a party of about a hundred Tories was laying on the other side of the creek. Leighton is believed to have sent them word. In a short time the Tories came & lay across the lane on each side of the house. Two of them then came near the house & fired on the Whigs. Sharp and Giles mounted their horses & charged through the Tories, & made good their retreat. Jolly and Crane attempted to run off through the field; Crane succeeded, but Jolly was shot through & killed immediately. I saw him the next morning Early; my mother heard the firing & went up in the morning. She sent [word? or me?] to Jolly's wife & got him buried &c. The four Whigs that remained in the house kept up a fight till night when they were forced to capitulate.

They were carried to Ninety Six & put in jail where old Hughes and his son both died. The others returned. Several Tories were killed & wounded in this engagement."[9]

No sooner had McJunkin's arm begun to heal than word came that a party of Tories had gotten word of his camp, so he was taken across the Broad River ". . . into the vicinity of the Rev. Dr. Joseph Alexander whose house . . . was a real Lazaretto for the sick and wounded of our army." Here McJunkin contracted smallpox, and when his mother came to act as his nurse, she contracted the disease and died.*

Charles Sims' wife and children were still refugees, and "She afterwards got with her children under the protection of Dr. Joseph Alexander, of York. He kept a sort of hospital, where he inoculated the Whig families who had been exposed to the small pox." In another version of the story, "My father heard of situation and came for us. He got some horses & took us to the house of Rev. J. Alexander, York District. Here this new parson innoculated us all with the small pox. The matter [pus] was taken from Maj. Jos. McJunkin."[10]

McJunkin's travails seemed endless. He returned to his father's house, only to be taken prisoner on 9 May in another Tory sweep of the country-side. On the march ". . . other prisoners were taken, some of whom were killed on their knees begging for quarter." At Wofford's Iron Works, McJunkin was summarily sentenced to hang and the noose was around his neck when a messenger rode up to warn that a Whig patrol was nearby. The prisoners were marched toward Ninety Six, and on the march ". . . no epithets were too abusive or insulting to be applied to him with the greatest freedom and frequency."

Near Ninety Six the party halted and McJunkin lay on the ground nursing his damaged arm when a party of Tories rode up. A man that he thought was Bloody Bill Cunningham drew his sword and rushed at him, only to draw back at the last moment, saying "I was mistaken in the man."

At Ninety Six McJunkin was tried for "killing one of His Majesty's subjects—the man who broke his arm." In his defense McJunkin dissem-

---

*Continentals benefited from the new practice of smallpox vaccination, and in the disruption of war smallpox and many other infectious diseases were rampant. At this time some non-medical practitioners were performing dangerous vaccinations.

bled, showing his arm and arguing that a man with a broken arm could not have pursued and killed the Tory. He was acquitted of murder, but tossed into the prison where he would suffer until being paroled in mid-May.[11]

HOBKIRK'S HILL, 25 APRIL 1781

Cornwallis' main army was in desperate condition after Guilford Courthouse, and he had turned reluctantly east toward Wilmington to take up winter quarters where he could be resupplied by sea. Greene followed cautiously in his wake. With the onset of milder spring weather in early April Greene moved south, hoping to lure Cornwallis after him, but the British army was in no condition to pursue. Loyalist outposts in South Carolina would have to fend for themselves.

Lord Francis Rawdon had led the British left flank at Camden, and Cornwallis' movement into North Carolina left Rawdon as *de facto* commander-in-chief in South Carolina. Most of Rawdon's troops were Loyalist militia dispersed among the arc of outposts around Charleston; the largest was the garrison at Camden, Rawdon's headquarters, with about 900 men.

Greene detached Harry Lee's dragoons to cooperate with Francis Marion and eliminate some of the smaller British posts. Fort Watson, a small stockade with a garrison of 120 redcoats and Loyalist militia, on the Santee River, was the first victim. On 16 April Lee and Marion first tried to force the garrison to surrender by cutting them off from a nearby water supply. When that failed (the garrison quickly dug a well), one of Marion's officers, Major Hezekiah Maham, designed a sort of siege tower of pine logs that could be pre-fabricated off site. On the night of 22 April the Patriots erected the tower.*

On 23 April sharpshooters began to snipe at the garrison from the top of the tower, driving the defenders off the walls. The garrison surrendered the same day.

Greene hoped to carry Camden by surprise, but found the garrison alerted and the defenses manned. He retreated a short distance to the north and took position on Hobkirk Hill, a linear ridge with his left (eastern) flank anchored on a poorly drained flat-bottomed ravine. The aggressive

---

*Maham's design was later used at the better-known siege of Ninety Six, 22 May–18 June.

A mine or tunnel (the only such work constructed during the war) and structures like this replica Maham Tower at Ninety Six National Historic Site were used during the May–June 1781 siege. Patriot militiamen sniped at British cannon crews, and Thomas Young and William "Squire" Kennedy sniped at Loyalist water parties from one of these towers.—AUTHORS

Rawdon wanted to deal with Greene before Marion and Lee arrived, and at mid-morning on 25 April attacked Greene's larger force. Greene's pickets bought him enough time to form a battle line along the ridge with units, from left to right, the 2nd Maryland, 1st Maryland, 1st Virginia, and 2nd Virginia. Rawdon advanced on a narrow front and Greene ordered his units to wheel inward and encircle the British flanks.

Yet again fortune deserted Greene. The commander of the rightmost company of the 1st Maryland was killed and the regiment stopped to reform; then the commander of the 2nd Maryland was mortally wounded, so both of Greene's wings began to withdraw. The situation was clearly falling apart, so Greene ordered a general retreat, covered by his only intact units, the 1st Virginia and William Washington's dragoons.[12]

It was a humiliating tactical defeat. Greene briefly considered abandoning the campaign, but as was typical of him, he persevered. Rawdon had won the victory, and his overall casualties were lighter: 39 killed, 210 wounded, and 12 missing as opposed to 321 killed, wounded, and captured for Greene. But again the British had suffered losses they could not replace without a recruiting pool. Rawdon began a slow but systematic abandonment of all the outlying posts that had once been thought necessary to

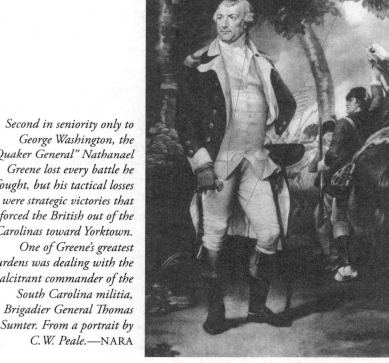

Second in seniority only to George Washington, the "Quaker General" Nathanael Greene lost every battle he fought, but his tactical losses were strategic victories that forced the British out of the Carolinas toward Yorktown. One of Greene's greatest burdens was dealing with the recalcitrant commander of the South Carolina militia, Brigadier General Thomas Sumter. From a portrait by C. W. Peale.—NARA

screen the vital ports of Charleston and Savannah. Greene had for all practical purposes already won the war, but there was more bloodshed to come.

On the day of Rawdon's victory Cornwallis began his march northward toward Virginia. Young William Sims had recovered from his smallpox inoculation, and his father decided to take them back to extended family who lived farther north. "When we recovered my father put us in a wagon & carried us to Virginia. We travelled along after Lord Cornwallis's army about fifteen miles, in the rear of it."[13]

ORANGEBURG, 10–11 MAY 1781

On 8 May Francis Marion had laid siege to the British depot of Fort Motte, a fortified plantation on Buckhead Hill garrisoned by redcoats, Hessians, and Loyalist militia. Thomas Young: "After I had recovered somewhat from my wound, I joined Col. Brandon's party, amounting perhaps to 50 or 60 men—among them were Capt. Ben. Jolly, Wm. Giles, afterward Capt. Giles. We proceeded down Broad & Congaree rivers, leaving Granby on our right, & arrived at Buckhead after the siege of that place had been commenced." The company remained at the siege only a day. "A party of us were sent on to the siege of Orangeburg."[14]

Orangeburg was garrisoned by about seventy Tory militia and fifteen uniformed Provincials (estimates vary). Orangeburg was a fortified hamlet, the civilian population largely descendants of the original German, Swiss, and Dutch founders. Recognizing its vulnerability, Rawdon had ordered it abandoned but Patriots had intercepted the courier.

Declining to attack stronger Fort Granby, Sumter decided to eliminate the Orangeburg post. Sumter had cadged a six-pounder (57mm) cannon from Greene, but the heavy cannon was unwieldy on the march. Impatient as ever, Sumter left the Second Spartans and others to manage the cannon, and rode ahead with a large force of mounted militia to invest Orangeburg on 10 May. The garrison retreated into a fortified brick building, and a standoff ensued.

Accounts of the fight are confused and contradictory. Thomas Young's account is brief but probably the most reliable: "In the morning the rest of the troops reached the place with a three pounder.* The main body of us marched down the road, & drew the whole attention of those engaged in the defence of the house. The house was a two story brick building, & the Tories who defended it were in the second story. They shot at us, & hallooed furiously as we passed on. When we were beyond the reach of their balls, we waited till our canon had got near enough at another point to play upon the house. It was discharged three times & a flag was hung out."

In his pension statement Young was terse: "The tories were lodged in a brick house, and kept up a monstrous shouting and firing to very little purpose. As soon as the piece of artillery was brought to bear upon the house, a breach was made through the gable end; then another, a little lower; then about the centre, and they surrendered."[15]

The scribe who recorded William Grant's pension declaration itemized his statements: "4th) Afterward in the Spring of 1781 Genl. Sumter called

---

*Most sources say a six-pounder.

on the minute men, and Capt [William] Grant being out on duty at Neils Mills, Col Brandon ordered this applicant he being first lieut to collect the volunteers and to go with him the Col. to join General Greene at the Congaree Fort. Applicant did collect his men and went under Col. Brandon to Congaree Fort, sometime after their arrival, Genl. Greene ordered General Sumter to take Col. Brandons Regt. and attack the Fort at Orangeburg. Applicant went with Brandon & Sumter & they took the Fort (the Old Jail) and eighty Tories & some British prisoners, commanded by Col. Fisher."[16]

Samuel Otterson had briefly participated in the siege at Buckhead, then "The day before that place surrendered, I was sent with my Company under General Sumter to Orange-Burgh, which latter place surrendered after the fire of three field pieces [three rounds?] on our part. One of the enemy was kill & none of our detachment were kill nor wounded except one or two who were struck by dead balls* without any Injury."[17]

Some accounts say that the Loyalists immediately surrendered to the cannon fire, but several veterans suggested an actual infantry attack. Thomas Petty: ". . . in the next expedition his capt. Was Robert Montgomery & the Regiment was at that time commanded by Col. Brandon who after that time became a general—the Col. was the highest in command at the taking of Orangeburg—he also recollects Maj. Snipes who commanded the front guard in which applicant was stationed on that day. . . ."[18]

At any rate Sumter by some accounts captured 28 Provincials, 55 Tory militia, and a generous quantity of supplies.

Thomas Young described more tempting booty. "Here we found a quantity of rum & sugar, but the common soldiers received none of it, but a gill of rum to a man.† One man who was set to guard the sugar, filled his pockets with it, & this was all of that article that was of any benefit to us, & we at that time needed that article very much, as were in pressing need of provisions. Col. Wade Hampton was the commander who is said to have made private property of the spoils on this occasion."

Marion and Lee had by that time taken Fort Motte, so the Patriot militia was dismissed or reassigned. William Grant: ". . . about this time Genl.

---

*A projectile with insufficient velocity to kill or injure; sometimes called a spent bullet.
†An Imperial gill of the era was equivalent to 4.8 liquid ounces/142ml.

Marion had taken Wrights Bluff—Greene the Congaree Fort—They were then sent home to collect more men and ordered to meet at 96 where Genl. Greene intended to besiege that fort and drive the Enemy from the back country. . . ."[19]

Some men remained to garrison Orangeburg. John Davidson: "That General Greene ordered a detachment to be formed of Four men from each captain's company—and all under the command of Col. Roebuck & Leut. Col. Farr [of Brandon's regiment] to proceed to Orangeburgh C. H. [Courthouse]—for the purpose of guarding with greater security the Jail at that place—in which were confined a number of prisoners—that he was one of the four men—taken from the company of Capt. Pharis [Faris]— and was placed under the immediate command of Lieut. Latimer [Francis Lattimore] of Capt. Thompsons company—and then marched to Orange-burgh C. H. where he remained in the aforementioned service for the space of two months. then the prisoners were sent by order of Genl Greene to his Head Quarters. . . ."[20]

The often chaotic militia organization in this phase of the war became looser still. Men—even senior officers—might elect to individually partic-ipate in some adventure. Thomas Young detached himself on one mission to capture badly needed horses. "I then joined a party of dragoons under Capt. Boykin, at the Bacon's Bridge, in the low country. It was a most haz-ardous expedition, and required great courage and prudence. Capt. Boykin had both. We went to the hotel and called for the hostler. Capt. Boykin drew his pistol, cocked it, and told him if he did not open the stable door, he would shoot him dead. You may rest assured he did not long consider about it! They got three very fine animals: two stallions and a gelding. Neither Giles nor I got a horse, and we were in not very good humor, as we knew we should have to go back at so rapid a pace that our nags could not stand it. Sure enough, after one day and night's travel, our horses began to fail, and we resolved to take the woods; but Boykin begged us to try and keep up, and as we soon should come to another billet of horses, we should have the first choice. Well, next day we did come upon a fine lot of horses, wild as devils. Giles and I went in, and I soon caught a yellow sorrel mare. Giles, who was an excellent judge of horse flesh, was struck with her form, and said to me, 'Young, if you will let me have that mare, I will help you catch any horse in the lot!' I gave her to him, and picked me out a bay mare. Time proved that Giles was correct in his judgment, as the yellow mare was never caught in a chase, or beaten in a race afterwards. We were all now well mounted, and pushed off to join our detachment above.

"When we arrived at Granby, we were nearly all discharged."[21]

As men were released from service, companies were consolidated. Private Simon Davis: ". . . by orders of Colonel Brandon who Dispatched two captain's companies consolidated on horseback Captain Grant and Captain Price to go on an express expedition against the Tories down to a place called Ninety Six. . . ."[22]

SECOND SIEGE OF AUGUSTA, 22 MAY–6 JUNE 1781

Augusta, commanded by "Burnfoot" Brown at its main defensive position, Fort Cornwallis, was another linchpin of the British defensive strategy. In May Greene turned his attention upon it. Andrew Pickens maneuvered his large Patriot militia force between Augusta and Ninety Six to prevent reinforcement. On 16 April the first contingents of Patriot militia arrived at Augusta and set up a fortified camp nearby, but Brown considered his garrison too weak to sortie out and attack. By 15 May more Patriot militia had arrived to close the ring, and Greene had instructed Harry Lee to break off activities around Ninety Six and join Pickens with his dragoons.

On 21 May the Patriots attacked George Galphin's Indian agency post 12 miles (19km) south of the town, capturing 126 men—many of them badly needed British redcoats—and military supplies intended for the Creeks. On 23 May the Patriots attacked Fort Grierson, a stockade a half-mile away along the river. When a sortie from Fort Cornwallis failed, Grierson attempted to break out and reach the main position. The families of the Georgia Patriot militiamen under Elijah Clarke had suffered under Tory and Creek raiders operating out of Augusta for years; they massacred Grierson's entire garrison.

Fort Cornwallis was a different matter, and Lee suggested a Maham Tower. The 30-foot structure was likely built in defilade provided by a nearby house that prevented Brown's cannons from striking it. On 1 June Pickens' single cannon, manhandled to the top of the tower, began to rake the interior of the fort. Brown attempted to have a spy burn the tower, but failed.

On 5 June, after weeks of travail, Brown surrendered. Mindful of his own reputation, "Burnfoot" stipulated that he would personally surrender only to the handful of Continentals in Pickens' command. He had good cause. The families of Clarke's Georgia men had been the primary victims of Brown's sadistic raids, and ". . . the militia could, with difficulty, be restrained from acts of blood and violence. All the firmness of the officers was necessary to control or to quell them; and, at last it has been seen, that it became necessary to march the prisoners off, under a strong guard of South Carolina militia and North Carolina regulars, to insure their safety."[23]

The noose was tightening around Charleston.

THE SECOND SIEGE OF NINETY SIX, 22 MAY–19 JUNE 1781

The fortified village at Ninety Six was the linchpin of British strategy. It was a logistics base, recruiting depot, prison, launching point for both full-scale operations and Loyalist raiders, and a communications nexus sitting at the junction where the Whitehall Road to the west met the north-south road connecting Charleston to Island Ford and the Cherokee towns. It was the most heavily fortified position outside of the coastal cities. Loyalist Lieutenant Colonel John Cruger commanded a powerful garrison of some 400 New York and New Jersey Volunteers, and about 200 Loyalist militia. The latter were "all desperate men" who had committed various crimes against the local Patriot families. The Volunteers were uniformed Loyalists trained and equipped to the standard of British Regulars. Cruger also had a trio of wheeled three-pounder (47mm) cannons.[24]

The village had long been surrounded by a log stockade, but the industrious Cruger utilized slave labor under the direction of British engineer officer Lieutenant Henry Haldane to continuously improve the position. By 1781 the village proper—including the large brick jail, courthouse, and a dozen houses—was surrounded by an improved five-sided log stockade, a surrounding ditch, and an abatis.[25]

The northeast corner of the stockade was anchored on the formidable Star Fort, a twelve-foot earthen berm with seven salients, surrounded by a dry moat. The position's one weakness was the water supply, a small spring and creek at the base of a steep slope to the west of the village. To secure this the garrison constructed the Stockade Fort, also known as Holmes' Fort. The log and earth structure with two blockhouses sat on the west side of the creek, and dominated the spring and creek bottom. The fortified jail, a brick structure on the east side of the stream, must have been quite impressive, as one Patriot held prisoner described being chained in the top-floor cell, thirty feet (9m) square and forty-five feet (14m) above the ground. British Lieutenant Anthony Alaire was briefly quartered in the town in 1780 and joyfully described ". . . the constant view of Rebels peeping through the grates, which affords some satisfaction to see them suffer for their folly."[26]

The jail and Stockade Fort were mutually supporting. The village and Stockade Fort were connected by a covered way, a trench with dirt berms on either side that provided protection for people going for water and moving between the two positions.*

The meticulous Cruger left nothing to chance. Anticipating the arrival of Greene's army he stripped the surrounding Whig communities of useful provisions, destroyed anything not confiscated, and instructed Bloody Bill Cunningham's partisans to disperse into small bands and waylay Greene's foraging parties. Cruger also divested himself of useless mouths; Joseph McJunkin was paroled ". . . but meeting Greene near 96 and being anxious that he should carry that place returned with him to give my assistance so far as I was able in my crippled state."[27]

Greene had at his disposal about 850 Continentals and 200 militia, far too few to storm the position. The militia would play an ancillary role. The militia numbers may have been greater. Present were at least ten of Brandon's Second Spartan companies under William Grant (joint command with Thomas Price), Robert Montgomery, two William Youngs (both led Ranger companies), Samuel Otterson, John Thompson, John Putman, George Anderson, Thomas Blassingame, and George Aubrey.

One private, John Bearden, illustrates the perpetual fluidity of the militia organization, and their diverse duties. ". . . about one week before the Siege of Ninety Six that he was marched to that place, a drafted soldier, and was in the Engagement at that place, he says he was there transferred from Captain Blassingame's company to Volunteers under Captain John Putman and was marched through the country in different directions in

---

*The configuration of the town stockade is from Johnson, *Sketches of the Life and Correspondence of Nathanael Greene, Volume II*, p. 141. The configuration is at odds with later descriptions.

Search of a band of tories under the command of a tory captain by the name of Jesse Gray. . . ."[28]

Polish-born Colonel Tadeusz Kosciuszko supervised a traditional siege operation, in which the Patriots had little experience. On 22 May the Patriots began construction of trenches on the northeast, but too close to the walls of the Star Fort. The aggressive Cruger sortied under cover of cannon fire and slaughtered the sappers to a man while a party of slaves hastily refilled the trenches and carried captured Patriot tools back inside the fort.

Thomas Sumter was not at all pleased to have "his" militia usurped by Greene. On 26 May Greene drafted one of his typically courteous replies to Sumter. "Col. Branum [Brandon, annotation by Lyman Draper] on his return home, called upon this place and told me he had your orders to bring back a part of the militia to your aid below. For particular reasons I have desired him to join us, with all the forces he can collect, at this place, to expedite the reduction of it, as soon as possible—my motives I will explain to you more fully hereafter. I am sorry to break in upon your arrangements, but I flatter myself you will be persuaded it is for the good of the service at large, tho' it may be a little inconvenient to you for a time."[29]

Kosciuszko began more systematic zigzag approach trenches with parallels, protecting the sappers with gabions (dirt-filled baskets), and Cruger countered with nocturnal forays to disrupt the work. About 3 June the Patriots installed forty-foot tall Maham Towers that allowed riflemen to fire over the fort's parapet, temporarily silencing Cruger's cannon. Cruger attempted to burn the towers with red-hot cannon shot, and when that failed he raised the fort's parapets with sandbags. The towers were soon abandoned.*

After the fall of Orangeburg most of Brandon's men had been marched to Granby and discharged. Three chose to go to Ninety Six to join the companies already there. Thomas Young: "Col. Brandon, Major [Benjamin] Jolly and myself, resolved to make an excursion to 96—where the siege was then going on.

---

*Sketch maps like the 1952 version reproduced in Pancake, *This Destructive War*, p. 211, and the National Park Service's replica tower and supporting interpretations at the Ninety Six National Historic Site, indicate a single tower north of the Star Fort. Johnson's 1822 *Sketches of the Life and Correspondence of Nathanael Greene, Volume II*, p. 141 and accompanying text gave no specific location and specifically indicated

"Here I remained during the siege. As we every day got our parallels nearer the garrison, we could see them very plain when they went out to a brook or spring for water. The Americans had constructed a sort of moving battery, but as the cannon of the fort were brought to bear upon it, they were forced to abandon the use of it. It had not been used for some time, when an idea struck old Squire Kennedy (who was an excellent marksman) that he could pick off a man now and then as they went to the spring. He and I took our rifles and went into the woods to practice at 200 yards. We were arrested and taken before an officer, to whom we gave our excuse and design. He laughed, and told us to practice no more, but to try our luck from the battery if we wanted to, so we took our position, and as a fellow came down to the spring, Kennedy fired and he fell; several ran out and gathered round him, and among them I noticed one man raise his head, and look round as if he wondered where that shot could have come from. I touched my trigger and *he* fell, and *we* made off, for fear it might be *our* time to fall next."[30]

The garrison was reduced to sending slaves at night to bring back pails of water, and an old well was reopened inside the Star Fort.

Cruger stubbornly refused to surrender, even when on 12 June Pickens arrived and paraded the captives from Augusta outside the fort. Lighthorse Harry Lee's troops were assigned to occupy positions on the west side of the fortress. Efforts to set fire to the village with flaming arrows were thwarted when Cruger ordered the roofs removed, and an ill-advised effort by Lee to set fire to the abatis failed when the small group assigned the mission was annihilated by the defenders.

Kosciuszko began construction of a mine to tunnel under the north-eastern side of the fort, but the work was never completed.[31]

Greene was now a man in a hurry. He was advised that Lord Rawdon, with three redcoat regiments fresh from Ireland, was marching toward Ninety Six. Marching through the brutal heat, one regiment alone recorded over fifty heat-related deaths, but Rawdon pressed on. Greene had dis-

---

towers, plural. The fact that an abandoned tower was later briefly reoccupied and used to snipe at Tory water carriers in the creek bottom indicates that at least one was placed within line of sight of where the covered way crossed the stream. Towers placed to the west would also have been more suited to long-range sniping at the crews of Cruger's cannons that were firing northeast at the Patriot siege works.

patched letters urging Sumter to concentrate and join him to confront Rawdon, but by chance rather than skill Rawdon's column slipped past Sumter and Marion's main forces; he suffered only minor delaying attacks by small detachments of Sumter's scattered militia and William Washington's dragoons. A messenger won through the Patriot lines to advise Cruger that help was at hand.

It was now or never for Greene and at noon on 18 June a Patriot cannonade announced the general assault on the north side by the Continentals. Harry Lee's troops easily occupied the Stockade Fort; it had been abandoned under cover of darkness on the previous night.

A forlorn hope rushed in to cut away the abatis around the Star Fort, followed by men equipped with hooked poles to pull down the sandbags. For forty-five gory minutes the assault troops struggled with the defenses under fire from loopholes in the sandbag wall until the Continentals gained a foothold on the parapet. Various accounts differ, with the Loyalists and Harry Lee concurring that defenders sallied and attacked both flanks of the assault party, with men clubbing and stabbing at each other in the dry ditch.

Greene soon realized that even if he took the town he would be too depleted to face Rawdon. Cruger declined a truce to allow Greene to recover the Patriot dead but, confident in his victory, offered to return the Patriot dead and assured Greene of good care for his captured and wounded.

Greene's army was decimated, and Sumter soon reported that much of his militia had departed en masse. On 19 June Greene marched away from Ninety Six toward the high hills of the Santee where his troops could lie up over the coming "fever months." Rawdon briefly pursued, but his own depleted troops could not catch up. Captain Samuel Otterson: ". . . at the siege under General Greene the militia at this place was commanded by Brigadier General Henderson. after a siege of some weeks the British General Lord Rowden came to reinforce the garrison & General Greene raised the siege & retreated over Broad river pursued by the British as far as [the] Enoree [River]."[32]

Rawdon realized he could no longer hold Ninety Six, and marched back toward Camden, harassed by Patriot militia. On 8 July Cruger burned the remaining structures and followed Rawdon, escorting any Loyalists who wished to leave. Greene had lost another battle and won another strategic victory.

The militia scattered and resumed their internecine war. Thomas Young: "After the siege of 96, I returned to my old neighborhood, and was engaged in various scouting expeditions till peace was declared. I was on a scouting expedition to Mudlick, under Col. Brandon. We were all mounted. We saw two spies, before we came upon the tories, and pursued them to the creek. Col. Brandon sent out Major Jolly with a flank guard to prevent their outflanking us—they were on the opposite side of the creek, and commanded the ford, so that we could not cross. Jolly and I approached very near; so near that a cousin of mine, William Young, hailed us and inquired who commanded. A good deal was said to keep us engaged. Young waved his sword to me several times, and hallooed to me to go away; a moment after we were fired upon by a party who had crept up the creek through the bushes. A shot went under Jolly's horse's belly, and another shaved my horse's forelegs. We returned the fire, but did no damage, save putting a ball through Young's horse's nose. We then retreated, under the hope that they would pursue us, but they did not.

"This same cousin of mine had offered a hundred guineas to any man who would bring me into 96. In one of our excursions we heard of a band of tories being concealed in a very dense thicket, over on Sandy River; it was said they had a great deal of plunder."[33]

On another occasion "A party, of which I recollect Col. Brandon, Col. Casey, Col. Hughes, and Major Jolly, were members, went to attack them. We got there early in the day, and it was not long before we had possession of the place. In the fight I took a little fellow, by the name of Tom Moore, prisoner. I ran him for some distance, shot at him, and broke his arm. When I took him back Tom Salter wanted to kill him, because Moore had once had him prisoner, and would in all probability have killed him, if he had not escaped. I cocked my gun, and told them no! he was my man, and I would shoot the first one who harmed him. During this skirmish I witnessed rather an amusing scene between Col. Hughes and a tory. Hughes had dismounted to get a chance to shoot at some fellow through the bushes, when a tory sprang upon his horse and dashed sway. Hughes discovered it in time, fired, and put a ball through the hind tree of the saddle and the fellow's thigh. The tory fell, and Hughes got his horse. In this excursion we got a great deal of plunder, which had been concealed by the tories.

"Once after this, I was taken by a party of 'Outliers' (a name given to the Greys), the most notorious and abandoned plunderers and murderers of that gloomy period. On account of the kindness I had once shown to one of them while a prisoner, in my charge, I was set at liberty without being hurt."

TORY RAIDS

The British presence in the back country might be in decline, but for Patriot and Tory partisans it was a desperate period of settling scores. It is impossible to determine timing of many of these small, bloody skirmishes. Richard Brandon was killed in one such skirmish, his last day of service listed as 25 June 1781.[34]

Christopher Brandon: "I can now call to memory the flush of determination that appeared in his [William Kennedy Sr.'s] face whenever he knew the enemy were near. On one occasion a scouting party of Tories and British crossed Broad River, and began to plunder the women and children of every thing they possessed. One of Kennedy's runners came to where myself and two others were out-lying—for we could not stay at home for fear of being massacred by the Tories. On being informed of the place of rendezvous which Kennedy had appointed, we mounted our horses and set off at half speed to join him. It was a hot day. We [illegible] a small cowpath through the dense forest. We stopped at a small branch that crossed our path for our jaded horses to drink. The moment we stopped, I heard the crack of a rifle, and at the same moment the brains of one [of my] comrades were spattered by the ball, over the bosom of my shirt and in my face. The ball of the unseen Tory had passed clear through his head, and grazed my cheek. He fell stone dead from his horse into the brook beneath. Myself and the other survivor spurred our horses at full gallop, and as we fled the unseen enemy, more than a dozen rifles were fired at us from behind the trees, but we escaped uninjured.

"We reached Kennedy at his [illegible] and with a party of fifteen or twenty set out in pursuit of the Tories. We had passed through their midst without knowing it, and having heard the galloping of our horses, they had lain in wait for us. We came up with them a few minutes before sunset. Kennedy's horse was as well trained as himself, and at the word *who[a]*, would instantly stop. The Tories were plundering a house a few rods* from the public road, and we were first attracted by the cries of the women and the children. The sentinel fired as we neared the house and gave the alarm, and instantly the Tories mounted and fled. Our party divided, and each pursued his man at full speed. I being young, Kennedy had directed me to stay near him and to fire only when he told me. The leader of the party, whose name was Neal, was pursued by Kennedy. He fled through an open field toward the woods at some distance off. Kennedy kept the road in pursuit for some distance, running nearly parallel with the fugitive for the purpose of coming to an open place in the hedge row of bushes that partially obstructed the view. Coming to an open place, he said *who[a]* to his horse, and as quick as thought I heard the crack of his rifle. Neal fell from his horse shot through. When we came up to where he lay, he was stone dead. The distance of Kennedy's fire was one hundred and forty yards. More than one-half the party of Tories were killed—*not one* taken prisoner—for that occurred but seldom; the rifle usually saved us that trouble. We took all their booty, returned it to the distressed women and children."[35]

Another, more questionable, episode near Brandon's Fair Forest base also involved Kennedy. "On the heights at Fair Forest Shoal was an old stockade post or block-house. Many tragic incidents occurred there, and in its neighborhood. A Tory, whose name has been forgotten, had with his band, done much mischief in that region; and among other unpardonable sins, had killed one of Wm. Kennedy's dearest friends. The latter learned that the culprit was within striking distance, and called his friends together, who went in search of him. The two parties met some two or three miles from the block-house, where a severe contest ensued. The tories were routed; the leader, who was the prize Kennedy sought, fled. Kennedy, Hughes, Sharp, McJunkin and others pursued. The chase was one of life or death. The tory approached the bank of Fair Forest at a point, on a high bluff, where the stream at low water was perhaps twenty or thirty yards over [wide], and quite deep. The fleeing Loyalist, hemmed around by his pursuers on the cliff, just where they aimed to drive him, hesitated not a moment, but spurred his horse and plunged over the bank, and into the

---

*One rod = 16.5 feet/5m.

stream below—a fearful leap. His pursuers followed, and at the opposite bank they made him their prisoner.

"Their powder being wet by its contact with the water, they resolved to take their captive below to the block-house and hang him. When they arrived there, the officer in command would not permit him to be disposed of in that summary manner, but ordered him to be taken to Colonel Brandon's camp, a considerable distance away, to be tried by a court martial. Kennedy was placed at the head of the guard, but the Tory begged that Kennedy might not be permitted to go, as he apprehended he would take occasion to kill him on the way. Evidently intending to make an effort to escape, he did not wish the presence of so skillful a shot as Kennedy. His request, however, was not heeded. He took an early occasion to dash off at full speed, but Kennedy's unerring rifle soon stopped his flight, and his remains were brought back to the foot of the hill near the block house, and there buried."[36]

Greene was relatively inactive in the summer, so in August some men were given leave to visit their homes. Local Tories on the west side of the Broad River banded together and killed several of them in nocturnal raids, then fled back across the river. "Col. Brandon happened to be in Chester at the time of these outrages. He accordingly rapidly pursued the fugitive tories, and early one morning came [illegible] their camp. The Tories were engaged in cooking their breakfast and did not even have sentinel on post. Brandon charged their camp—killed and wounded [illegible], and completely routed their entire band."

In the melee ". . . Col. B. came in contact with a tory by the name of John Houston from Chester Co., S.C. and aimed a blow at his head with his broad sword, but the sword glanced cutting out one of his eyes and leaving a deep wound in his face. Houston fell bleeding profusely and was left on the battle field apparently dead. After the contest was over and each party had retired, one of Col. B's men visited the battle ground and found Houston still alive weltering in his own blood. He was cared for and recovered from his wound, and was known during the balance of his life as 'one eyed John Houston' . . . Col. Brandon bent his broad sword when he struck John Houston over the head and had to straighten it before he could use it again."[37]

EUTAW SPRINGS, 8 SEPTEMBER 1781

Eutaw Springs was a pleasant settlement that boasted cool, clear springs, about thirty-five miles (56km) northwest of Charleston. Nathanael Greene's intelligence suggested that as the British withdrew into Charleston they intended to establish an outpost there, probably in part to serve as a base for foraging parties. Learning that the British had been reinforced, Greene advanced cautiously, waiting for Marion to join him.

Part of the Second Spartans joined Greene. Private Simon Davis: "My Next Tower [tour] must have been in 1781. I was called out by Captain William Grant and Major Jolly for a tower of three months we was marched down Broad River to the mouth of Sandy River where we joined some other forces. from there we marched down the River to where Columbia now stands where we met with more forces. from that place we was marched Down the River within Twenty-five Miles of the Utaw Springs, where we joined the Main Army under the command of General Green and Colonel Washington."[38]

The late summer heat and humidity were debilitating to both armies. Lieutenant William Grant, Jr. of Jolly's battalion was called upon to raise a company. He ". . . joined Col. Lee's Corps of Horse and went on to McCord's Ferry with him under Major Jolly he was there taken sick and was appointed Officer of the Sick and left there with a promise of support & assistance. After remaining there some time and obtaining no support the applicant discharged all the sick who were living and all that could went home. He went home & was sick all the next winter was out not less than two & a half months."[39]

In the pre-dawn hours of 8 September Greene set out to attack the British. The British commander, Lieutenant Colonel Alexander Stewart, was completely oblivious to Greene's approach. Stewart: ". . . the Americans had way-laid the swamps and passes in such a manner as to cut off every avenue of intelligence," and Lee's dragoons had captured a large scouting party during the night.[40]

In the wooded country Greene's front line was composed of four battalions of militia, one of them Jolly's from the Second Spartans. The main line was three brigades of Continentals, with Harry Lee's Legion and State troops screening the flanks, and Washington's dragoons and more Continentals as a reserve. The flankers clashed with British parties protecting a 300-man "rooting party" who were digging sweet potatoes. The militia drove off the protecting troops and captured a number of foragers.[41]

About this time Stewart was belatedly warned of the danger by two deserters from Greene's army. Meeting resistance from a small force that Stewart rushed forward to delay him, Greene paused to issue a rum ration and realign his troops, with the militia as forward skirmishers. Jolly's battalion from the Second Spartans would be under Andrew Pickens on the extreme left flank, advancing through the swampy bottoms along Eutaw Creek. Jolly had at least four companies under Captains Joseph Hughes, Robert Montgomery, George Avery, William Grant, Sr., and possibly George Aubrey.[42]

The British defensive line was uncharacteristically drawn up in the woods, necessary since the large British camp occupied most of the open fields near Patrick Roche's plantation house and gardens. Apprehensive, Stewart instructed his subordinates to form a last-ditch defense on the house, squarely in the path of the Second Spartans.

The Patriot militia line fought with unprecedented discipline, going toe-to-toe with superior numbers of British infantry. Militia had seldom exhibited such abilities, and an astonished Greene later wrote to Inspector General Friedrich Steuben that "such conduct would have graced the veterans of the great King of Prussia." But the British artillery, exhaustion of their ammunition—seventeen rounds per man—and a British bayonet charge eventually forced the Patriot militia back.

Surprisingly, the battle in which the militiamen performed so far above expectations figures very little in memoirs. Simon Davis remembered only that ". . . there I saw more men slaughtered than I ever saw before or since. in the wing I was in the ground was almost covered with the dead and dying."[43]

Greene threw his main force of Continentals against the British, forcing Stewart to commit his reserve, and eventually pushing the enemy back toward last-ditch positions around the house and gardens. Despite a disastrous cavalry charge by Washington on the Patriot left, the British were driven back in disarray. Unfortunately the passage through the British camp disclosed its riches, and the Continentals stopped to plunder the liquor supplies. Their officers found themselves advancing on the house and gardens virtually alone, and were fired upon with devastating effect.

The British cavalry rallied and counterattacked, and the disorganized Patriot cavalry proved ineffective: the British swept through the confused Continentals in the camp. This was likely the point at which Colonel Washington was wounded and captured. Private John Cain of Jolly's battalion: "I can also recollect Col. Washington at that battle. I saw him taken prisoner by the British his horse was shot down in the old fields [as] they were called, and he was taken. General Pickens I recollect was wounded also in the breast, a ball the force of which was nearly spent struck him in the breast and lodged. I saw the ball taken out, but he did not fall off his horse."[44]

British infantry made a brief foray out of the positions around the house and gardens, capturing the unprotected Patriot artillery and recovering their own captured guns. Seeing victory slip away, Greene accepted the bitter pill and ordered a general withdrawal of seven miles.

James Hall had been wounded. "I well remember this day for I received a wound in my right wrist which destroyed the Joint and has left me a cripple to this day—orders came for all the wounded to go to the hospital in the high hills of Santee, but by the entreaties of my officers I was allowed to return home."[45]

Stewart executed a skillful withdrawal to link up with reinforcements, and the capture of the Patriot artillery was a point of prestige. Greene returned the next day to find Stewart gone and the dead unburied (usually a "prerogative" of the victor). A brief pursuit toward Charleston was futile.

Both sides could—and would—claim a tactical victory, but it was in fact another devastating strategic defeat for the British. They were forced to break or abandon some 1,000 muskets, and destroy considerable precious supplies. Patriot losses were much greater than the British, but Stewart's manpower losses were irreplaceable, including 500 prisoners, largely among the foraging party initially surprised.* The assumption of British superiority with the bayonet had proven false when they fled in the face of Continental bayonets.

---

*Modern sources vary considerably, with about 80–85 killed, 350 or so wounded, and nearly 700 captured or missing. See for example O'Kelley, *Nothing but Blood and Slaughter, Volume 3* (p. 342), and Savas and Dameron, *A Guide to the Battles of the American Revolution* (p. 328) for summaries.

Most importantly, the British were now firmly locked inside their self-managed prison at Charleston.

HAYES' STATION AND THE "BLOODY SCOUT," 19 NOVEMBER 1781

Bloody Bill Cunningham was one of the most embittered and recalcitrant Tories. Probably in retaliation for Governor Rutledge's ill-advised decree that all Tory families were to be evicted from the state and their property seized, and Whig partisans preying upon Tory families, Cunningham led about 300 Tories on one final spasm of violence. The Bloody Scout was a two-month rampage of often pointless mayhem, launched from Charleston. Sweeping through the region his men murdered individual Patriots, burned homes and property, and picked off small garrisons.

The residents of James Williams' Little River district had for years suffered the depredations of raiders from Ninety Six, and probably thought the war all but over. On 19 November 1781 Cunningham set the long-dead Williams' house and barns ablaze, thereby alerting the small garrison at Edgehill Station, an old two-story forted house. The Patriot garrison took refuge in the house until Cunningham's men set the roof ablaze, forcing surrender after Cunningham promised treatment as prisoners of war.

The garrison submitted to being tied, but Cunningham then ordered them hanged from a fodder pole (a vertical pole supporting a haystack). Fourteen-year-old Joseph Williams wailed, "Oh! brother Daniel, what shall I tell mother?" Cunningham replied, "You shall tell her nothing, you damned Rebel suckling!" Then he ran Joseph through with his sword. After Colonel Hayes and seventeen-year-old Daniel Williams were slowly strangled, the pole broke. In frustration Cunningham and his men set upon the others, hacking and stabbing; the enraged Cunningham hacked at the bodies until he collapsed from exhaustion. Sixteen were killed, some mutilated beyond recognition, and a dozen others left for dead.

On 7 December Cunningham and his men captured a convoy of wagons carrying corn to the Patriot army. The leader of the convoy was John Pickens, the youngest brother of General Andrew Pickens. Cunningham and fifty of his men went one way, while the rest of his men took their prisoners into the lower Cherokee towns. Colonel Robert Anderson tried to intercept the "Bloody Scout" and release the prisoners. He failed.

"The Cherokee scalped John Pickens and then burned him to death on a pile of light-wood while Cunningham's Tories watched with pleasure. A.L. Pickens wrote of the oft described stoic Andrew Pickens, 'General Pickens on learning of his brother's death was said to have wept like a child.'"[46] Other prisoners taken in the Bloody Scout were also turned over to the Cherokee to be tortured to death, for which the tribe would pay dearly.[47] Pickens made an immediate retaliatory raid on the town where his brother was killed, but the Cherokee had not seen the last of Pickens.

CHAPTER 17

FINIS IN THE SOUTH, 1782

Humanity has won its battle.
Liberty now has a country.
—MARQUIS DE LAFAYETTE

BY EARLY 1782 THE BRITISH CAUSE IN AMERICA WAS obviously lost.

After the Guilford Courthouse debacle Cornwallis had marched his decimated army to the port of Wilmington, North Carolina where they could be resupplied from the sea. Harassed by Patriot forces, he then turned north into Virginia, arriving with about 1500 men at Petersburg in late May of 1781. Far from victoriously "rolling up" the rebellion from the South, Cornwallis was now trying to survive.

In February of 1781 Washington had sent a Patriot force of some 1200 Continentals under the young French-born Major General the Marquis de Lafayette, joined by another 1200 French troops, to counter Benedict Arnold's British forces already in the state. British forces in Virginia, and a handful of reinforcements sent south by Sir Henry Clinton, swelled Cornwallis' force to some 7500 men. Through the summer months Lafayette shadowed Cornwallis as he marched and raided throughout eastern Virginia. With an army "not Strong enough even to get Beaten," Lafayette stubbornly declined to be cornered and destroyed, giving battle only when temporary advantages allowed. For Cornwallis the only bright spot was when the threat from one of Tarleton's raids drove the Virginia state government out of Charlottesville, and Governor Thomas Jefferson only narrowly avoided capture. Clinton's orders were ambiguous, but Cornwallis turned east toward the Chesapeake Bay and the perceived safety of the Royal Navy. On 1 August 1781 he took up a defensible position at York-town, on the peninsula formed by the James and York Rivers, with an out-lying position on Gloucester Point across the York.

Offshore the Royal Navy lost the Battle of the Virginia Capes to a French fleet on 5 September, severing Cornwallis' communications by sea. Sensing an opportunity, Lafayette proposed that Washington move the main Patriot army south, and French control of the sea allowed rapid trans-port of a large Franco-American force. By mid-September Washington arrived with over 17,000 American and French troops to bottle up Corn-wallis.

The brief siege of Yorktown resulted in the 19 October surrender of 8000 British and Hessian soldiers and sailors, 144 cannon, and 46 ships stranded in the rivers.

At the surrender ceremony British musicians played "The World Turned Upside Down." It truly was a turning point. The British Parliament had turned against the war, but like most wars it stubbornly refused to end.

In the far South, British and Loyalist forces remained penned into the coastal cities of Savannah and Charleston. A few British-held islands were used to graze cattle, but they ventured into the mainland countryside only to forage for food, fodder, and firewood. Major General Alexander Leslie, the garrison commander in Charleston, ordered many of the garrison's horses slaughtered for want of feed.

On 11 July the British evacuated Savannah, with Patriot forces slowly moving into the city to avoid fighting with the retreating British.

The problem of course was that the British garrison in Charleston still needed supplies. Nathanael Greene declined to let the British purchase food since he needed it for his own troops. British raids on coastal rice plantations and storage sites continued, with skirmishing between Patriot and British detachments.

Inland, a bitter cycle of reprisals was fought out as Whigs plundered Tory homes and Loyalists retaliated. Loyalist partisan leaders continued to launch retaliatory raids from the sanctuary at Charleston. Lieutenant Colo-nel Benjamin Thompson led the largest of these raids, plundering, seizing much-needed food, and attempting to assassinate Nathanael Greene.

Die-hard Loyalists had moved west into Cherokee territory, among them the much-wanted Thomas Waters. The Patriots had largely spent the summer months growing crops and rebuilding ravaged communities, but clearly something had to be done to stop the continual Cherokee raids fomented by the Tories. In mid-September Andrew Pickens decided to eliminate the threat once and for all, but was hampered by a severe shortage of ammunition, often as little as six rounds per man.

Few Tories were as persistently or nastily vengeful as Bloody Bill Cunningham. While the Patriots were preoccupied with the expedition against the Cherokee, Cunningham seized the opportunity to launch what was destined to be the last of his sorties from Charleston. As was his practice he split his raiders up into smaller parties with instructions where and when to rendezvous. The usual Patriot guard companies were left behind to deal with such a contingency, and Captain William Butler's company of the Lower 96th District Regiment set off in pursuit of Cunningham. Butler had served in the First Spartans, and his father had been killed by Cunningham's men. Taking a Cunningham relative hostage, they forced him to guide them to Bloody Bill's camp near Lorick's Ferry on the Saluda River.

Though surrounded, the Loyalists managed to scatter, closely pursued by the Patriots. Most of Cunningham's men were cornered against the river and either killed or captured, but he managed to escape by swimming his powerful horse to safety. Cunningham returned to the refuge of Charleston, but was never able to recruit another band of raiders.[1]

With the British eliminated, the Patriots now turned to eliminating the Cherokee threat, and the Loyalist exiles who had been urging the tribe to attack the frontier settlements. Compared to the bitter fighting of the previous Cherokee wars, the struggle was anti-climactic.

Like many militiamen, William Addington "Reenlisted a third time and received a commission under Capt Young, and received a commission as lieutenant, and marched the company as such and pursued the Indians through Georgia into N Carolina on the Tennessee River. Gen Pickens was chief in command. Benj. Jolly Major, Thos. Brandon Col. Killed three Indians in the Tennessee River and one white man, and took two Indians prisoner, and returned to S Carolina."[2]

Andrew Pickens marched into Cherokee territory at the head of a sizeable militia force, but with the intent to stop the continual spiral of reprisals let it be known that ". . . no Indian woman, child or old man, or any unfit to bear arms should be put to death on pain of death to the perpetrator. . . ." The expedition burned several towns.

After a skirmish near the Cherokee town of Sauta, a brave escaped by diving into a ravine with his rifle. Pickens' horsemen couldn't follow, and fired into the ravine to no avail. "A militiaman identified only as Parata, jumped into the ravine with his rifle and sword. He and the brave came within 30 yards of each other as they fired and dodged from tree to tree. The warrior charged and swung his rifle at Parata who parried with his saber and yelled 'Now, damn ye—it's my turn.'

"They continued to swing their weapons at each other. Finally, Parata sliced the brave's throat with his saber, and the Indian went down. Parata cursed with each blow as he decapitated the warrior. General Pickens said loudly, 'Parata acts like a fool.'

"Parata climbed out of the ravine with his own weapons and the brave's rifle and shot pouch. He haughtily said, 'General you 'lacked' [liked] to have lost the best soldier you have.'

"Andrew Pickens gave Parata a stern glar and turned away with a 'Huh!'"[3] After moving swiftly to capture one town Pickens released prisoners with a message: "I did not blame the Indians so much as the white men that were amongst them who encouraged them or assisted them in the war. . . ." Pickens let it be known that he would halt and give the tribes two days to release hostages and any seized slaves. Then he would ". . . destroy as many of their towns & as much of their provisions as possible & if they wished to fight they knew where to find me."[4]

But the Cherokee had by now had their fill of fighting.

At least one of Brandon's companies participated in the campaign and the memories are not quite so simple. Abel Kendrick recalled that, "In 1782 I was drafted for a twelve months tour against the Cher[okee] Indians, was under the command of Lieutenant Henley and [Lt.] Col. [Benjamin] Kilgore; at the end of said tour which was spent in marching from one Indian town to another, I returned home after suffering with hunger and fatigue excessively."[5]

Devastated by Pickens' punitive campaign, on 17 October a delegation of Cherokee chiefs led by *Tuksi* (Terrapin) met with Pickens and Elijah Clarke and agreed to a truce. One of the conditions was that the tribe would turn over specific Tories who had fled into the mountains; six were turned over as a gesture of good faith, but Thomas Waters fled the region.[6]

Since August the British had grown increasingly desperate for troops to oppose the French in the Caribbean. The British commander agreed not to destroy the city of Charleston or its facilities if Patriot forces allowed the British to depart unopposed. On 14 December 1782 the British evacuated Charleston. They took with them about 5,000 freedmen and slaves who had voluntarily come over to the British. Slaves captured from the rebels were considered seized property, and were returned to bondage.

The end of an official British presence in South Carolina by no means ended the fighting. Die-hard Loyalists continued the struggle, but they were now common criminals under the law. Like many, despite his crippled arm, Joseph McJunkin continued in action: ". . . after the British did leave Charleston the Tories at repeated times committed great depredations and I was out repeatedly—"[7]

In the end, the war in the South just subsided to a slow boil as each side grew increasingly weary of the bloodshed, or in the Tories' case just abandoned hope.

A final agreement with the Cherokee, the Treaty of Long Swamp Creek, was signed in May 1783 in Augusta. Georgia was the true beneficiary, as the Cherokee relinquished huge tracts of land between the Savannah and Chattahoochee Rivers, and it established the boundary between Georgia and Cherokee territories in modern Tennessee and North Carolina. The treaty is notable as the first one signed between a native tribe and the new United States.

Some tribesmen refused to acknowledge the treaty and would continue to resist white encroachment. Violence would flare up within the year. The most famous leader of resistance was the Cherokee war chief *Tsiyu Gansini* ("He who drags his canoe"), or Dragging Canoe to the whites. With his followers he moved west and south, and inspired future leaders like Sequoyah and the Shawnee Tecumseh, who would trigger the next war between the tribes and the United States, the Red Stick War of 1813–1814.[8]

Wars are notoriously easy to start and hard to end. Negotiations between the United States and its allies—France, Spain, and the Dutch Republic—and Britain commenced in April 1782. The Americans and British haggled over control of eastern Canada (one of Benjamin Franklin's goals), and the British finally prevailed. Britain returned Florida to Spain (but without a clear northern or western boundary), and Spain returned the Bahamas, Grenada, and Montserrat to Britain. More haggling ensued over details such as control of smaller islands, colonial trading privileges, and fishing rights. For the United States, key provisions were acknowledgement as an independent nation, establishment of the US—British North American (Canadian) border, free access to the Mississippi River shared with Britain, fishing rights in the rich Grand Banks waters, appropriate property restitution, and that the US Congress would "earnestly recommend" the restoration of the rights of Loyalists who chose to remain in the United States.

Needless to say, many of these agreements would never be honored. Domestic strife between Whigs and Loyalists continued, with the native tribes attacking both. The British stalled evacuation from what was now American territory in the Great Lakes region, and the European powers, particularly Spain, continued to jockey for position in North America. The stage was already being set for the next round of warfare.

The Treaty of Paris (actually a complex of inter-related treaties) was not ratified by all parties until 3 September 1783.[9] But the fighting never truly ended.

EPILOGUE

The American Revolution was a
beginning, not a consummation.
—WOODROW WILSON

THE WAR LEFT MARKS THAT HAD YET TO BE WASHED AWAY with blood. In a typical incident a Tory named Love was tried for murder; he had participated in a massacre during the Bloody Scout when prisoners were placed into a ring and hacked to bits; Love personally dispatched the wounded. When an innocent verdict was pronounced, based on the terms of a general amnesty, a contingent of Whigs marched into the courtroom, seized Love, and lynched him. The sheriff, ordered by the judge to quell the riot, replied, "It is more than my life or yours is worth to attempt it." Even the governor proved powerless to punish the killers.[1]

Many Loyalists pledged their allegiance to the new nation and quietly became model citizens. Some fled to British colonies in the West Indies, and many settled in Canada. Those with a bounty on their heads fled west to be absorbed into Indian tribes, or to British territories. Bloody Bill Cunningham went to Spanish Florida, only to be arrested when the British relinquished Florida in 1783; the Spanish recommended imprisonment in a mining (i.e. death) camp, but he was instead deported to Cuba. He sought restitution from the Crown for lost property; awarded only a pittance, he died in 1787 on Nassau.

Burnfoot Brown continued to stir up trouble among the Creeks from his exile in British Florida. Displaced again, to the Bahamas, Brown clashed with the Crown government, ironically over the lack of representative gov-

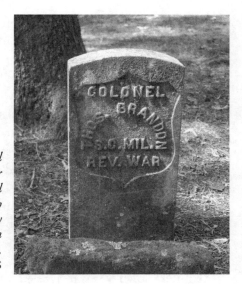

Following the Revolution, Colonel Thomas Brandon became a Brigadier General of Militia, served as a civil judge, and as a member of the South Carolina state legislature. With many others of his regiment, he was buried in the Old Union Cemetery near Union, South Carolina.—AUTHORS

ernment. He died a successful plantation owner on Saint Vincent in 1825.[2]

Joseph Hughes had seen too many of his family brutally killed, and simply continued killing those Tories he thought needed killing. In one judicial proceeding the judge inquired if a notorious Tory was indeed dead, and if so, when he died. Summoned to testify, Hughes stated that he was indeed dead, since he had shot him after the war. As an elderly man he moved to western Alabama, where by chance he encountered a tough old Tory refugee named Radcliff. Hughes' son-in-law grew alarmed when Hughes confronted Radcliff, who had a sizeable retinue of devoted slaves and Indians, saying, "I ran you, sir, from Chester District and nothing but an accident saved your life. I am a good mind to make way with you now. Hop about now, or I'll do it yet." Radcliff was "thoroughly cowed, and was annoyingly obsequious" for the duration of Hughes' stay.[3]

Thomas Brandon continued to occupy the Fair Forest Creek properties seized from Fletchall under "Sumter's Law." This controversial practice was repudiated by the State Legislature, Brandon lost ownership, and the property was up for auction. Brandon was the winner. Some have said it was because, given Brandon's reputation for violence, others were afraid to bid against him. An early news clipping said that "Fletchall had been very obnoxious, as a leading Kingsman, and the feeling among the citizens was—as it was in great degree owing to Gen. Brandon's energy and bravery—they were rid of Fletchall's presence, he should come into possession of the confiscated land, and no one bid against him at the sale." Brandon purchased several such properties, among them the Brown's Creek estate of dead Tory John Mayfield from Mayfield's son.

Brandon's violent reputation may be exaggerated. He went on to become a brigadier general of militia, Justice of the Court (essentially a Justice of the Peace, with petty criminal and civil jurisdiction), County Ordinary (administering probate of estates and guardianships, sometimes called the "orphans court"), and served in both houses of the State Legislature. He died in February 1802 at age sixty, and was buried with appropriate military honors alongside many former members of his regiment. His grave, and others, are now marked by simple stones in the Old Union Cemetery in Union, SC, placed by the Daughters of the American Revolution.[4]

Samuel Clowney was renowned for his Presbyterian piety and his dry wit. When his son (later Congressman) William Kennedy Clowney, was away at college he repeatedly wrote home for money, prompting his father to observe that "William Clowney will never scratch a rich man's head."[5]

William Kennedy, Sr., "industrious, intelligent, and devoutly pious," became a State Legislator and Elder of the Presbyterian Church, but never let a slight pass unanswered. "Grossly insulted" by a former Tory at the courthouse, he summoned one of his sons from home. "'Thomas,' said the old man, 'I want you to whip that rascal.' No sooner said than Thomas entered on the job and finished it up in good style to the satisfaction of the old man, not however, without suffering in the flesh himself . . ." since Thomas ended up with a prominent scar on his head.[6]

Thomas Young made good on his pledge of revenge. "He took prisoner and hung his brother's murderer within a few rods of where his brother was born. A few years ago, passing near the old soldier's house, I called to see him. Although trembling with the weight of years, he pointed to the tree upon which he hung the murderer of his brother, and his eyes grew brighter as he told the story." The wound suffered after Cowpens ". . . left a deep indentation in the skull . . . which, although it healed, at times gave him severe pain to the end of his life."[7]

For most of the militia veterans "the thanks of a grateful nation" was something they would never live to see. Most had not only fought a war for independence, but had paid for it from their own pockets. Robert Long: "Not expecting any advantage but Liberty for the above service has kept no memorandum of it save his memory." Some, like William Young, had lost everything for which they had worked and fought so long and hard: ". . . at the end of which peace was made when the this declarant found him self without either money or anything else but his hand & it occupied by a Tory as all the rest of his property had been taken by the Tories & put to their uses the Tory who had his land in possession was named Howell."[8]

Through a system of restitution the State of South Carolina reimbursed some men for loss of personal property like horses and saddles. Between 1789 and 1832 Congress passed a series of increasingly benevolent pension acts, and in 1806 granted pensions for service in the militia. The complex application process required arduous travel to appear before a magistrate, grilling in court depositions (many of which served as the basis for this work), presentation of long-lost commissions or discharge papers never issued in the chaos of war, assembling supporting statements from other veterans scattered across the country, and the patience of Job as the application wended its way through the bureaucracy. Many died during the course of the process. Others with years of documented service, like Abel Kendrick and James Collins, were arbitrarily denied pensions for reasons the modern researcher is unable to fathom.

Many of the militiamen moved south and west into Georgia, Tennessee, and the new Mississippi Territory—present-day Alabama and Mississippi—some to claim veterans' land grants. As restless as their ancestors, a few eventually settled as far west as Louisiana and Texas. As middle-aged men some fought again in the Red Stick War and The War of 1812.

Not content with having birthed a new nation, they were intent upon raising it to maturity.

APPENDIX A

THE MANY VERSIONS
OF COWPENS

THE PREPARATIONS ON THE NIGHT BEFORE THE BATTLE of
Cowpens were chaotic, final tactical dispositions were not made until the last
moment, the battle was short, and many of the participants recorded their
accounts years or even decades later. Historians have continued to parse these
written accounts, to overlay the attitudes and beliefs of their own eras (much
of it romanticized or hero-worshipful), and to examine events in excruciating
detail. The result is a variety of conflicting versions of this momentous battle.
Interestingly, one of the simplest descriptions was recorded two days after the
battle by Daniel Morgan.[1]

We have drawn upon Morgan's version of events using the sparse topographic detail to fix a known position: "The light infantry commanded by Lt.
Col. Howard, and the Virginia Militia under Major Triplett, were formed on
a rising ground," clearly the first low rise to the west of the Green River Road.
The initial dispositions of Morgan's other troops were then described in terms
of relative direction and distance (specified in paces, usually defined as about
30 inches) from this main formation. Morgan's description is relatively simple,
describing a sort of V with the open end toward the advancing British. Morgan, however, placed Brandon ("Brannon") and Thomas's South Carolina militia on the extreme right, in contradiction of the men in the units.

This simple disposition would at first have masked the fire of Howard's
Continentals, not a significant issue given the short effective range of their
muskets. It would also have helped accomplish Morgan's tactical goal. Morgan
had commanded both militia and Continentals and knew that the militia
would not stand to face British bayonets. Their retreat would goad the British
into a headlong pursuit and disrupt their unit cohesion as they struck
Howard's more steadfast Continentals and Virginia militia.

Certain aspects of Morgan's description ring quite true, in that he
described retiring ". . . in good order, about fifty paces, formed and advanced
on the enemy and gave them a brisk fire, which threw them into disorder."
This would accord with accounts that described the British infantry advancing

blindly in disorganized pursuit, only to be confronted by withering volleys from Howard's troops on a reverse slope.

Morgan also does not describe the complex battle of movement and encirclement described by many subsequent authors. His description suggested a simpler folding in of the extended Patriot wings and attack by Patriot cavalry from the flanks and rear to encircle the British, very much like the Carthaginian tactics at Cannae (216 B.C.).

In his later years Samuel Hammond provided two contradictory sketch maps of the dispositions at Cowpens. The first and more complex map was drawn up as a preliminary based on oral orders promulgated by Morgan on the night before the battle; it does not from Hammond's own description represent dispositions during the fight. The second, labeled "Second View of the Two Armies After the Retreat of the American Militia," depicts, like Morgan's description, a simpler tactical disposition. Like Morgan, Hammond depicts a fairly orthodox situation, with the British arrayed in a linear formation astride the Green River Road, MacArthur's 71st Regiment of Foot committed on the British left, "Tarleton's charge" (presumably the 17th Light Dragoons) confronting Washington's cavalry on the British right, and a "horse reserve" (Legion dragoons) to the left rear. The American line is extended to overlap both British flanks, with Washington's dragoons in a position to sweep into the British right flank and rear.[2]

Hammond's second map is also suggestive of Cannae. It indicates that the British front was relatively narrow, perhaps drawn in when units closed up as the result of heavy casualties, or perhaps as part of Tarleton's intention to crush the Patriot center. In either case the Patriot forces are poised to close the flanking wings and execute an encirclement, with cavalry ready to push into the British rear. This map is in accord with the remembrances of the men in Pickens' brigade (including Brandon's command) since it depicts the brigade on the extreme Patriot left confronting the British 17th Light Dragoons.

Two additional maps are preserved, the so-called "Pigree map" and the "Clove map." Who drafted the maps and when are unclear; a cover letter associated with the Clove map was dated 15 February 1781, was written by a Major of Engineers, and dealt primarily with construction of a blockhouse. The associated name appears to be spelled "Colonel Pigree Quarter M. Gene [missing]" on that map, and clearly "Colonel Pigrin" on the Clove map.[3]

The Clove map is a barely legible graphic depiction of Morgan's written account. The Pigree/Pigrin map is a more detailed representation of the course of battle which depicts the skirmishers falling back into the second or militia line, and the militia line in turn withdrawing to the flanks of the Continentals. The slight topographic rise is apparently depicted as a set of crude hachures. Again the position of many units is inconsistent with those in participants' accounts, for us most notably showing "Col. Brannon" on the Patriot extreme right.

In the early nineteenth century, maps of the battle grew ever more fanciful, with one well-known map depicting the Patriot position with its rear and left (eastern) flank against the Broad River (the river is 5 miles away, to the north).[4]

In more recent years useful analyses involved efforts such as the Army Command and General Staff College's battlefield staff ride.[5]

More recent historians have based analyses of the battle on the older sources, and incorporated additional detail from sources like pension records to elaborate upon the simplistic period accounts of the senior officers.[6]

For Cowpens the definitive example of rigorous battlefield analysis is the work of Lawrence Babits. An historian with military experience and a background as a military re-enactor, Babits undertook a more rigorous and in part mathematical analysis that emphasized viewing the battle in terms of established eighteenth-century military drill and procedures.[7]

The inherent problem in this approach is that as George Patton and many others have pointed out, "Battle is an orgy of disorder." Eighteenth-century drill was an effort to impose order upon chaos, where individual men stumbled over the dead and wounded, fumbled the complex reloading procedure, were paralyzed, or fled in panic. The more disciplined infantry of the American Civil War, or even the red-coated long-service British infantry of the late Victorian era (probably the most battle-hardened and rigorously-disciplined "old sweats" the modern world has seen), using reliable breech-loading Martini-Henry rifles, could not maintain consistent volley fire for more than a few minutes of intense combat.

To expect the militia, with no formal drill, at best ill-disciplined, and using an astonishingly motley assortment of weapons, to have executed highly-disciplined rotating volley fire by battalions is unrealistic, so formulaic analysis of the militia's actions is unrealistic. We have also interpreted specific incidents differently in light of the militia's typical behaviors, and personal accounts.

All such minor differences aside, Babits provides the best framework for understanding this complex battle.

ENDNOTES

CHAPTER 2

1   Robert Long FPA S7157.
2   Leyburn, *The Scotch-Irish: A Social History*, p. 32-33. Originally founded as Charles Town, by the time of the Revolution the spelling had evolved to Charlestown, and by the early nineteenth century to the modern spelling of Charleston. By the time some veterans filed pension claims, the Charleston spelling was in common use. Hereafter the modern spelling is used except in direct quotation of period documents.
3   http://www.ancestryireland.com/irish-presbyterianism/presbyterian-ancestors/seceders-non-subscribers-and-covenanters/
4   Leyburn, *Scotch-Irish: A Social History*, p. 143–148.
5   Frazer, *The Steel Bonnets*, p. 4.
6   Durham, *Border Reiver: 1513–1603* p. 6.
7   Leyburn, *The Scotch-Irish: A Social History*, p. 32-33.
8   Durham, *Border Reiver 1513–1603*, p. 7.
9   Durham, *The Border Reivers*, p. 13.
10   Ibid, p. 13.
11   Ibid, p. 7.
12   Ibid, p. 33.
13   Leyburn, *The Scotch-Irish: A Social History*, p. 32–33.
14   Blethen and Wood, *From Ulster to Carolina*, p. 6.
15   Ibid, p. 6.
16   http://www.bbc.co.uk/history/british/plantation/planters/es10.shtml
17   http://en.wikipedia.org/wiki/Battle_of_the_Boyne
18   Leyburn, *The Scotch-Irish: A Social History*, p. 158–175.

CHAPTER 3

1   Howe, *The Scotch-Irish and Their First Settlements on the Tyger River and Other Neighboring Precincts in South Carolina: A Centennial Discourse delivered at Nazareth Church, Spartanburg District, South Carolina September 14, 1861*, p. 12.
2   Leyburn, *The Scotch Irish*, p. 216-217.
3   Saye, *The Memoirs of Major Joseph McJunkin*, p. 2; Howe, *The Scotch-Irish and Their First Settlements on the Tyger River*, p. 12.
4   Draper, *Kings Mountain*, p. 479.
5   Webb, *The Centenary of Catholicity in Kentucky*, p. 21.
6   Bass, *Ninety Six*, p. 25.

7   Hooker, *The South Carolina Back Country on the Eve of the Revolution*, Locations 759, 775, and 1097 in e-book edition.

8   Ibid, Location 1062.

9   There is no clear published description of the Cherokee concept of balance; the best exposition is presented in displays at the Museum of the Cherokee in Cherokee N.C.

10 Bass, *Ninety Six*, p. 42.

11 *South Carolina Newspapers: The South Carolina Gazette 1760, No. 1330*, p. 7.

12 Bass, *Ninety Six*, p. 45.

13 *South Carolina Newspapers: The South Carolina Gazette 1760, No. 1330*, p. 66. Fort William Henry appears to be a reference to Edward Musgrove's Fort on the Enoree, later renamed in honor of Governor William Henry Lyttleton.; see http://www.northamericanforts.com/East/sc-north.html#ott

14 R.L. Gage, *Revolutionary Incidents IV, Christopher Brandon*.

15 Bass, *Ninety Six*, p. 48.

16 *South Carolina Newspapers: The South Carolina Gazette*, p. 49.

17 Edgar, *Partisans & Redcoats*, p. xii.

18 Richard J. Hooker, *The South Carolina Back Country on the Eve of The Revolution*, Location 3255 of 6151 of e-book edition.

19 Ibid, Location 730 of 6151 of e-book edition.

20 Edgar, *Partisans and Redcoats*, p. 14.

21 Richard J. Hooker, *The South Carolina Back Country on the Eve of the Revolution*, e-book location 4116.

22 "Coffell" is the name found in Hooker and Scoggins' work, but Schofield is the name of the commander cited by Bass. Early in the Revolution Tories were called Schofieldites or Scoffolites. At least one family history notes a Loyalist Colonel Coffel said to be the son of a Schofield.

CHAPTER 4

1   Walter Edgar, *Partisans and Redcoats*, p. 27.

2   John Drayton, *Memoirs of the American Revolution From Its Commencement To The Year 1776*, p. 194.

3   John Drayton, *Memoirs*, p. 216–217.

4   It certainly might be argued that these penalties were often not enforced in areas of any given colony with a large Loyalist population.

5   John Drayton, *Memoirs*, p. 286.

6   Ibid, p. 256.

7   John Buchanan, *The Road to Guilford Courthouse*, p. 92.

8   Ibid, p. 92.

9   Robert Bass, *Ninety Six*, p. 81–82.

10 John Drayton, *Memoirs*, p. 311–313.

11 John S. Pancake, *This Destructive War*, p. 74.

12 John Buchanan, *The Road to Guilford Courthouse*, p. 96–97.
13 James H. Saye, *Memoirs of Major Joseph McJunkin*, p. 5.
14 John Landrum, *Colonial and Revolutionary History of the Upper Country of South Carolina*, p. 52.
15 John Buchanan, *The Road to Guilford Courthouse*, p. 98.
16 Matthew Patton FPA S18153.

CHAPTER 5
1   William Kenedy FPA S2695.
2   Gordon, *South Carolina and the American Revolution*, p. 37.
3   Ibid, p. 47.
4   Drayton, Memoirs of the American Revolution. . . ,Vol. II, p. 332.
5   Charles Brandon FPA S3086.
6   Dean, *A Demand of Blood*, Location 1885.
7   Ibid.
8   Saye, *Memoirs of Major Joseph McJunkin*, p. 6-7.
9   The Hannon story is found with slight variations in a number of sources: see also http://boards.ancestry.com/surnames.hannon/88/mb.ashx ; for a more balanced look at both sides of the issue see http://hendersonheritage.com/early-county-formations-and-revolutionary-war/
10 See Hoeft Family website, http://www.genealogy.com/ftm/h/o/e/Kim-M-Hoeft/WEBSITE-0001/UHP-0909.html
11 Landrum, *Colonial and Revolutionary History of Upper South Carolina*, p. 87.
12 See York County Library Digital Collections, https://dspace.ychistory.org/bitstream/handle/11030/69958/00000601.pdf?sequence=1
13 There are many versions of stories relating to the fate of the Hampton family. A summary of some stories along with information regarding the probable location of the Hampton home is found at http://gaz.jrshelby.com/hampton-massacre.htm; see also Bass, *Ninety Six*, p. 135, and the York County Digital link listed above provides newspaper articles/reprints dealing with the Hampton family.
14 Landrum, *Colonial and Revolutionary History of Upper South Carolina*, p. 97.
15 Drayton, Memoirs of the American Revolution..., Vol. II, p. 366.
16 Wayne Lynch, *Captain McCall & Alexander Cameron in the Cherokee War*, Journal of the American Revolution, April 22, 2013, available online at http://all thingsliberty.com/2013/04/captain-mccall-and-alexander-cameron-in-the-cherokee-war/
17 Bass, *Ninety Six*, p. 135.
18 Drayton, Memoirs of the American Revolution..., Vol. II, p. 366.
19 Reynolds, *Andrew Pickens: South Carolina Patriot in the Revolutionary War*, p. 68.
20 Drayton, Memoirs of the American Revolution..., Vol. II, p. 354.
21 Samuel Otterson FPA S25344.

22 James Hall FPA W25471. In Hall's pension record he names Thomas Brandon as his captain on this campaign. It seems more probable that he forgot whether Brandon or Jolly was captain, as Joseph McJunkin and Samuel Otterson name Brandon as a major in this campaign, and he is designated as a major in the *Journal of Arthur Faries*. Jolly apparently succeeded Brandon as captain of his company.

23 O'Neal, *Revolutionary Incidents,* unpaginated.

24 Drayton, Memoirs of the American Revolution…, Vol. II, p. 351.

25 Drayton, *Memoirs of the American Revolution…*, Vol. II, p. 352.

26 O'Kelley, Patrick, "Rebuttal: The Patriot View of the Cherokee Indian Campaign of 1776, p. 58, in southerncampagn.org magazine, Volume 5, No. 1, 2008. http://southerncampaign.orgJudge then, what feelings such a man must be possessed of; who, in the place of hatenting to save and revenge his country, can content himself with doing nothing. Vol 5, No. 1, pdf, p. 58.

27 Gordon, *South Carolina and the American Revolution*, p. 52–53; Bass, *Ninety Six*, p. 137.

28 Drayton, *Memoirs of the American Revolution*, Vol. II, p. 368.

29 Samuel Otterson FPA 25345.

30 William Young FPA S4742. William Young was born in Pennsylvania, and apparently a son of Thomas Young, Sr. by his first wife. Young's second wife, Catherine, was the sister of Thomas Brandon and the mother of Major Thomas Young.

31 Joseph Hughes FPA S31764.

32 William Young FPA S4742.

33 See battle site maps at http://gaz.jrshelby.com/coweechee.htm; Bass, *Ninety Six,* p. 141–142.

34 O'Neal, *Memoir of Major Joseph M'Junkin, The Magnolia, or Southern Apalachian*, Vol. II, No. 1 (Jan. 1843).

35 Drayton, *Memoirs of the American Revolution, Vol. II*, p. 365–356.

36 Joshua Palmer FPA S2192; William Young FPA S4742; Joseph Hughes FPA S31764.

37 Joseph McJunkin FPA S118.

38 Wayne Lynch, *Captain McCall & Alexander Cameron in the Cherokee War*, Journal of the American Revolution, April 22, 2013, available online at http://allthingsliberty.com/2013/04/captain-mccall-and-alexander-cameron-in-the-cherokee-war/

39 O'Neall, *Memoir of Joseph M'Junkin of Union. The Magnolia, or Southern Apalachian*, Vol. II, No. 1 (Jan. 1843).

40 James McCracken FPA W4716.

41 Robert Bass, *Ninety Six*, p. 147–149.

42 Joseph Hughes, FPA S31764.

43 Logan, *A History of the Upper Country of South Carolina, Vol. II*, p. 2.

44 William Beard FPA 2981.
45 Samuel Otterson FPA 25345.
46 Joseph McJunkin FPA S18118.
47 John Jolly FPA W9276.

CHAPTER 6

1   Bass, *Ninety Six*, p. 154.
2   Logan, *A History of the Upper Country of South Carolina, Vol. II*, p. 2.
3   There was a Cherokee Ford on the Broad River in South Carolina, but there was also a Cherokee Ford on the Savannah.
4   Thomas Davis FPA S1509.
5   Bass, *Ninety Six*, p. 163.
6   Mayfield Crane FPA S30356.
7   Matthew Patton FPA S18153.
8   Gordon, *South Carolina and the American Revolution*, p. 68.
9   Gordon, *Ibid*, p. 68.
10 Simon Davis FPA S6784.
11 Aaron Guyton FPA W21237; Simon Davis FPA S6784; Matthew Patton FPA S18153; William Kelly FPA W7.
12 Joseph Hughes FPA S31764.
13 Unless otherwise noted the general framework of the 1779 Savannah Campaign is from Wallace, *The American Revolution in the Southern Colonies*, p. 110–125.
14 Samuel Mayes FPA W2140.
15 Abel Kendrick FPA R5861; William Young FPA S4742.
16 Johnson, *Traditions and Reminiscences*, p. 288.
17 Undated letter "Major L.T. Sims Traditions of Union District," Draper, *Manuscript Collection*, 15VV, p. 218–219.
18 Shadrach Gibbs FPA S10740.
19 Samuel Mayfield FPA S16930.
20 Abel Kendrick FPA R5861; Lewis Turner FPA W11667; Samuel Mayfield FPA S16930; William Young FPA S4742.
21 John Jeffries Narrative, in Draper, *ManuscriptCollection*, 23VV, p. 254–258.
22 Mahlon Pierce FPA S3663.
23 John Jeffries Narrative, in Draper, *Manuscript Collection*, 23VV, p. 254–258.
24 Henry Deshasure FPA S16362. The inconsistency of spelling Brandon's name is typical. The various clerks who recorded Deshasure's depositions spelled Henry's name in three different ways.

CHAPTER 7

1   A lengthy description of the siege, its precursors and aftermath, are provided in Johnson, *Traditions and Reminiscences*, p. 246–279.
2   Johnson, *Traditions and Reminiscenses*, p. 251–252, provides details such as British

use of booby-trapped incendiary carcasses, and the city's fire-fighting efforts.

3   Joseph Hughes FPA S31764.

4   Matthew Patton FPA S18153.

5   The following summary is based primarily on a talk by Jim Piecuch at the 2013 Bobby Moss Symposium. See also Piecuch, *Three Peoples, One King.*

6   Tarleton, *A History of the Campaigns of 1780 and 1781*, p. 30–31.

7   For a version more sympathetic to Tarleton, see Piecuch, *Massacre or Myth? Banastre Tarleton at the Waxhaws, May 29, 1780.*

8   Johnson, *Traditions and Reminiscenses*, p. 265–268, quotation and italics by Johnson.

9   Saye, *Memoirs of Major Joseph McJunkin*, p. 10–11.

10 Saye, Memoirs of Major Joseph McJunkin, p. 11.

11 Gage, *Memoir of Major Thomas Young*, p. 2.

12 See for example http://gaz.jrshelby.com/brandonsdefeat.htm; Aaron Guyton FPA W21237.

13 Including Richard Addis FPA S1594.

14 Samuel Otterson FPA S25344; Aaron Guyton FPA W21237; Saye, *Memoirs of Major Joseph McJunkin*, p. 11.

15 Saye, *Memoirs of Major Joseph McJunkin*, p. 11; Gage, *Memoir of Major Thomas Young*, p. 2.

16 Saye, *Memoirs of Major Joseph McJunkin*, p. 11; Aaron Guyton FPA W21237.

17 Draper, *Manuscript Collection*, VV23, p. 256.

18 Draper, *Manuscript Collection*, 23VV 266; Saye, *Memoirs of Major Joseph McJunkin*, p. 11.

19 Logan, *A History of the Upper Country of South Carolina, from the Earliest Periods to the Close of the War of Independenclettere, Volume II*, p. 40.

20 William Sims letter in Draper, *Manuscript Collection*, 22VV, p. 266–267; *S. T. Sims, Traditions of Union District*, p. 220–225.

21 Joseph Hughes FPA S31764.

22 Angelica Mitchell Nott, *Traditions of the Revolutionary War*, in Draper, *Manuscript Collection*, 23VV, p. 269.

23 Gage, *Memoir of Major Thomas Young*, p. 12; Christopher Brandon FPA S9288.

24 Gage, *Revolutionary Incidents IV Christopher Brandon*, p. 382; Christopher Brandon FPA S9288.

25 Baxley, *Battle of Mobley's Meeting House*, p. 25.

26 William Kenedy FPA S2695.

27 Saye, *Memoirs of Major Joseph McJunkin*, p. 11–12.

28 Joseph McJunkin FPA S18118, S25344; the pension statements of Joseph Hughes FPA S31764, and Samuel Otterson S25344 corroborate the McJunkin account.

29 Aaron Guyton FPA W21237.

30 John Jefries narrative in Draper, *Manuscript Collection*, 23VV, p. 254-258.

31 Angelica Mitchell Nott, *Traditions of the Revolutionary War,* in Draper, *Manuscript Collection,* 23VV, p. 267–271.

32 Draper, *Manuscript Collection,* 1DD, p. 130–132; apparently a transcript of a newspaper article written by Samuel Hammond's son Abner for the *Charleston Courier* over the period 1858–1860.

33 Angelica Mitchell Nott, *Traditions of the Revolutionary War,* in Draper, *Manuscript Collection,* 23VV, p. 269. Waters account from O'Neall, *The Annals of Newberry,* p. 182–183; retold in other accounts including Lewis, *Miss Ann Kennedy.*

34 Collins, *Autobiography of a Revolutionary Soldier,* p. 41.

35 Logan, *A History of the Upper Country of South Carolina, from the Earliest Periods to the Close of the War of Independence, Volume II,* p. 41; this version also appears verbatim in Undated letter "Major L.T. Sims Traditions of Union District," Draper, *Manuscript Collection,* 15VV, p. 233.

36 For a sympathetic portrayal of Huck, see http://home.golden.net/~marg/bansite/friends/huck.html.

37 Jones, *The Theological, Philosophical and Miscellaneous Works of the Rev. William Jones,* p. 356; Ellet, *Women of the American Revolution Volume III,* p. 179. For an analysis of the war as a religious conflict see http://allthingsliberty.com/2013/09/presbyterian-rebellion/

38 Ellet, *Women of the American Revolution Volume III,* p. 225–226 (Strong), 218–219 (Simpson).

39 Union County Historical Foundation, *A History of Union County,* p. 73.

40 Joseph Hughes FPA 31764; Samuel Otterson FPA S25344.

41 Saye, *Memoirs of Major Joseph McJunkin,* p. 13; Saye, *Revolutionary Reminiscenses Related by Major Thomas Young.*

42 Draper, *Revolutionary Reminiscences related by Christopher Brandon, Manuscript Collection,* p. 233.

43 Gage, R. J., *Memoir of Major Thomas Young,* p. 10.

44 Draper, *Revolutionary Reminiscences related by Christopher Brandon, Manuscript Collection,* p. 233.

45 Saye, *Revolutionary Reminiscenses Related by Major Thomas Young;* Gage, *Memoir of Major Thomas Young,* p. 10.

46 Gage, *Revolutionary Incidents IV Christopher Brandon, of Union District, S. C.,* p. 382; Saye, *Revolutionary Reminiscences related by Christopher Brandon,* p. 233.

47 Gage, *Revolutionary Incidents IV Christopher Brandon, of Union District, S. C.,* p. 382–383.

48 Scoggins, *The Battle of Stallions' Plantation,* p. 1.

49 Draper, *Revolutionary Reminiscences related by Christopher Brandon.*

50 Scoggins, *The Battle of Stallions' Plantation* provided a summary of several accounts and their discrepancies, such as placing the battle either late at night or near dawn. Scoggins included a lengthy and seemingly detailed account recited by Christopher Brandon and preserved by Draper, which illustrates why Draper

should not be considered a "primary source." Detailed reading of Draper's papers indicates a complex story. Congressman Daniel Wallace was ill for a protracted period, so his elderly neighbor—Brandon—sat with him, entertaining him with stories. Wallace later wrote down these tales from memory, garbling many details, such as calling Stallings "Patterson." He was writing to the historical fiction author William Gilmore Simms, and forthrightly described how many of these tales would make good fictional plot elements. In 1871 Draper hand copied the letter, adding his annotations of recognized errors. The copy of Wallace's letter, with Draper's annotations, is in Draper, 16VV p. 197–198.

51 The quotations from Young are from Gage, *Memoir of Major Thomas Young*.
52 The quotations by Brandon are from Gage, *Revolutionary Incidents IV. Christopher Brandon,* p. 382–383.
53 Lemuel Carroll interview by Draper nearly a century later, Draper, *Manuscript Collection,* 16VV p. 70–71, as quoted by Scoggins, *The Battle of Stallions' Plantation,* p. 5.
54 Lemuel Carroll interview, Draper, *Manuscript Collection,* 16VV p. 70–71; see Scoggins, *The Battle of Stallions' Plantation,* p. 5.
55 Lewis, *The Olden Times*; Lewis, *Miss Ann Kennedy.*
56 Gage, *Revolutionary Incidents IV. Christopher Brandon,* p. 382–383. Note that Thomas Young, who at the time of his interview was quite aged, reversed the sequence of events placing Reid/Reed's death after the Stallions fight.
57 Lemuel Carroll interview, Draper, *Manuscript Collection,*16VV p. 70–71; see Scoggins, *The Battle of Stallions' Plantation,* p. 5.
58 Saye, *Revolutionary Reminiscences related by Christopher Brandon.*
59 Wallace, *Incidents of the Revolution,* p. 187–188.

CHAPTER 8

1 O'Neall, *Memoir of Joseph McJunkin,* p. 9.
2 The general outline Huck's ill-fated campaign, unless otherwise noted, is from Edgar, *Partisans and Redcoats,* and the much more detailed Scoggins, *The Day It Rained Militia.*
3 Collins, *Autobiography of a Revolutionary Soldier,* p. 24; Saye, *Memoirs of Major Joseph McJunkin,* p. 13.
4 There are numerous sources for Huck's comments as part of local lore; see Edgar, *Partisans and Redcoats,* p. 73–74, or Bailey, *Commanders at Kings Mountain,* p. 203.
5 Collins, *Autobiography of a Revolutionary Soldier,* p. 24–25.
6 Saye, *Memoirs of Major Joseph McJunkin,* p. 14.
7 Lewis, *The Olden Times.*
8 Ibid; also Lewis, *Miss Ann Kennedy.*
9 Unless otherwise noted, the following account is derived from Scoggins, *The Day It Rained Militia,* p. 102–122.

10 Ellet, *Women of the American Revolution, Volume I*, p. 242–243.

11 Collins, *Autobiography of a Revolutionary Soldier*, p. 26.

12 Jacob Brown, FPA W333.

13 Joseph McJunkin, FPA S18118.

14 Samuel Otterson FPA S25344.

15 Saye, *Memoirs of Major Joseph McJunkin*, p. 14; O'Neall, *Memoir of Joseph McJunkin of Union*, p. 7.

16 The following account is from Salley, *Col. William Hill's Memoirs of the Revolution*, p. 11–12.

17 Letter dated 9 August 1780, Clark, *State Records of North Carolina, Volume 14*, p. 540.

18 O'Neall, *Memoir of Joseph McJunkin of Union*, p. 8.

19 Joseph McJunkin, FPA S18118.

20 O'Neall, *Memoir of Joseph McJunkin of Union*, p. 8.

21 Ibid; also John Adair FPA W2895 as quoted in Scoggins, *The Day It Rained Militia*, p. 162.

22 Pancake, *This Destructive War*, p. 97; Sumter quote from letter dated 9 August 1780, Clark, *State Records of North Carolina, Volume 14*, p. 541.

23 Tarleton, *A History of the Campaigns of 1780 and 1781*, p. 94–95.

24 Letter dated 9 August 1780, Clark, *State Records of North Carolina, Volume 14*, p. 541.

25 Jacob Brown FPA 333.

26 Saye, *Memoirs of Major Joseph McJunkin*, p. 14.

27 Jacob Brown, FPA W333.

28 Gordon, *South Carolina and the American Revolution*, p. 91.

29 Gates and his political machinations have been the subject of numerous studies; for a brief introduction see http://en.wikipedia.org/wiki/Horatio_Gates

30 Clark, *State Records of North Carolina, Volume 14*, p. 550, 553.

31 Saye, *Memoirs of Major Joseph McJunkin*, p. 14–15.

32 William Smith FPA W22272.

33 Salley, *Colonel William Hill's Memoir*, p. 16.

34 Moore, *The Life of Gen. Edward Lacey*.

35 Johnson, *Traditions and Reminiscences*, p. 519. Inexplicably, Draper in *King's Mountain and Its Heroes* said that Samuel Hammond's account of Musgrove's Mill is fraudulent. An interesting account of Draper's use or misuse of sources, and his bias against Hammond, can be found at http://archive.org/stream/musgrovemillhisto1unse/musgrovemillhisto1unse_djvu.txt, in Appendix C, p. 82

36 Johnson, *Traditions and Reminiscences*, p. 519.

37 Buchanan, *The Road to Guilford Courthouse*, p. 141

38 Bailey Anderson FPA S30826; Joseph Hughes FPA S31764; William Kenedy FPA S2695 (Kenedy's captain would have been Benjamin Jolly; Joseph Hughes took command of this company for the first time at Cow pens); Joseph McJun-

kin FPA S18118.

39 The date of the Battle of Musgrove's Mill has been disputed, and Williams' report added to the confusion as he states that they marched from the Broad River on 17 August, but that the Tories were reinforced on the night of the 18th. See Graves, *Backcountry Revolutionary*, p. 196. Samuel Hammond recalled that their group left McDowell on the 16th. See Johnson, Traditions and Reminiscences, p. 519. Joseph McJunkin FPA S18118, weighs in with another date, 20 August.

40 Johnson, *Traditions and Reminiscences*, p. 519.

41 Graves, *Backcountry Revolutionary*, p. 197.

42 Johnson, *Traditions and Reminiscences*, p. 520.

43 Ibid, p. 521.

44 Ibid, p. 521.

45 The Indian halloo later became known as the "Rebel Yell." To get an idea of what it sounded like, go to http://www.smithsonianmag.com/videos/category/3play_1/what-did-the-rebel-yell-sound-like/

46 Draper, *King's Mountain*, pp. 110–111. There is some question as to whether Brandon or his Lieutenant Colonel, James Steen, egged Tinsley on.

47 Edward Doyle FPA S2216.

48 Graves, *Backcountry Revolutionary*, p. 197.

49 Hiatt, *Musgrove's Mill Historic Site, Historic Resource Study*, Appendix C, p. 82. Apparently Draper discounted Hammond's account of the battle, because he found it unlikely that word of both Gates' and Sumter's defeats could have arrived at one time.

50 Johnson, *Traditions and Reminiscences*, p. 522.

51 The following account is from Collins, *Autobiography of a Revolutionary Soldier*, p. 41–47.

52 Tarleton, *A History of the Campaigns of 1780 and 1781*, p. 115.

53 A detailed account of the siege is Rauch, *An Ill-timed and Premature Insurrection—The First Siege at Augusta, Georgia September 14–18, 1780*, p. 1–18.

54 McCall, *History of Georgia*, p. 486.

55 For a more detailed account see Scoggins, *The Battles of Stallions' Plantation and Bigger's Ferry*, p. 13–16.

56 Collins, *Autobiography of a Revolutionary Soldier*, p. 49.

CHAPTER 9

1 Roosevelt, *The Winning of the West, Volume II, From the Alleghenies to the Mississippi 1777–1783*, location 8296 to 8303 in the e-book version. Roosevelt's work provides a few interesting insights. He correctly assessed the weaknesses of the ill-disciplined militia, but attributed the King's Mountain victory almost entirely to the "horse-riflemen" from west of the mountains, and his assertion that the weaker men of the eastern lowlands were predominantly Tory, is demonstrably false.

2   Dunkerly, *The Battle of King's Mountain*, p. 98–122.

3   Draper, *King's Mountain*, p. 591–593.

4   Graves, *Backcountry Revolutionary*.

5   Draper, *King's Mountain*, p. 277; Park Service placards see Graves, *Backcountry Revolutionary*, p. 6–7.

6   Draper, *King's Mountain*, p. 522. The source for Graves' mention of the letter to Gates is unclear; see Graves, *James Williams*, p. 41. Graves does however give a good explanation of how and why militia numbers were often exaggerated.

7   Graves, *Backcountry Revolutionary*, p. 7–8.

8   Draper, *King's Mountain*, p. 270 attributes this to "Narrative of Major Thomas Young, drawn up by Col. R. J. Gage, of Union County, and published in the *Orion* magazine, Oct. 1843." Authors' version—from a transcript provided by Michael Scoggins—is subtly different in wording, and is attributed to R. J. G., *Memoir of Major Thomas Young, A Revolutionary Patriot of South Carolina, Part 2*.

9   Allaire, *Diary*, p. 506 -507 in Draper, *King's Mountain*.

10 For a brief summary of Ferguson's career, see http://en.wikipedia.org/wiki/Patrick_Fergusan, and more detail in Buchanan, *The Road To Guilford Courthouse*, p. 194–202.

11 Roosevelt, *The Winning of the West, Volume II, From the Alleghenies to the Mississippi 1777–1783*, location 7727 in the e-book version. Roosevelt does not provide documentation, but his analysis is consistent with local folklore, and the fact that Ferguson was well-enough regarded that his American foes later erected a large monument at his burial site.

12 For analysis of Cornwallis' growing disenchantment with Ferguson and the militia in general, see Bass, *Ninety Six*, p. 225, and Buchanan, *The Road To Guilford Courthouse*, p. 195.

13 Ross, *Correspondence of Charles, First Marquis Cornwallis, Volume 1*, p. 58–59.

14 Small detachments were also at Thicketty Fort, Wofford's Ironworks, and on the Pacolet River, Draper, *King's Mountain*, p. 169.

15 Ibid; Draper cites several older sources. Buchanan, *The Road To Guilford Courthouse*, p. 208 gives the name as Phillips but we have used Draper's original spelling.

16 See for example Draper, *King's Mountain*, p. 295; Roosevelt, *The Winning of the West, Volume II*, location 7830.

17 Buchanan, *The Road To Guilford Courthouse*, p. 208; Roosevelt, *The Winning of the West, Volume II*, location 7853.

18 Draper, *King's Mountain*, p. 176.

19 Ibid, p. 348.

20 Shelby, *Battle of King's Mountain* ("Gov. Shelby's Pamphlet"), reproduced in Draper, *King's Mountain*, p. 564. This part appears factual, but in some matters the reader should bear in mind that the pamphlet was produced as part of the nasty post-war Shelby-Sevier debate over Campbell's role.

21 Graves, *Backcountry Revolutionary*, p. 5.

22 alley, A. S. Jr., *Col. William Hill's Memoirs.*

23 Ibid; see also Draper, *King's Mountain*, p. 221; contrast to Shelby, *Battle of King's Mountain.*

24 Draper, *King's Mountain*, p. 217–221.

25 Ibid.

26 Moore, *The Life of Gen. Edward Lacey*, p. 16–17.

27 Benjamin Merrell FPA S8891; John Moor FPA W4935; William Pelham FPA R8080.

28 Elisha Parker FPA S11354, as recorded by Will Graves. See http://revwarapps.org/s11354.pdf

29 Draper, *King's Mountain*, p. 223–224.

30 Dunkerly Robert M., *The Battle of King's Mountain—Eyewitness Accounts*, p. 91.

31 Moore, *The Life of Gen. Edward Lacey*, p. 17.

32 Dunkerly, *The Battle of King's Mountain—Eyewitness Accounts*, p. 54–55.

33 Draper, *King's Mountain*, p. 225–226.

34 Draper, *King's Mountain*, p. 277 gave a more detailed breakdown, but his reliance upon Hill who "is silent in his narrative as to their strength" and contradicts his own comments on the previous page invite skepticism. Hill was in fact *not* silent, giving a very precise head count of 933; Salley, *Col. William Hill's Memoirs of the Revolution,* p. 22. Draper did, however provide a lengthy footnote describing possible sources of error in troop estimates.

35 Dunkerly, *The Battle of King's Mountain—Eyewitness Accounts*, p. 55.

36 Collins, *Autobiography of a Revolutionary Soldier*, p. 50.

37 Ibid, p. 50–51.

38 See Dunkerly, *The Battle of King's Mountain—Eyewitness Accounts*, p. 60. This is an excellent example of how Draper (*King's Mountain*, p. 224) elaborated upon the veterans' actual words; Draper's florid version is nothing like McBee's matter-of-fact statement.

39 See for example Dunkerly, *The Battle of King's Mountain—Eyewitness Accounts,* p. 91–95. Dunkerly correctly notes that in his book Draper edited these personal accounts heavily for dramatic effect. Dunkerly included the two conflicting statements by Young, "Thomas Young's Account" from Gage, *Memoir of Major Thomas Young,* p. 2–3 reads "As soon as we got something to eat, for we were very hungry and weary, we retired to sleep at random in the woods. I did not wake until broad daylight." In another interview with Reverend James H. Saye Young said that "We traveled on till late at night; we then lay down to sleep. . . ."; Draper *Manuscripts Collection,* 23 VV, p. 238. Most of Draper's embellishment occurred in the writing of his book, and in this case the Saye via Draper interview is more plausible. The Gage interview would place them still at the Cowpens on the morning of 7 October, conflicts with both Young and McBee's remembrance of crossing the Broad River near dawn of that morning, and would

require a very long march entirely in daylight.

40 Dunkerly, *The Battle of King's Mountain—Eyewitness Accounts*, p. 78–79.
41 Ibid, p. 40.
42 Salley, *Col. William Hill's Memoirs of the Revolution*, p. 22.

CHAPTER 10

1   Dunkerly, *The Battle of King's Mountain—Eyewitness Accounts*, p. 94; Draper, *King's Mountain*, p. 228.
2   Salley, *Col. William Hill's Memoirs of the Revolution*, p. 22.
3   Draper, *King's Mountain*, p. 229.
4   Dunkerly, *The Battle of King's Mountain—Eyewitness Accounts*, p. 94.
5   Draper, *King's Mountain*, p. 229.
6   Christopher Brandon FPA S9288.
7   Local lore has the Hambright name as a corruption of Hambrecht. There is some uncertainty about the name of the courier; Draper, *King's Mountain*, p. 233.
8   Several older sources as cited in Draper, *King's Mountain*, p. 233.
9   Dunkerly, *The Battle of King's Mountain—Eyewitness Accounts*, p. 94. Note that the sequence of events is not precisely as set forth by Draper, so we have chosen to use the sequence of events as described by the actual participants.
10 Collins, *Autobiography of a Revolutionary Soldier*, p. 51.
11 See Draper, *King's Mountain*, p. 288–290 for examples on nineteenth century speculation.
12 Salley, *Col. William Hill's Memoirs of the Revolution*, p. 23.
13 Draper, *King's Mountain*, p. 207–208.
14 Ibid, p. 238.
15 Collins, *Autobiography of a Revolutionary Soldier*, p. 52.
16 Draper, *King's Mountain*, p. 245.
17 Ibid, p. 249.
18 Collins, *Autobiography of a Revolutionary Soldier*, p. 52.
19 There are various versions of DePeyster's exact comment; this version is from Draper, *King's Mountain*, p. 246–247.
20 Draper, *King's Mountain*, p. 279.
21 Dunkerly, *The Battle of King's Mountain—Eyewitness Accounts*, p. 94.
22 Wallace, *Incidents of the Revolution*, p. 191; this was paraphrased by Draper, *King's Mountain*, p. 269.
23 Collins, *Autobiography of a Revolutionary Soldier*, p. 53.
24 Ibid, p. 52.
25 The assessment of three unsuccessful counterattacks is from sources cited by Draper, p. 272. Draper refers to sources describing Whig riflemen who "fell headlong over the cliffs" in these counterattacks, clearly confusing Brushy Ridge with the rocky pinnacles of King's Mountain proper. The discipline of the Loyalists

is from Draper, p. 279, but is drawn from the second-hand account of the son of a man in Sevier's command—who was not counterattacked.

26 Dunkerly, *The Battle of King's Mountain—Eyewitness Accounts,* p. 92, 94. The reader should note that Dunkerly gives two accounts by Young, one attributed to Thomas Young, the other to Major Thomas Young. The interviewer was using Young's postwar title of Major; he was a private at King's Mountain.

27 Saye, *Revolutionary Reminiscenses Related by Major Thomas Young* , in Draper, *Manuscript Collection,* 22VV, p. 241.

28 Ibid.

29 Draper apparently based this on a single secondary source; Draper, *King's Mountain,* p. 273.

30 Dunkerly, *The Battle of King's Mountain—Eyewitness Accounts,* p. 64.

31 Draper, *King's Mountain,* p. 287–288, 290.

32 Ibid, p. 280.

33 Collins, *Autobiography of a Revolutionary Soldier,* p. 52.

34 Draper, *King's Mountain,* p. 281–282.

35 Ibid, p. 283.

36 Ibid, p. 277.

37 Dunkerly, *The Battle of King's Mountain—Eyewitness Accounts,* p. 93.

38 Joseph Hughes FPA S31764; Draper, *King's Mountain,* p. 286.

39 Collins, *Autobiography of a Revolutionary Soldier,* p. 52–53.

40 Tarleton, *A History of the Campaigns of 1780 and 1781,* p. 165.

41 Dunkerly, *The Battle of King's Mountain—Eyewitness Accounts,* p. 82.

CHAPTER 11

1 Saye, *Revolutionary Reminiscenses Related by Major Thomas Young, in* Draper, *Manuscript Collection,* 23VV, p. 241.

2 Collins, *Autobiography of a Revolutionary Soldier,* p. 53–54.

3 Dunkerly, *The Battle of King's Mountain—Eyewitness Accounts,* p. 55.

4 Ibid, p. 82.

5 Draper, *Kings Mountain,* p. 316, cites a letter by Shelby.

6 Collins, *Autobiography of a Revolutionary Soldier,* p. 54.

7 Draper, *Kings Mountain,* p. 318–319.

8 Collins, *Autobiography of a Revolutionary Soldier,* p. 54; Draper, *King's Mountain,* p. 292, 320.

9 Dunkerly, *The Battle of King's Mountain—Eyewitness Accounts,* p. 48.

10 Ibid, p. 65.

11 Ibid, p. 82.

12 Allaire, *Diary,* in Draper, *Kings Mountain,* p. 510–512.

13 Gage, *Memoir of Major Thomas Young, A Revolutionary Patriot of South Carolina,* Part 2.

14 Dunkerly, *The Battle of King's Mountain—Eyewitness Accounts,* p. 83.

15 Draper, *Kings Mountain*, p. 328.

16 Ibid, p. 326. The tale—possibly apocryphal—originated with the embittered William Hill but was often repeated, as in Lewis, *The Olden Times.*

17 Draper, *Kings Mountain*, p. 326–327, 510.

18 Ibid, p. 331.

19 Draper, *Manuscript Collection*, 22VV, p. 242.

20 Draper, *Kings Mountain*, p. 329–339.

21 Ibid, p. 341, 511.

22 Dr.W.A. Moore letter, April 25 1870, Draper, *Manuscript Collection*, 14 VV, p. 78-80.

23 Gilbert and Gilbert, *Patriot Militiaman In The American Revolution 1775–82*, p. 49.

24 Draper, *Kings Mountain*, p. 341–343; Gage, *Memoir of Major Thomas Young*, p. 4.

25 Draper, *Kings Mountain*, p. 511.

26 Ibid, p. 348.

27 Collins, *Autobiography of a Revolutionary Soldier*, p. 54; Gage, *Memoir of Major Thomas Young, A Revolutionary Patriot of South Carolina*, Part 2.

28 Elisha Parker FPA S11354, as transcribed by Will Graves. See http://revwarapps.org/s11354.pdf

CHAPTER 12

1 Salley, *Col. William Hill's Memoirs*, p. 13.

2 Detailed accounts of this action are described in O'Kelley, *Nothing But Blood and Slaughter, Volume 2*, p. 355–360, and at http://www.carolana.com/SC/Revolution/revolution_battle_of_fishdam_ford.html. Quote from Salley, *Col. William Hill's Memoirs*, p. 14; some accounts infer that Sumter covertly pocketed the list to keep his men from executing Wemyss.

3 There is enormous confusion over Money's actual rank. Various sources list Money's rank from lieutenant to lieutenant colonel. His contemporary, Lieutenant Roderick McKenzie, in his *Strictures On Lt.Col. Tarleton's History*, refers to him as Major Money. Confusion probably arose from conflation with Major John Money, a British Army officer of the era who went on to become a general and pioneer balloonist. Baxley, *British Lt. John Money—63rd Regiment of Foot—Killed at Blackstock's Plantation November 20, 1780*, makes a convincing argument that Money was indeed a lieutenant, and therefore probably a trusted protégé of Cornwallis who was awarded a command far above his rank.

4 Reynolds, *Andrew Pickens*, p. 134, 170.

5 This and subsequent references by Hammond are from Johnson, *Traditions and Reminiscences, Chiefly of the American Revolution in the South*, p. 522–526.

6 William Grant FPA W1757.

7 John Calhoun FPA W8579.

8 Ibid.

9   British numbers from Tarleton, *History of the Campaigns of 1780 and 1781*, p. 177.

10   Moore, *The Life of Gen. Edward Lacey*, p. 22; Hammond quote Draper, *King's Mountain Papers*, 1DD, p. 273.

11   Moore, *The Life of Gen. Edward Lacey*, p. 22, fixes the date as two days before the Blackstock's battle.

12   Saye, *Memoirs of Major Joseph McJunkin*, p. 28.

13   Logan, *A History of the Upper Country of South Carolina, from the Earliest Periods to the Close of the War of Independence, Volume II*, p. 3–4.

14   William Beard FPA S2981.

15   Saye speculated that McJunkin's promotion resulted from the death of Lt. Col James Steen, with senior major William Farr promoted to fill Steen's billet, and McJunkin succeeded to Farr's billet; Saye, *Memoirs of Major Joseph McJunkin*, p. 28.

16   Samuel Otterson FPA S25344.

17   O'Neall, *Memoir of Joseph McJunkin of Union*.

18   Letter by Joseph F. Hart to Dr. Joseph Logan dated 1 November 1858(year is uncertain, Draper, *Manuscript Collection*, 15VV, p. 212–216.

19   Moore, *The Life of Gen. Edward Lacey*, p. 22–23.

20   The configuration of the battle site is reconstructed from (1) Tarleton's sketch map in the British National Archives, (2) archeological studies (Smith, *Research at Blackstock's Battlefield*), (3) lidar imagery (http://gaz.jrshelby.com/blackstocks.htm), (4) veteran's descriptions, (5) a description in a letter by Joseph F. Hart to Dr. Joseph Logan dated 1 November 1858(year is uncertain, Draper, *Manuscript Collection*, 15VV, p. 212–216),and (6) ground inspection by the authors.

21   Tarleton sketch map *Plan of Action at Black Stock's 21st Nov. 1780*, included in Cornwallis Correspondence files, British National Archives. This map is stamped item 366. Note that maps are filed separately from correspondence, and the maps were not included in Cornwallis's published correspondence.

22   Communication from Col. S. T. Sims to Lyman Draper, in *Draper Manuscript Collection*, 16VV, p. 336.

23   Draper, *Manuscript Collection*, 15VV, p. 212.

24   Tarleton, *History of the Campaigns of 1780 and 1781*, p. 179–180.

25   Ibid, p. 177.

26   Smith, *Research at Blackstocks Battlefield*, catalog of artifacts p. 17–20.

27   Saye, *Memoirs of Major Joseph McJunkin*, p. 28.

28   O'Neall, *Memoir of Joseph McJunkin of Union*.

29   Ellet, *The Women of the American Revolution, Volume 3*, p. 296–297.

30   John Calhoun FPA W8579; Brandon was frequently recalled (or recorded by interviewers) as Brannon.

31   Saye, *Memoirs of Major Joseph McJunkin*, p. 28.

32   Tarleton, *A History of the Campaigns of 1780 and 1781*, p. 178.

33   Col. S. T. Sims to Lyman Draper, in *Draper Manuscript Collection*,16VV, p. 336.

34 O'Neall, *Memoir of Joseph McJunkin of Union*.

35 Letter by Joseph F. Hart to Dr. Joseph Logan dated 1 November 1858 (year is uncertain, Draper, *Manuscript Collection*, 15VV, p. 214–215.

36 Col. S. T. Sims to Lyman Draper, in *Draper Manuscript Collection*, 16VV, p. 336.

37 Moore, *The Life of Gen. Edward Lacey*, p. 23

38 Tarleton, *A History of the Campaigns of 1780 and 1781*, p. 182.

39 Salley, *Col. William Hill's Memoirs of the Revolution*, p. 15.

40 Moore, *The Life of Gen. Edward Lacey*, p. 23.

41 Bass, *Gamecock*, p. 197. Otterson corroborated this account in Col. S.T. Sims to Lyman Draper, *Draper Manuscript Collection*, 16VV, p. 336. Gabriel Brown was the cousin of Jacob Brown who was married to Otterson's wife's aunt (both named Ruth Gordon). This was typical of the complex familial relationships within militia regiments.

42 McKenzie, *Strictures On Lt.Col. Tarleton's History*, p. 78.

43 Simon Davis FPA S6784.

44 McKenzie, *Strictures On Lt.Col. Tarleton's History*, p. 77.

45 Abraham Bolt Sr. FPA S9282

46 O'Neall, *Memoir of Joseph McJunkin of Union*.

47 Saye, *Memoirs of Major Joseph McJunkin*, p. 29.

48 Lewis Tuner FPA W11667.

49 Sumter was by all accounts delirious and had already surrendered command, so Log is clearly talking about Twiggs. Reuben Long Sr. FPA R6431. William Beard FPA S2981.

50 Johnson, *Traditions and Reminiscences, Chiefly of the American Revolution in the South*, p. 508.

51 Undated letter "Major L.T. Sims Traditions of Union District," in Draper, *Manuscript Collection*, 15VV, p. 220–226. Sims clearly confused the timing of events, referring to the period of Loyalist William Cunningham's Bloody Scout of late 1781. Draper's annotations indicate his decision to assign these events to the aftermath of the Second Siege of Augusta (1781), but the events are clearly garbled.

52 Saye, *Memoirs of Major Joseph McJunkin*, p. 29.

53 Tarleton, *A History of the Campaigns of 1780 and 1781*, p. 178–183; McKenzie, *Strictures On Lt.Col. Tarleton's History*, p. 73–74.

54 McKenzie, *Strictures On Lt.Col. Tarleton's History*, p. 78.

55 O'Kelley, *Nothing But Blood and Slaughter, Volume Two*, p. 366, 556. O'Kelley does not cite specific sources.

56 Saye, *Memoirs of Major Joseph McJunkin*, p. 29.

57 Tarleton, *A History of the Campaigns of 1780 and 1781*, p. 205.

58 Abel Kendrick FPA R5861; Lewis Turner FPA W11667.

CHAPTER 13

1 Johnson, *Traditions and Reminiscences, Chiefly of the American Revolution in the*

South, p. 526.

2　William Grant FPA W1757.

3　Lewis Tuner FPA W11667; John Calhoun FPA W8579.

4　Lewis Tuner FPA W11667.

5　Moore, *The Life of Gen. Edward Lacey*, p. 23.

6　Samuel Otterson FPA S25344.

7　Logan, *A History of the Upper Country of South Carolina, from the Earliest Periods to the Close of the War of Independence, Volume II*, p. 4.

8　Saye, *Memoirs of Major Joseph McJunkin*, p. 29–30.

9　Logan, *A History of the Upper Country of South Carolina, from the Earliest Periods to the Close of the War of Independence, Volume II*, p. 4–5.

10　Collins, *Autobiography of a Revolutionary Soldier*, p. 56.

11　Wallace, *Incidents of the Revolution*, p. 179–180.

12　O'Neall, *Memoir of Joseph McJunkin of Union*.

13　Lewis, *The Olden Times*.

14　Sims, S. T., *Traditions of Union District, (no date)*, handwritten transcript, 16VV, p. 220–221.

15　Saye, *Memoirs of Major Joseph McJunkin*, p. 29–30.

16　O'Neall, *Memoir of Joseph McJunkin of Union*, p. 11.

17　Gage, *Revolutionary Incidents IV Christopher Brandon, of Union District*, p. 383.

18　Letter, *Cornwallis Correspondence*, British National Archives, PRO 30/11/66, p. 33–34.

19　Letter, *Cornwallis Correspondence*, British National Archives, PRO 30/11/14 p. 364.

20　Ibid, p. 383–384.

21　Letter, *Cornwallis Correspondence*, British National Archives, PRO 30/11/109, p. 43.

22　Letter, *Cornwallis Correspondence*, British National Archives, PRO 30/11/66, p. 44–47.

23　Draper, *Manuscript Collection*, 7VV, p. 134–135.

24　There are a number of good biographies of Morgan. For a readily accessible summation, see http://en.wikipedia.org/wiki/Daniel_Morgan

25　As with Morgan, there are a number of good biographies of Greene. For a readily accessible summation, see http://en.wikipedia.org/wiki/Nathanael_Greene

26　Myers, *Cowpens Papers*, p. 9–12.

27　Lewis, The Olden Times. Draper, *King's Mountain* 15VV, , p. 127–128 gives a much elaborated version of this story.

28　Logan, *A History of the Upper Country of South Carolina, Volume II*, p. 5. As to Tory forces see for example O'Kelley, *Nothing But Blood and Slaughter, Volume Two, 1780*, p. 393.

29　Gage, *Memoir of Major Thomas Young*, p. 4.

30　Logan, *A History of the Upper Country of South Carolina, Volume II*, p. 5.

31 Myers, *Cowpens Papers*, p. 15. Not much information is actually known about these actions. For a summary see McGee, *"The better order of men" Hammond's Store and Fort Williams*.
32 Logan, *A History of the Upper Country of South Carolina, Volume II*, p. 5.
33 Johnson, *Sketches of the Life and Correspondence of Nathanael Greene Volume I*, p. 410–411.

CHAPTER 14

1   Johnson, *Sketches of the Life and Correspondence of Nathanael Greene Volume I*, p. 5.
2   Angelica Mitchell Knott, *Traditions of the Revolutionary War*, in Draper, *Sumter Papers*, 23VV, p. 267, 270; Greene's dispatch from Myers, *Cowpens Papers*, p. 19.
3   Joseph McJunkin FPA S18118.
4   Saye, *Memoir of Major Joseph McJunkin*, p. 38–39. McJunkin was disingenuous here, as on numerous occasions he interpreted dreams; see Draper, *Sumter Papers*, 23VV, p. 153.
5   Gage, *Memoir of Major Thomas Young*, p. 4.
6   Johnson, *Traditions and Reminiscences, Chiefly of the American Revolution in the South*, p. 527.
7   Myers, *Cowpens Papers*, p. 21.
8   Collins, *Autobiography of a Revolutionary Soldier*, p. 56.
9   Gage, *Revolutionary Incidents IV Christopher Brandon, of Union District*, p. 383.
10 Gage, *Memoir of Major Thomas Young*, p. 4–5.
11 Ibid, p. 5.
12 Gage, *Revolutionary Incidents IV Christopher Brandon, of Union District*, p. 383–384.
13 Gage, *Memoir of Major Thomas Young*, p. 5.
14 Ibid, p. 5.
15 Collins, *Autobiography of a Revolutionary Soldier*, p. 56–57.
16 Landrum, *Colonial and Revolutionary History of Upper South Carolina*, p. 275.
17 Morgan as quoted, *Ibid*, p. 275–276.
18 Johnson, *Traditions and Reminiscences, Chiefly of the American Revolution in the South*, p. 527; Gage, *Memoir of Major Thomas Young*, p. 6.
19 Landrum, *Colonial and Revolutionary History of Upper South Carolina*, p. 276–277.
20 Various memoirs cited by Babits, *A Devil of a Whipping*, p. 66–67,
21 Gage, *Revolutionary Incidents IV Christopher Brandon, of Union District*, p. 384.
22 Gage, *Memoir of Major Thomas Young*, p. 6.
23 Babits, *A Devil of a Whipping*.
24 Gage, *Revolutionary Incidents IV Christopher Brandon, of Union District*, p. 384.
25 Stewart, *Highlanders of Scotland, Volume II*, see section *Military Annals of the Highland Regiments, Fraser's Highlanders or Seventy-first Regiment* in the online

version (not paginated).

26 Feaster, *A History of Union County, South Carolina*, p. 79.

27 Gage, *Memoir of Major Thomas Young*, p. 6.

28 John Jolly FPA W976.

29 Stewart, *Highlanders of Scotland, Volume II*, as cited above.

30 Angelica Mitchell Nott, *Traditions of the Revolutionary War*, in Draper, *Sumter Papers*, 23VV, p. 271.

31 Stewart, *Highlanders of Scotland, Volume II*; Babits, *A Devil of a Whipping*, p. 77.

32 MacKenzie, *Strictures on Lt. Col. Tarleton's History*, p. 94.

33 Gage, *Revolutionary Incidents IV Christopher Brandon, of Union District*, p. 384.

34 MacKenzie, *Strictures on Lt. Col. Tarleton's History*, p. 99.

35 Collins, *Autobiography of a Revolutionary Soldier*, p. 57.

36 Logan, *A History of the Upper Country of South Carolina, Volume II*, p. 43–44.

37 Wallace, *Incidents of the Revolution*, p. 188–190.

38 Collins, *Autobiography of a Revolutionary Soldier*, p. 57.

39 Gage, *Revolutionary Incidents IV Christopher Brandon, of Union District*, p. 384.

40 Draper, *Sumter Papers*, 22vv, p. 244–245.

41 Stewart, *Highlanders of Scotland, Volume II*.

42 Johnson, *Sketches of the Life and Correspondence of Nathanael Greene Volume I*, p. 381.

43 Collins, *Autobiography of a Revolutionary Soldier*, p. 57.

44 Gage, *Revolutionary Incidents IV Christopher Brandon, of Union District*, p. 384

45 Gage, *Memoir of Major Thomas Young*, p. 6.

46 Ibid, p. 6–7.

47 Stewart, *Highlanders of Scotland, Volume II*.

48 Johnson, *Sketches of the Life and Correspondence of Nathanael Greene Volume I*, p. 382.

49 Ibid, p. 383–384.

50 Gage, *Revolutionary Incidents IV Christopher Brandon, of Union District*, p. 384.

51 Collins, *Autobiography of a Revolutionary Soldier*, p. 57–58.

CHAPTER 15

1 MacKenzie, *Strictures on Lt. Col. Tarleton's History*, p. 94; de Chastellux, *Travels in North America*, p. 236–237.

2 Myers, *Cowpens Papers*, p. 34–35.

3 Ibid, p. 36.

4 Gage, *Memoir of Major Thomas Young*, p. 7–8. Essentially the same story appears in Draper, *Manuscript Collection*, 22VV, p. 244.

5 Draper, *Manuscript Collection*, 22VV, p. 244.

6 Ibid, p. 244–245.

7 Gage, *Memoir of Major Thomas Young*, p. 8.

8 Draper, *Manuscript Collection*, 22VV, p. 245.

9   Gage, *Memoir of Major Thomas Young*, p. 8.

10 Draper, *Manuscript Collection*, 22VV, p. 246.

11 Gage, *Memoir of Major Thomas Young*, p. 8.

12 Samuel Otterson FPA S25344; Myers, *Cowpens Papers*, p. 26.

13 Stewart, *Highlanders of Scotland, Volume II*.

14 Samuel Otterson FPA S25344; Christopher Brandon FPAS9288-.

15 William Kenedy FPA S2695.

16 Samuel Otterson FPA S25344; Christopher Brandon FPA S9288; John Albritton FPA S31517; Richard Addis FPA S21594; John Biddie (or Biddy) FPA S10374; Abraham Bolt Sr.FPA S9282.

17 For a brief summary with very good maps see Konstan, *Guilford Courthouse 1781*. For a more detailed analysis see Buchanan, *The Road to Guilford Courthouse*, p. 334–358.

18 Buchanan, *The Road to Guilford Courthouse*, p. 348.

19 Buchanan, *The Road to Guilford Courthouse*, p. 349; Tarleton, *A History of the Campaigns of 1780 and 1781*, p. 225–226.

20 The remark is quoted in slightly different forms in various sources, but the sense is the same.

CHAPTER 16

1   Joseph McJunkin FPA S18118, second deposition, Charles Tankersly FPA W4602.

2   Captain William Young FPA S4742.

3   Private Samuel Smith FPA S21988; Joseph McJunkin FPA S18118, second deposition; Charles Tankersly FPA W4602.

4   Wallace, *Incidents of the Revolution*, p. 179–180.

5   Saye, *Memoir of Major Joseph McJunkin*, p. 34–35.

6   Article from the January 1843 issue of the *Magnolia*, as quoted in Saye, *Memoir of Major Joseph McJunkin*, p. 37.

7   Saye, *Memoir of Major Joseph McJunkin*, p. 37–38.

8   Matthew Patton FPA S18153; some accounts have Roebuck captured at Mudlick Creek on 2 March, which seems implausible. Saye, *Memoir of Major Joseph McJunkin*, p. 34–37, has Roebuck and others captured when Tories raided homes on 10 March. We have used Patton's account since he was taken with Roebuck.

9   William Sims Narrative in Draper, *Manuscript Collection*, 23VV, p. 265–266. Analysis of pension records suggests some ambiguity about the exact date of this event.

10 Ibid, p. 266–267.

11 Saye, *Memoir of Major Joseph McJunkin*, p. 37–38. The date of his capture is from his pension application, FPA S18118

12 A very clear description of the battle can be seen at http://militaryhistory.about.com/od/AmRev17781783/p/American-Revolution-Battle-Of-Hobkirk-S-Hill.htm, with a good map at http://www.hobkirkhill.org/battlemaps.aspx

13   Narrative of William Sims, Draper, *Sumter Papers*, 23VV, p. 267.

14   This and subsequent quotes by Young are from Draper, *Sumter Papers*, 22VV, p. 246–247.

15   Gage, *Memoir of Major Thomas Young*, p. 8.

16   William Grant FPA W1757; Grant's original deposition is included in his widow's file.

17   Samuel Otterson FPA S25344.

18   Thomas Petty FPA S1710.

19   William Grant FPA W1757.

20   John Davidson FPA S31639.

21   Gage, *Memoir of Major Thomas Young*, p. 8–9.

22   Simon Davis FPA S6784.

23   Johnson, William, *Sketches of the Life and Correspondence of Nathanael Greene Volume II*, p. 137.

24   A brief summary of the siege is provided in Pancake, *This Destructive War*, p. 209–216. The account given here is derived primarily from Johnson, *Sketches of the Life and Correspondence of Nathanael Greene Volume II*, p. 138–155.

25   Alaire, *Diary*, in Draper, *King's Mountain*, p. 498–499.

26   Ibid, p. 499; description of the jail from Smith, *Historical perspectives at Ninety Six*, p. 63.

27   Joseph McJunkin FPA S18118.

28   John Bearden FPA S2991. Gray was one of the more notorious Tory raiders; see http://www.carolana.com/SC/Revolution/loyalist_leaders_sc_william_cunningham.html

29   Draper, *Sumter Papers*, 7VV, p. 306.

30   Gage, *Memoir of Major Thomas Young*, p. 9.

31   The tunnel is still preserved. See photos at http://www.foxcarolina.com/story/25271391/revolutionary-war-tunnel-preserved-explored-in-ninety-six

32   Samuel Otterson FPA S25344.

33   Gage, R. J., *Memoir of Major Thomas Young*, p. 9–10.

34   This date from Richard Brandon's posthumous stub indent X2341.

35   Wallace, *Incidents of the Revolution*, p. 181–184. There are alternative versions of this story, all essentially similar, including Lewis, *The Olden Times*, which is a version passed along to Lewis's wife, who was descended from William Kennedy Sr. and his wife Mary Ann Brandon Kennedy. Draper, *King's Mountain*, p. 130–131, in a much-elaborated version cited a letter from Congressman Daniel Wallace to novelist William Gilmore Simms. In the letter Wallace made factual errors and was suggesting plot elements for fiction.

36   Draper, *King's Mountain*, p. 132–133. Draper's slightly different original transcription appears in Daniel Wallace, *Revolutionary Incidents*, p. 194–195.

37   Lewis, *The Olden Times*.

38   Simon Davis FPA S6784.

39 William Grant Jr.FPA W1757.
40 Unless otherwise noted the description of the battle is from Johnson, *Sketches of the Life and Correspondence of Nathanael Greene Volume II*, p. 220–237.
41 Greene, *Gen. Greene to the President of Congress*, letter in Southern, *Voices of the American Revolution*, p. 237–242.
42 Simon Davis FPA S6784, James Hall FPA W25471, Joseph Hughes FPA S37164, John Whelchel FPA W6498, and Aaron Guyton FPA W21237.
43 Simon Davis FPA S6784. In addition to those mentioned by name in the text at least 14 other named individuals are placed in the battle by pension records, but offer no significant details.
44 John Cain FPA W3510.
45 James Hall FPA W25471.
46 Reynolds, *Andrew Picken*, p. 296.
47 Drawn primarily from Wyman and Goldsmith, *Commemorating The Massacre at Hayes Station and the Little River Regiment*, p. 3–5. See also O'Kelley, *Nothing but Blood and Slaughter . . . Volume Three 1781*, p. 397–400; O'Kelley's account differs slightly. Other details from Pancake, This Destructive War, p. 88, and Bailey, *Commanders at King's Mountain*, p. 322–323.

CHAPTER 17
1 This brief account is drawn from http://www.carolana.com/SC/Revolution/revolution_loricks_ferry.html; O'Kelley, *Nothing But Blood and Slaughter, Volume 4, 1782*, p. 95–96; and Gordon, *South Carolina and the American Revolution*, p. 170–174.
2 William Addington FPA W5598.
3 Reynolds, *Andrew Pickens*, p. 299.
4 Reynolds, *Andrew Pickens . . .* , p. 23–24.
5 Abel Kendrick FPA R5861.
6 See for example O'Kelley, *Nothing But Blood and Slaughter, Volume Four, 1782*, p. 90.
7 Joseph McJunkin FPA S18118.
8 For a brief biography of Dragging Canoe see https://en.wikipedia.org/wiki/Dragging_Canoe
9 See extended summary and consequences of the treaty at https://en.wikipedia.org/wiki/Treaty_of_Paris_(1783)

EPILOGUE
1 O'Neall, *Annals of Newberry*, p. 235–236.
2 https://en.wikipedia.org/wiki/Major_%E2%80%9CBloody_Bill%E2%80%9D_Cunningham; https://en.wikipedia.org/wiki/Thomas_Brown_(loyalist)
3 Logan, *A History of the Upper Country of South Carolina, Volume II*, p. 42.
4 Draper, *King's Mountain*, p. 469; Lewis, *The Olden Times*, although Lewis badly

garbled the story of Brandon's funeral, rendering it almost comic.
5   Lewis, The *Olden Times*.
6   Ibid.
7   Wallace, *Incidents of the Revolution*, p. 192–194.
8   Robert Long FPS S7157; William Young FPS S4742.

APPENDIX A
1   Myers, *Cowpens Papers*, p. 24–28.
2   Johnson, *Traditions and Reminiscences*, p. 526–530.
3   Both maps are on microfilm at National Archives I, Microcopy Group 859, roll 82. Babits (*A Devil of a Whipping*, p. 182) speculated that both were drafted by a Major Edward Giles.
4   A useful summary of maps is the website *A Miniature History of the Revolution—Cowpens: Battlefield Maps*, http://miniawi.blogspot.com/2009/06/cowpens-battlefield-maps.html
5   Moncure, *The Cowpens Staff Ride and Battlefield Tour*.
6   See for example Babits, *A Devil of a Whipping*; Brown, *King's Mountain and Cowpens*; Bearss, *Battle of Cowpens: A Documented Narrative and Troop Movement Maps*.
7   Babits, *A Devil of a Whipping*.

INDEX